The Society Tale in Russian Literature

From Odoevskii to Tolstoi

Edited by

Neil Cornwell

AMSTERDAM - ATLANTA, GA 1998

∞ The paper on which this book is printed meets the requirements of "ISO 9706:1994, Information and documentation - Paper for documents - Requirements for permanence".

ISBN: 90-420-0329-4   100153037X
©Editions Rodopi B.V., Amsterdam - Atlanta, GA 1998
Printed in The Netherlands

TABLE OF CONTENTS

INTRODUCTION

> ... she talks so much better than most of the people in
> society. I hope you don't mind my saying that, because I
> have an idea that you are not in society. You can imagine
> whether I am! Haven't you judged it, like me, condemned it,
> and given it up? Are you not sick of the egotism, the
> snobbery, the meanness, the frivolity, the immorality, the
> hypocrisy?
>
> (Henry James, *The Princess Casamassima*, 1886, ch. 34)

A firm definition, if not more than one, of the *svetskaia povest'* (society
tale) may well emerge, or be confirmed, as the essays in this volume
unfold. Without imposing anything too firm at this stage, it might be
emphasized that we are dealing with a predominantly *dvorianskaia
literatura* (or aristocratic literature), at least as far as the earlier half of
the nineteenth century is concerned; or – to put it in another language –
the term 'society tale' denotes above all the literary outpourings, or the
creative consciousness, of what Tolstoi would have recognised as *les
deux cents familles* of Russian society. In English literature we may
think first of Jane Austen or, considerably later, of Henry James. What
kind of development of this type of fiction took place in Russian
literature? That is something we expect to establish in the course of the
essays that follow.

Russian prose seemed to pause in the first two decades of the
nineteenth century, mesmerized perhaps by the travel letters of
Karamzin and the journeys of Radishchev, or halted in its tracks,
possibly, by Karamzin's abandoned proto-*Bildungsroman* of 1803,
called (almost as though in anticipation of Lermontov) *Rytsar' nashego
vremeni* (*A Knight of Our Time*), and his subsequent permanent plunge
into history. History, indeed, in imitation of French and English models
– most notably Walter Scott – seemed to dominate much of the prose
fiction in Russia of the first quarter of the nineteenth century. Yet,
within little more than half a century, and inside a period stretching
from Lermontov's *Geroi nashego vremeni* (*A Hero of Our Time,* 1840)
to, let us say, the novels of Turgenev and Goncharov that had appeared
by the end of the 1850s, there had become firmly established a
phenomenon that we now think of as the nineteenth-century Russian
(realist) novel. Certain features of this artistic development will be

repeatedly referred to throughout the contributions to follow. European models and influences apart (and much could be said on these, from Sterne and Goethe, to Constant and Balzac), the Russian novel as we know it evolved largely through a process of amalgamation and mutation. The seedbed consisted of a number of more or less literary prose forms that were the common currency of these formative years and, in particular, I would here suggest, of the melting-pot decade of the 1820s: a decade in which little prose of lasting value was produced, but in which were rudely fashioned the building blocks of what were to be the grandiose edifices that followed. Among these literary forms we may number the adventure tale (often historical and/or military, variously romantic and occasionally Gothic), the travelogue (or travel notes, often epistolary), the essay genre (historical, philosophical, aesthetic or critical, and journalistic), the 'familiar letter' (so termed by William Mills Todd) and, of course, the society tale. Visualize an amalgam of these forms and, arguably, you will have envisaged the Russian novel; conceive of a sufficient expansion in scale and chronology, and you might even divine *Voina i mir* (*War and Peace*)!

The society tale in Russia, in the 1820s and 30s, arose and evolved as part of the development of romantic prose in Russia. This is the generally accepted, if slightly simplistic, view expressed by R.V. Iezuitova, in her essay, '*Svetskaia povest'*' (in the collection *Russkaia povest' XIX veka*, published in Leningrad in 1973, edited by B.S. Meilakh).[1] The earliest practitioners, well within the 1820s, were Vladimir Odoevskii, Bestuzhev-Marlinskii (originally Aleksandr Bestuzhev, who was allowed to publish under the penname 'Marlinskii' as a Decembrist exile) and Orest Somov. This was seen as a period in which the previous forms of inspiration for prose fiction, drawn from books and from nature, began to give way to a renewed interest in the machinations of (high) society. Such a process soon coincided with what is seen by Elizabeth C. Shepard, in the other seminal essay on the society tale (published in *Russian Literature* in 1981), as 'the innovative argument in Russian prose fiction of the 1830s'; the 'discovery' of the nineteenth century as a new era, and the

---

[1]Details of studies of general relevance, including those by Iezuitova and Shepard, are given in the Select Bibliography to the present volume (and, as applicable, in the notes to individual essays).

consequent awareness of progress and modernity, led to an emphasis in literature on observation and analysis (taking precedence over imagination and invention). The raw material for a more realist approach to fiction was readily available in society itself.

Many of the practitioners of the society tale in Russia had impeccable credentials for knowing society from the inside: Odoevskii was a prince (*kniaz'*) and V.A. Sollogub a count (*graf*); Pushkin and Lermontov, too, were well-connected aristocrats. The driving attitude towards society was critical, whether coming from the 'repentant noblemen' themselves, from interlopers of lower or mixed rank, or from the women who were, or might well have been, its victims. Odoevskii despised the ballroom and the card table and, in his *Pestrye skazki* (*Variegated Tales*, of 1833), set about the drawing room:

> No, gentlemen, you do not know society! You do not know its vital province – the drawing rooms! ... Oh, if you should stumble upon the veritable wound of the drawing rooms – it would not be cold laughter that would greet you; you would sadly hold your breath, or a wailing and a gnashing of teeth would break out from their marble walls.[2]

His friend Evdokiia Rostopchina wrote in 1839 of the need to investigate society 'with the scalpel of the scientist and the intuition of the poet', in order 'to de-gild the tinsel, to expose the mirage, to incinerate the dream' (quoted by Iezuitova, p. 177). Drawing rooms are, of course, frequented by society's creatures; Ivan Panaev, writing in 1834, is totally scathing on the *svetskii chelovek* (the society personage, the *beau*, or the man-about-town):

> The society personage is a creature who breathes only the atmosphere of the drawing rooms; merely think of depriving him of this atmosphere and he will be destroyed, he will perish ... The society personage gyrates aimlessly every day around the lie, around scandal, pomposity, prejudice, caprice, fabrication – in a word, around the entire fleamarket of pitiful human worthlessness and, finally, gets stupefied from his gyrations.[3]

If the society tale was ever the dominant form in Russian prose, its heyday was undoubtedly the 1830s, although even then other styles of fiction, exploited by Pushkin and Gogol' in particular, as well as by

---

[2] V.F. Odoyevsky, *Pyostryye skazki*, edited by Neil Cornwell, Durham, University of Durham, 1988, pp. 81-2 (and quoted by Iezuitova, p. 171).
[3] I.I. Panaev, *Spal'nia svetskoi zhenshchiny* (quoted by Iezuitova, p. 179).

Odoevskii and Marlinskii themselves, still seem more prominent. The society tale, as well as existing as a (diachronically) transitional form between Russian romanticism (a complex enough mix in itself)[4] and realism, was a (synchronically) tangential style that bordered on or blended with other sub-genres, or was written by the exponents of other, more widely discussed, forms. As indicated above, the military tale, historical fiction, the Gothic (or fantastic), travel notes and sketches of various types (including the social-satirical *feuilleton*, derided for its superficiality by more serious figures) all come into play as period styles. Shorter fictional works were generally (if not exclusively) the order of the day. It is by no means coincidental that, for instance, Marlinskii wrote military, Gothic and exotic forms of romantic fiction (for which he is today mainly remembered) as well as the occasional society tale; similarly, Odoevskii is certainly as equally known for his mystical-philosophical and fantastic fiction as for his society tales. Indeed, the styles in question frequently overlapped, both in these writers and in others. Marlinskii and Odoevskii also wrote historical fiction, as, of course, did Pushkin. Pushkin's *Pikovaia dama* (*The Queen of Spades*), cited by several contributors to this volume for its society tale elements, is at least as readily categorizable as a military tale and as a tale of the Gothic fantastic.[5] Lermontov's celebrated novel, *Geroi nashego vremeni* (*A Hero of Our Time*) includes among its constituent episodes (alongside travel, adventure and military prose) what is frequently regarded as the finest example of the society tale, 'Kniazhna Meri' ('Princess Mary').

Iezuitova and Shepard both confine themselves very largely to considering shorter works of prose fiction and to works produced in the decade of the 1830s. However, Pushkin's *Evgenii Onegin* – a 'novel in verse' written from 1823-1830 – is clearly regarded by several contributors to the present volume as being of vital importance to any real understanding of the society tale (as of much else in the development of Russian literature): in terms of plotlines and functions,

---

[4]For detailed discussions of the complexities of Russian romanticism (in addition to works included in the Select Bibliography) see Lauren Leighton, *Russian Romanticism*, The Hague, Mouton, 1975; Robert Reid (editor), *Problems of Russian Romanticism*, Aldershot, Gower, 1986; and Lauren Gray Leighton (editor), *Russian Romantic Criticism: An Anthology*, New York, Greenwood Press, 1987.

[5]For a survey of the large number and variety of readings accorded this work, see Neil Cornwell, *Pushkin's 'The Queen of Spades'*, London, Bristol Classical Press, 1993.

and of character types. The other key formative work here emphasized is Griboedov's classic verse comedy *Gore ot uma* (*Woe from Wit*: written between 1820 and 1824, published in censored form in 1833, and in full only in 1860). Griboedov and Odoevskii (the former perhaps more the godfather and the latter a natural one) seem to emerge as fathers of the genre, by virtue of their work from the first half of the 1820s.

The term '*svetskaia povest'*' is traced by Iezuitova (p. 172) to a review of stories by N.F. Pavlov, published in 1835 (and its validity was soon questioned by Belinskii). Pavlov, Nikolai Polevoi, Panaev and Aleksandr Vel'tman all published society tales, as (naturally enough, in many estimations) did the rising generation of women writers: Nadezhda Durova, Evdokiia Rostopchina, Elena Gan [or Hahn], Mariia Zhukova and Karolina Pavlova. By the late 1830s, the popularity of this type of tale was such that it was giving rise to a flood of inferior imitations (for details, see Iezuitova, pp. 182-4). The inbuilt formulaic quality of the society tale no doubt contributed to its lack of longevity. Even in the cases of its more accredited exponents, in Iezuitova's view (p. 182), 'the most interesting works in an artistic sense, as a rule, were [their] first attempts'. By 1841, when V.A. Sollogub published his emblematic *Bol'shoi svet* (*High Society*), the form – at least in the stricter sense employed by Iezuitova and Shepard – had had its day; this very story, in Iezuitova's opinion (p. 199), contained nothing new and embodied 'an undoubted symptom of the incipient withering away of the society tale'. The Lermontov connection does, however, give this tale a greater interest than this comment would suggest.

So what did happen to the society tale? Iezuitova's answer is that the advances made by the authors of the *svetskie povesti* were 'assimilated by Russian prose as a whole and the demand for a special sub-generic form faded' (ibid.). While this may undoubtedly be true, it remains possible to flesh out this assimilation more fully and this is a challenge taken up in several of the essays which follow. Many of the elements of the society tale, and, for that matter, many of the ingredients of the melting pot from which the society tale had itself emerged, enjoyed a continued prominence within vastly larger-scale works by Dostoevskii and Tolstoi, while the debt of Goncharov and Turgenev to the society-tale form is at least equally clear. *Anna Karenina*, for instance, is here presented by more than one contributor as, whatever else it may be, a prime example of the society tale writ large.

Dostoevskii, too, absorbed the society tale into his novelistic armoury and its impact is noted here on works stretching from *Bednye liudi* (*Poor Folk*) to *Idiot* (*The Idiot*), while an unassailable case can be made for seeing in his short novel *Igrok* (*The Gambler*, 1866) a revisitation of the pot-boiling society tale formula. Foma Fomich, the Tartuffe-like protagonist of Dostoevskii's *Selo Stepanchikovo i ego obitateli* (*The Village of Stepanchikovo*, 1859), it might be worth remembering, was himself supposedly writing a society tale. By then, of course, the *svetskaia povest'* – at least as traditionally envisaged – was long since *passé* as a sub-genre. Furthermore, Foma Fomich was in large measure a parodic portrait of Gogol' – apart from anything else, the one great master of Russian prose in this period *not* really to have engaged with the society tale.

Society-tale scenes and motifs long continued to reverberate through the Russian novel. One has only to think of the masked ball in Belyi's *Peterburg* (*Petersburg*, 1913), or the Sventitskiis' Christmas party in *Doctor Zhivago* (1957), to see that this tradition survived, at least into turn-of-the-century settings. In the post-revolutionary era, the tradition is parodied in historiographic metafictional form by Satan's ball in Bulgakov's *Master i Margarita* (*The Master and Margarita*), while the Berlin settings of Nabokov's Russian novels reproduce a variant emphasis on émigré society. Even in the Soviet Union, the society tradition was carried on, after a fashion, under socialist realism and was later developed in a different style in, for instance, the Moscow novellas of Iurii Trifonov.

According to Iezuitova (p. 173):

> At the base of the society tale lies a psychological drama of love intrigue, the action of which unfolds in a society milieu and the protagonists of which (or, at least, one of them) belong to this milieu.

Again, evidence offered by the essays in this volume confirms that this is, generally speaking at least, the case. However, additional factors are also thrown up: power play, social status and financial preoccupations assume a particular importance. These can be adduced through attention to 'chronotope' (the intersection of time and place), plot function, motif and motivation (*motivirovka*). Setting (*topos*) in the society tale is therefore of the essence: both in the wider, or exterior, sense (urban, provincial or colonial; society's modish haunts within Russia, or fashionable foreign spas), and in a narrower, or interior one (the ballroom, the salon and the boudoir), as well as points of intersection (the threshold and the street), or means of transition (the carriage or, later, the train). The essays in this collection deal with both the major figures and several of the more minor literary players, concentrating on individual authors or texts (in Part I) and on more thematic or general approaches (in Part II), as well as broaching later developments and generic questions. It is hoped that these studies will help stimulate research into further aspects of the genre and its place in the development of Russian prose, as well as into authors and texts here touched upon only in passing.

One of the main achievements of the society tale, most commentators would now agree, is its pioneering role in the raising of consciousness over questions of gender. This involves, as all our essays to a greater or lesser extent reveal, a fuller and more questioning analysis of the treatment of female characters in fiction, through their role and prospects in society (that is to say, a highlighting of the *zhenskii vopros*). It also points up, as indicated above, the contributions to this body of fiction made by the women writers of the period – *zhenskie pisatel'nitsy*, only recently rediscovered, republished and re-assessed. At a time when prose fiction by women writers is establishing itself as a leading force in the new Russian literature (through contemporary society narratives from Tat'iana Tolstaia, Liudmila Petrushevskaia and others), it is less than totally edifying to hear Boris Yeltsin's view voiced abroad that Russian boys will continue to dream of becoming cosmonauts, while Russian girls will continue to dream of marrying them! One might begin to wonder just how far, for all its tale-telling, Russian society has really come since the 1830s.

This collection is based on the proceedings (with extra contributions added) of a symposium on 'The Society Tale' held at the University of Bristol in July 1996 (under the auspices of the Nineteenth-Century Studies Group of the British Association of Slavonic and East European Studies).

The editor is grateful for the generous and invaluable efforts of Birgit Beumers in the final preparation of this volume.

VLADIMIR ODOEVSKII AND THE SOCIETY TALE IN THE 1820s AND 30s

NEIL CORNWELL

It has become a commonplace of Odoevskii criticism to say that he enjoyed three almost discrete literary careers.[1] The first took place during the era of the Liubomudry and the publication of the almanac *Mnemozina*, in Moscow in the first half of the 1820s (and was interrupted by the events of 14 December 1825). The second, coinciding with much of Odoevskii's Petersburg period, extended from the late 1820s until the publication of his *Sochineniia* (*Works*) in 1844 – during which decade and a half he wrote almost all the works for which he is now remembered. And the third comprised a late flurry, in a minor key, back in Moscow in the 1860s. With regard to the society tale, as with much else, the second, or major, period of Odoevskii's literary career is generally, and not surprisingly, held to be the most important: the period which gave us *Kniazhna Mimi* (*Princess Mimi*) and *Kniazhna Zizi* (*Princess Zizi*), as well as a number of shorter works in that style and a number of unfinished projects, some at least of which were coloured in a distinctly society tale (*svetskaia povest'*) hue.

Before considering the works of the 1830s, however, it is worth looking more closely than has been usual at the somewhat precocious fictional endeavours of Odoevskii's early period.[2] Arguably, their artistic immaturity notwithstanding, some of these works may, from the generic perspective of our present preoccupation, take on an interest, and perhaps even an importance, that has seldom been recognised.

Until and unless a viable link emerges that would bridge the works of social setting of the eighteenth century (which are generally assumed to have arisen largely from an impulse to imitate or follow French trends

---

[1] See for instance Ch. Vetrinskii, 'Chelovek trekh pokolenii', in his *V sorokovykh godakh: istoriko-literaturnye ocherki i kharakteristiki*, Moscow, 1899.

[2] For a brief general account of Odoevskii's writing of this period, see Neil Cornwell, *The Life, Times and Milieu of V.F. Odoyevsky 1804-1869*, London, Athone Press / Athens, Ohio, Ohio University Press, 1986, pp. 31-7.

of salon literature, often theatrically based) and those of the 1820s
(arising once again from a largely French-inspired post-Enlightenment
penchant for an instructional didacticism that often included elements
of social satire), the era of the early 1820s will remain as appearing to
have fostered the beginnings of the society tale – at least in the sense
that we are here using and understanding the term. Again, drama is to
the fore, with Griboedov and Shakhovskoi featuring as the most
prominent exponents, but the social elements were quickly spreading
into both verse and prose. In the case of prose fiction, this led to what
we are calling the *svetskaia povest'*. Vladimir Odoevskii, in the early
1820s, certainly appears to have been among the first writers to break
this path in Russian prose. Not all commentators, though, have chosen
to emphasize his work in terms of the 'society tale' as such: the phrases
'nravopistael'nye povesti' ('novellas of manners') and *'prosvetitel'skii
realizm'* ('educational realism') have also been applied.[3]

When Belinskii reviewed Odoevskii's *Sochinenia* in three volumes
of 1844, from which virtually the whole body of his work of the 1820s
had been omitted, he stressed the historical importance and the novelty
to Russian literature of Odoevskii's contribution from this period – by
then long neglected, and by now totally forgotten. He praised the rather
skimpy and schematic apologues as something completely new in
Russian literature and went so far as to reprint the texts of two of them
in his review article.[4] In addition to the apologue (which may be
considered an alternative term for 'fable' – often, but not always, of the
'beast' variety – but, in Odoevskii's case, unlike that of Krylov, written
in prose), was cultivating the form of what we may now consider the
proto-society tale. The first significant works of this type, published as
early as 1822-3 (when their author was about eighteen), were a series
appearing under the title, or in some cases the subtitle, of *Pis'ma k*

---

[3]See for example N.M. Mikhailovskaia's articles, 'Nravopisatel'nye povesti V.F.
Odoevskogo', in *Voprosy istorii i teorii literatury*, VI, Cheliabinsk, 1970, pp. 3-16; and
'Prosvetitel'skii realizm 20-kh godov XIX veka (o proze pisatelia)', in *Problemy
metoda i stilia*, Cheliabinsk, 1976, pp. 117-31.

[4]V.G. Belinskii, 'Sochineniia kniazia V.F. Odoevskogo', *Polnoe sobranie sochinenii*,
vol. 8, Moscow, 1955, pp. 297-323 (reprinted with cuts in V.F. Odoevskii, *Poslednii
kvartet Betkhovena*, Moscow, 1982). On Belinskii and Odoevskii, see Neil Cornwell,
Vladimir Odoevsky and Romantic Poetics: Collected Essays, Oxford, Berghahn Books,
1998 (which includes a revised version of the article first published in *The Slavonic
and East European Review*, 62, 1, 1984, pp. 6-24).

luzhnitskomu startsu ('Letters to the Luzhnitskii Elder'), published in *Vestnik Evropy*.[5] The 'Luzhnitskii starets' was a pen-name of that journal's proprietor, M.T. Kachenovskii, also professor of aesthetic theory and archeology. It was the publication of these 'Letters' that first drew Griboedov's attention to the young Odoevskii (he being too a distant relation of the Odoevskii cousins).

Griboedov was curious as to the authorship of these anonymously published letters and his uncovering of this led to a close friendship over a number of years (though one of a lesser intensity than that between Griboedov and Aleksandr Odoevskii). Vladimir Odoevskii met Griboedov at Moscow musical evenings, certainly in 1823 if not before, and they shared a deep scholarly interest in musical theory.[6] Odoevskii subsequently claimed to have heard almost the whole of *Gore ot uma* (*Woe from Wit*) recited even before it had been committed to paper, and a number of pre-revolutionary critics drew comparisons between early Odoevskii works and *Gore ot uma*, in particular between Odoevskii's protagonist Arist and Griboedov's Chatskii – some even identifying the young Odoevskii himself as a prototype for Chatskii.[7] Odoevskii, it is certainly the case, leapt in print to Griboedov's defence in the critical controversy over *Gore ot uma*.[8] In the 1830s, he signalled further his own debt to Griboedov by using the names of two of the latter's minor characters for his main contributions to the genre of the society tale, the *povesti* (or novellas) *Kniazhna Mimi* and *Kniazhna Zizi*.

A figure named Arist was the protagonist of a number of Odoevskii's early attempts at the society tale, including *Dni dosad* (*Days of Vexation*) and *Strannyi chelovek* (*The Strange Man*), both parts of the 'Luzhnitskii starets' series. It was indeed the figure of Arist and the title and concept of the '*strannyi chelovek*' that prompted

---

[5]This series was published in *Vestnik Evropy*, 1822: nos. 9-10, pp. 302-10; 11-12, pp. 305-12; 13-14, pp. 140-46; and 20, pp. 280-98; and 1823: nos. 9, pp. 34-45; 11, pp. 206-16; 15, pp. 219-26; 16, pp. 299-311; 17, pp. 24-48; and 18, pp. 104-25 (see bibliography to Cornwell, 1986, cited in note 2 above, p. 375).

[6]On Odoevskii and Griboedov, see Cornwell, 1986, pp. 234-37 and passim.

[7]For a list of nineteenth-century commentators who made such a suggestion, see Cornwell, 1986, p. 293, note 33.

[8]V.F. Odoevskii, 'Zamechaniia na suzhdeniia Mikh. Dmitrieva o komedii *Gore ot uma*', *Moskovskii telegraf*, 3, 10, 1825, pp. 1-12 (reprinted in *A.S. Griboedov v russkoi kritike: sbornik statei*, Moscow, 1958; and in V.F. Odoevskii, *O literature i iskusstve*, Moscow, 1982).

suggestions of the role played by Odoevskii in establishing an early prototype of the 'superfluous man' (along with Griboedov's Chatskii, Venevitinov's unfinished *Vladimir Parenskii*, and on to Onegin; and Lermontov's early dramatic attempt, also entitled *Strannyi chelovek*.[9] Arist, it should be said, is a sharp-witted and highly educated figure, normally assumed to be something approaching an authorial alter ego, whose interests in literary, musical and philosophical matters make him 'strange' to the philistine aristocratic society surrounding him, interested only in the perennial round of society balls and intrigue, cards and honours lists.

Arist, like an even earlier Odoevskii hero, the student of the unpublished 'Dnevnik studenta' ('The Diary of a Student', 1820-21), is drawn to an inner world of books and manuscripts, while keeping a ready tongue with which to combat his adversaries; finally he withdraws to a life of study and contemplation in the country, despairing of the idleness, vanity and ignorance pervading the society drawing-room. Society personages bear names reminiscent of characters from the comedies of Fonvizin and Griboedov – names which not infrequently recur in other Odoevskii works: Graf Gluposilin, Kniazhna Pustiakova and the money-lender Protsentin. Conversations are mounted on science, opera, Russian folksong and Schellingian philosophy (by this time flavour of the month at the Raich circle and taken here by Odoevskii's fictional 'society automata' to be 'Japanese'). Both ignorance and artificial conventions are attacked, especially Odoevskii's particular *bête noire*, the society ball. An older man, one Ernestov, acts as Arist's foil and conversation partner, being of somewhat like mind but of considerably greater 'experience'; in trying to reconcile Arist to the social scene he plays something of the demonic tempter: '[Ernestov's] smile seemed to me like Satan's smile when he tortures a sinner', we are told.[10]

While Arist may have been of some consequence in the development towards the superfluous man in Russian literature, of greater interest, arguably, to the theme of the society tale is the story *Elladii*, published in *Mnemozina* II in 1824, and subtitled '*kartina iz*

---

[9]See B.T. Udodov, *M.Iu. Lermontov: khudozhestvennaia individual'nost' i tvorcheskie protsessy*, Voronezh, 1973, pp. 519-25.
[10]*Vestnik Evropy*, 18, 1823, p. 118. English translations are my own, unless otherwise stated.

svetskoi zhizni' ('a picture from high-society life').[11] *Elladii* is thin in
both plot and characterization, its narrative method a pallid version of a
barely personalized and largely withdrawn first-person narration, which
depends almost entirely on 'telling', rather than 'showing'. The
plotline involves surrogate parentage, star-crossed lovers, cheating at
cards, suggestions of near incest, and societal intrigue based on malice
aforethought, mischievous marriage-making and dowry-seeking.
Finally, the villain, one Dobrynskii, facilitates what is to be a less than
happy ending by means of a death-bed confession of his transgressions,
having been fortuitously and gratuitously crushed by frightened horses:
he dies and his accomplices beg forgiveness; the heroine recovers from
a threatening inherited illness to marry another, while the sensitive
eponymous hero, mortified by the machinations enacted against him,
sinks into madness and melancholy.

While the artistic level of this tale might well in the normal way
continue to preclude it from serious notice, there are both intrinsic and
extrinsic factors that may render it worthy, for present purposes at
least, of some attention. Internally, one can point – with such
characterization as there is – to two types of *strannyi chelovek*. The
negative version, incongruously named Dobrynskii (who happens to
have a sidekick called Khrabrov), is introduced first in a positive light,
but with references to 'his extremely penetrating eyes' and his 'ever
ironic smile'.[12] His similarly studious but positive counterpart Elladii,
who is equally ill at ease in society, is graced with a 'contemplative
gaze' across which there not infrequently 'steals a mocking smile' (p.
106). Such characteristics of *ennui*, superfluity or 'outsiderdom'
become the stock in trade of future strange and superfluous types, both
in Odoevskii's mature works and more particularly in the cases of
better known figures created by subsequent Russian writers. Of
historical significance, one might suggest, is the – at first sight perhaps
– surprisingly high esteem in which Belinskii, in his writings of the
1830s and 40s, held Odoevskii's prose of the 1820s. *Elladii*, indeed, he
lauded as the first real *povest'* of Russian reality; admitting however
that the story itself was 'weak'.[13]

---

[11]*Mnemozina*, II, 1824, pp. 94-135 (reprinted as *Mnemozina: Sobranie sochinenii v
stikhakh i proze, I-IV*, Hildesheim, Georg Olms, 1986).
[12]Ibid., p. 101.
[13]Belinskii, *Pol. sob. soch.*, vol. 8, p. 300.

Belinskii was not so misguided a critic as to claim great artistic merit for such a work as *Elladii*, but he did discern in it the first attempt at depicting Russian society, not in the usual unrealistic idealized way, but as the author actually saw it. Belinskii also detected a certain originality and freshness in the composition of *Elladii* and in the feelings about society that the author was trying to arouse. Odoevskii's view of *bol'shoi svet* (high society) was indeed a critical one (particularly so in his somewhat 'angry young man' pre-Decembrist days); however, his critique was based rather on the excesses, weaknesses, philistinism and immorality of individuals rather than any real criticism of the social structure. Greed, card-playing and malicious lying are the motivating forces in *Elladii*; the plot a mere contrivance of sentimentalism and sub-melodrama. The story, then, compares unfavourably with, but points the way towards, Odoevskii's principal society tales of the 1830s, *Kniazhna Mimi* and *Kniazhna Zizi*. Furthermore, if Belinskii read with some admiration the youthful Odoevskii's works (either when of tender years himself and/or retrospectively, as the case may be) it seems reasonable to suppose that neither might their impact, at the time, have been entirely lost on other actual or budding literary figures.

Odoevskii's work of the 1830s contains much with a society-tale setting, including the frame elements of both his completed and major cycles, *Pestrye skazki* (*Variegated* – or 'Motley' – *Tales*) and *Russkie nochi* (*Russian Nights*). Such settings can embrace either the familiar *bol'shoi svet*, as in these works, or a more restricted depiction of the idealistic intelligentsia (as they later came to be known) of the 1820s, as in the story *Novyi god* (*New Year*). In addition, many of Odoevskii's fantastic/Gothic stories also take place in the contemporary, or near-contemporary, *haut monde*, notably *Kosmorama* (*The Cosmorama*) and *Zhivoi mertvets* (*The Live Corpse*), to name but two. The same can be said of several of the individual stories within *Russkie nochi* – a formal eccentricity in itself, as a philosophical novel-cum-frame-tale.[14] Furthermore, there are lesser known curiosities, such as the novelistic fragment, *Katia, ili istoriia vospitannitsy* (*Katia, or the Story of a*

---

[14]For an examination of the form of *Russkie nochi*, see Cornwell, 1998, cited in note 4 above (which includes a revised version of the article first published in *Essays in Poetics*, 8, 2, 1983, pp. 19-55).

Young Ward) and Odoevskii's only completed play, quaintly entitled *Khoroshee zhalovan'e, prilichnaia kvartira, stol, osveshchenie i otoplenie* (*A Good Salary, a Decent Appartment, Board, Lighting and Heating*, of 1837). The play develops a Tartuffe (or Stepanchikovo)-like situation, in which an unpricipled tutor takes over a household (over decades, in a highly extravagant chronology), to indulge his criminal activities.

Katia, published in 1834 and bearing the subtitle 'A fragment from a novel', deals with what Odoevskii calls 'the life of our middle class', the wards (*vospitanitsy*) from the lower orders, brought up 'charitably' by the more 'benevolent' elements of the aristocracy; such unfortunates are normally destined 'to spend their whole span in eternal celibacy, or to get married to some clerk of the fourteenth class'.[15] The story contains much social detail and a potentially interesting plotline develops between the eponymous heroine and a male ward of artistic proclivities (one Vladimir), whereupon the narrative abruptly breaks off. Surviving drafts for a continuation, however, suggest that Odoevskii intended to turn Katia not into a victim, but into a rich and ruthless financial wheeler-dealer ('*otkupshchitsa-milionersha*').[16]

As already suggested, *Zhivoi mertvets* (written 1838, published 1844, and a tale of mixed genre), can be considered, amongst other things, a society tale, albeit of a somewhat phantasmagoric nature; with *Kosmorama* this qualification is even more essential. Other stories of the period of an approximate society nature include *Chernaia perchatka* (*The Black Glove*, 1838), a didactic tale directed against English ideas and upbringing (such as Benthamism and English methods of estate management); and *Svidetel'* (*The Witness*, 1839), a short work reviving the theme of the duel, carried over from *Kniazhna Mimi* and no doubt re-elevated to consciousness by the death of Pushkin (as well as being of probable interest to Dostoevskii at a much later stage). A little-known candidate for consideration here is the story *Dusha zhenshchiny* (*A Woman's Soul*, 1841), which could be read almost as a tasteless tongue-in-cheek epilogue to *Kniazhna Zizi*. This work (not reprinted since 1844) comprises a confrontation between the soul of a society lady, just deceased, and her 'guardian spirit', who narrates her past life in the second person. The heroine of this

---

[15]V.F. Odoevskii, *Sochineniia v dvukh tomakh*, vol. 2, Moscow, 1981, p. 46.
[16]See ibid., p. 348.

somewhat unusual version of the society tale with a metaphysical setting – or rather her soul – is eventually condemned, despite having lived a life of apparent self-sacrifice (fidelity to a loathesome arranged marriage, the rejection of lovers), for 'the pride of humility' (*'gordost' smireniia').*[17]

Odoevskii's society tales of this period are therefore in many ways a recognizable continuation of the main trends of his fiction of the 1820s: the tone is frequently 'instructional' (or educational); the setting is predominantly the salon and the ballroom; the subject matter is mainly society intrigue (or 'drawing-room secrets'); under scrutiny are the mores of aristocratic society and such associated factors – becoming by now increasingly prominent – as the 'women's question' (*zhenskii vopros*). This theme is in any case the dominant one in his two principal society tales, to which we now turn.

Kniazhna Mimi (of 1834) is Odoevskii's most outspoken attack on the destructive, hypocritical and sterile aspects of *svetskaia zhizn'*, or *le beau monde*. It is, however, better known to many for its compositional quirks: the interposing of the digressive authorial 'Predislovie' (preface) about two thirds of the way through the story; and the comments on the anomalous state of the Russian literary language vis-à-vis salon French. The main artistic weakness is the hasty and melodramatic dénouement (a fatal duel and the wasting away in shame of a second hapless victim, the Baroness), merely summarised in an abrupt conclusion. The main interest lies in the relatively sophisticated attempt at the psychological portraiture of the vicious eponymous protagonist, Mimi, and in the treatment of the female question.

While Odoevskii may be criticized with late twentieth-century hindsight for investing one of his more elaborate characterizations in an unambiguously negative female figure, the elevation by a male writer of albeit such a character to a position of centrality was in itself unusual at this stage in such works of Russian fiction.[18] Furthermore, he may properly be justified in emphasizing the role played by certain *damy* (society ladies) as society's representatives, acting as guardians

---

[17]V.F. Odoevskii, *Sochineniia*, St Petersburg, 1844, Part III, p. 97.

[18]See Joe Andrew, *Narrative and Desire: Masculine and Feminine in Russian Literature, 1822-1849*, Basingstoke and London, Macmillan, 1993, pp. 50-84, for a less than totally sympathetic reading of Odoevskii's treatment of the female question.

of male hegemony in the policing of female purity for patriarchal benefit.

> There are actions which are prosecuted by society: the guilty perish, the innocent perish. There are people who sow misfortune with both hands, who arouse disgust for humanity in the souls of the high and gentle, who, in a word, triumphantly undermine the foundations of society, and society warms them in its bosom like a meaningless sun which indifferently rises both above the cries of hostile battle and above the prayer of the wise man.[19]

In any event, his overall attitude towards the position of women appears less hostile or indifferent than that of many other writers of his period. Odoevskii's stance on the position of women in society is perhaps not so very far from that to be adopted subsequently by Tolstoi, while (happily!) sparing us the latter's negative obsession with sexuality. There is criticism of the system of arranged marriage and of marriage in general as the only objective for women that is encouraged by society; those who miss out, like Mimi, may understandably turn bitter and will enjoy unlimited leisure in which to set themselves up as venomous arbiters of the so-called 'moral estate' ('*nravstvennoe soslovie*'). Mimi 'could have become either a good wife and a good mother of a family', we are told, 'or that which she had now become'; in any case, even at best, 'wives had a voice and power by virtue of their husbands'.[20]

Odoevskii's concern with female education, observable in a number of his works, appears to demonstrate that he, perhaps unusually progressively for a male writer of the 1830s, favoured a more positive alternative. His second major society tale of the 1830s, *Kniazhna Zizi*, was written in 1836 (in time to gain the approval of Pushkin) and published in 1839. In this work, more convoluted plotwise than its sister-tale *Knizhna Mimi* and again experimental in terms of narrative presentation (relying largely on dialogue and the epistolary form), Odoevskii provides a variant depiction of the unmarried woman. Princess Zizi (Zinaida) retains her integrity and wins through against the odds, taking on the legal system as well as her swindling and

---

[19]Odoevskii, *Sochineniia*, vol. 2, 1981, p. 257 (English translation by David Lowe, *The Ardis Anthology of Russian Romanticism*, edited by Christine Rydel, Ann Arbor, Ardis, 1984, p. 310).
[20]Odoevskii, *Sochineniia*, vol. 2, 1981, p, 222; *The Ardis Anthology of Russian Romanticism*, p. 287.

lecherous brother-in-law (who, though, it has perhaps to be said, is once again dispatched at the crucial moment through the agency of unruly horses – acting as *equus ex machina*).

Zizi, who is several times referrred to as '*strannaia*', a '*bol'shaia chudikha*' ('great eccentric') or a '*chudak*' (similarly 'eccentric':'*v nei mnogo strannostei*'; and '*v nei mnogo, mnogo strannogo*', we are told)[21] may be seen as Odoevskii's attempt to portray the arguably new type of a *strannaia zhenshchina* ('strange woman'), who is allowed, in a final plot-twist, to remain in a triumphant and even envied form of spinsterhood: still attracting the attentions of would-be admirers, at least until she removes her domino mask and shows her age. While such a portrayal might appear less than an ideal of liberation from a late twentieth-century perspective, it is at least striking for its period. The work is deliberately littered with literary references and clichés, furnishing it with a strong veneer of romantic pastiche; nevertheless, Odoevskii's consistent stress over a number of works on the *zhenskii vopros* as a strong part of his social, or societal, critique justifies overall the assertion that a serious element here underlies the generally tongue-in-cheek approach.

One of the few western commentators to examine *Kniazhna Zizi*, Lewis Bagby, remarks that the use of the word '*strannyi / strannaia*' here serves as a leitmotif for the ironic function of 'masking' and 'unmasking' in what is a complex narrative structure, self-consciously poised at a transitional point in the development of Russian fiction.[22] Pioneer as he was of the concept of the *strannoe*, Odoevskii failed to develop his younger version of the 'strange type' (*strannyi tip*) much beyond the period of his own youth, although the protagonists of such fantastic tales as *Sil'fida* (*The Sylph*) and *Salamandra* (*The Salamander*) do have certain claims in that direction. Zizi – his *strannaia zhenshchina* – apart, he preferred instead to develop the type of the somewhat less immediately appealing middle-aged male pedant and encyclopaedic alter-ego (another projection of his own personality, visible in life even in his younger years), such as Gomozeiko (of *Pestrye skazki* and other works), Faust (of *Russkie nochi*), and the

---

[21]['There is much strangeness in her'; 'there is much, much strangeness in her'] Odoevskii, *Sochineniia*, vol. 2, 1981, pp. 258-303.

[22]Lewis Bagby, 'V.F. Odoevskij's "Kniazhna Zizi"', *Russian Literature*, 17-3, 1985, pp. 221-42.

uncle in the second part of *Salamandra*. These figures therefore follow, in terms of Odoevskii's literary characters, his early-1820s prototype of the experienced mentor, Ernestov of *Elladii*.

Many of Odoevskii's literary endeavours may have been at least temporarily lost or neglected in transition, but his contribution to the society tale and its input into mainstream Russian fiction is not to be underestimated. Odoevskii's society tales, taken as a body of work, contain a considerable store of detail on Russian society of the first third of the nineteenth century. Many of them employ a retrospective chronology, stretching back over a number of years, with the occasional hint that 'now' things might have changed just slightly. An element of ambiguity or uncertainty is accentuated throughout by the employment of irony, eccentric modes of narration, schematic characterization, pastiche and other devices commonly found in European and Russian romantic prose. However, visible in these and other works (as indeed in the prose and longer poems of Pushkin) are the basic plotlines, dramatic situations, character types and configurations, albeit often in a relatively primeval form, that were to recur throughout Russian fiction for the rest of the century, from the work of the young Dostoevskii to the prose of Chekhov.

POINTING OUT THE POWER PARADOX: PUSHKIN'S SOCIETY TALE PARODIES

S. DALTON-BROWN

Vsia nyneshniaia literaturnaia nagota est' poslednii otblesk proshedshei deistvitel'noi zhizni ... nyneshniaia literatura ...est' kazn' ... Mozhet byt', nuzhno nashemu veku eto sil'noe sredstvo; mozhet' byt', ono, bespreryvno potriasaia ego nervy, probudit ego zasnuvshuiu sovest', kak telesnoe stradanie probuzhdaet utoplennika.

All this present-day literary nakedness is the remaining reflection of actual past life... present-day literature... is a punishment... Perhaps our age needs this strong means of expression; perhaps this method, constantly stunning the nerves, will awaken the age's sleeping conscience, just as bodily suffering awakens a drowning man.

V.F. Odoevskii, *Kniazhna Mimi* (1834)

The *svetskaia povest'*, that genre which developed in the late 1820s and 30s in Russia (dying out in the early 1850s), initially appears to be quite a simplistic literary form. It has very clearly defined conventions, such as four simple plot paradigms, four stock characters, five types of discourse, and a somewhat over-utilized stock of set phrases, tropes and settings.[1] The only unconventionality appears to lie in narrative types and structures, for on any list of 'society tales' one finds novels (even novels in verse, such as Pushkin's *Evgenii Onegin*, 1823-30); hybrid forms, such Karolina Pavlova's *Dvoinaia zhizn'* (*A Double Life*, 1848), a novel with poetic inserts; short stories and tales with dialogue represented in the form of stage speeches.[2] Narrative retardation is another favoured device, the prime example of which is Odoevskii's

---

[1] Carol Ayers distinguishes five types of social discourse, or social strategies, for communication: gossip, education (moral maxims), declarations of love, letters and natural conservation. See C.J. Ayers, 'Social Discourse in the Russian Society Tale', unpublished PhD dissertation, University of Chicago, 1994, pp. 65-6. See also O. Tsvetkov, 'Aspects of the Russian Society Tale of the 1830s', unpublished PhD dissertation, University of Michigan, 1984.

[2] V.G. Belinskii refused to accept that such a genre as the *'svetskaia povest''* existed; see his *Polnoe sobranie sochinenii*, Moscow, 1953-9, vol. 2, p. 133.

Kniazhna Mimi (*Princess Mimi*, 1834), in which the preface is placed two-thirds of the way through the text.[3]

The society tale focuses on the glittering world of the Russian aristocracy, usually depicted against a St Petersburg background of salons and theatres (although foreign spas or Moscow are also used), often interspersed with contrasting scenes of country life. The basic plot involves a naive heroine (or naive hero), whose passion for the hero/ine is either thwarted, due to his lack of status or wealth, or minor impediments such as her own married condition; or it is defeated by vicious society gossip, or by the cynicism of the loved one, who turns out to have been corrupted by society and is therefore incapable of returning her/his passion. This simple plot conflict between heart and society is then decorated with copious depictions of ball scenes, dresses, often duels, and intermixed with references to and portraits of leading society figures of that period, leading the reader to assume that the text is in part merely an amusing trifle, a nineteenth-century fictional form of today's gossip column.

The function and purpose of the society tale is not quite as easy to determine. It is not merely written to amuse, and, indeed, the often rather interminable conversational sections and the cliché-ridden nature of many of the texts render them somewhat less than witty. They do provide a good opportunity for social criticism; these heartless, glittering figures who move against the background of an artificial world in which only money and social status count are clearly not real people, but automatons, who have sold their souls for status and who are bored, jaded and incapable of feeling. The central concern of the society tale appears to be that of providing an unhappy love story as a means of exposing society's heartlessness. With few exceptions, such as Aleksandr Marlinskii's *Ispytanie* (*The Test*, of 1830), and Elena Gan's *Nomirovannaia lozha* (*The Numbered Box*, 1840),[4] the *svetskaia povest'* ends with love defeated and malicious society still supreme.[5] Love, the most powerful part of the society tale, is constantly rendered

---

[3]A point made by Neil Cornwell, in his *The Life, Times and Milieu of V.F. Odoyevsky*, London, The Athlone Press, 1986, p. 53.

[4]A point made by V. Korobin, 'Sredi bol'shogo sveta', in *Russkaia svetskaia povest' pervoi poloviny XIX veka*, Moscow, 1990, p. 7.

[5]Rather surprisingly, for they demonstrate love's impotence and defeat rather than celebrate it, *svetskie povesti* have appeared in, for instance, a collection entitled *Russkaia romanticheskaia povest'*, Moscow, 1980.

impotent in a society in which marriage, essential for any kind of social power for women, nearly always denies them the opportunity for emotional self-expression. This imparts a rather titillating atmosphere to many society tales; the heart, or rather, the flesh is, it seems, willing, for hero and heroine are constantly described in terms of blushing cheeks, heaving bosoms and piercing glances and all the other physical clichés of the genre; but the genre itself is weak, and, losing its nerve, takes refuge in voyeurism, refusing to permit passion to run unbridled.

The society tale, in fact, acts as a warning to women who, although seduced by the beckoning tide of the passions, will generally find that emotional indulgence leads to destruction. However, this does not make the genre particularly happy with itself. The society tale, albeit it seems so glittering and playful (the word '*svet*', used both in the sense of light, and of the fashionable world, is mentioned constantly, and there is frequent reference to shining diamonds and champagne glasses, to the whiteness of marble furnishings and gauzy dresses), is a darkly troubled genre. Passion puts dangerous tears in the social fabric and is naive and idealistic, yet most society men and women clothe themselves in propriety – not through any particular sense of moral virtue, but purely through caution and self-concern. Even 'honour', that so-called central pillar of society, appears rather shaky when viewed closely; honour appears to derive from bad temper, spleen, and possessiveness towards women.

Society-tale writers have of course attempted to transcend the limitations of the genre, or to utilize them consciously in order to offer rather more defensible ideas. Other 'messages' to the reader, beside the cynical creed defined above, can be found in most society tales, which either offer an educative lesson, point out the limits of rationalism, use humour to show how farcical the pursuit of social status is, or dig deeper, into the psychological motivations of the (usually rather one-dimensional) hero and heroine, in order to see how such an artificial social environment can have been created. Pushkin is the writer most known for transcending the society tale's conventions for the purposes of parody. His intent is, as always with Pushkin, both playful (for the genre does lend itself beautifully to parody) and serious.

In the novel *Evgenii Onegin* (1823-31), the stories *Vystrel* (*The Shot*), from *Povesti Belkina* (*The Tales of Belkin*, 1830), and *Pikovaia dama* (*The Queen of Spades*, 1833), Pushkin takes various society-tale conventions (such as the naive heroine, the foppish lover, the duel, the society ball or scene of revelry, the love-letter, the declaration scene and the midnight assignation) and parodies them, in order to underline his concern with a familiar theme, one glimpsed in many other of his works – *Mednyi vsadnik* (*The Bronze Horseman*) being the prime example – that of power and powerlessness. The central paradox of the genre is one he underlines and exploits, showing that social power is gained only at the cost of emotional impotence; and, also, that social power is ephemeral, for society men and women are weak, passive, impotent, or (adding perhaps another layer of paradox) at the mercy of their passions – but not the passion of love; rather, they lust for wealth and status.

The three texts referred to above are not the only texts in which Pushkin demonstrates his interest in the society-tale genre. His *svetskie* texts include the three fragments, 'Gosti s"ezhalis' na dachu' ('The guests were arriving at the dacha ...', 1828-30), 'Roman v pis'makh' ('A Novel in Letters', 1829), 'Na uglu malen'koi ploshchadi' ('In the corner of a small square ...', 1830-1), as well as the draft for a novel 'Russkii Pelam;' ('A Russian Pelham', 1834-5),[6] and the unfinished *Egipetskie nochi* (*Egyptian Nights*, 1835), in all of which he outlines the conventions which he is later to parody. A brief discussion of *svetskaia povest'* conventions in the above texts, and in tales by other *svetskie* writers, serves as a counterpoint to Pushkin's later treatment of them in terms of the theme of power and powerlessness.

a) the warned, disillusioned and 'chained' heroine

The major figure in any society tale is the naive heroine (or, occasionally, a naive hero), who is educated through her contact with the 'real' world of society, which proves to be quite unlike her

---

[6]Pushkin's 'Russkii Pelam', written in 1834-5, but published only in 1841, the title of which obviously derives from the Victorian novelist Bulwer Lytton's archetypal society tale (*Pelham*, published in England in 1828), hardly exists, apart from a set of outlines for a tale based in part on incidents from the life of Pushkin's friend Fedor Orlov, whose somewhat indecorous activities Pelam assists in, or bears witness to. See S. Driver, *Pushkin. Literature and Social Ideas,* New York, Columbia University Press, 1989, for a discussion of this fragmentary text. Another possible 'society tale' is Pushkin's *Arap Petra Velikogo* (*The Blackamoor of Peter the Great,* 1829), which does contain scenes of society life, albeit during the Petrine age.

romantic preconceptions of life. The turning of the text into a young lady's primer in which the only lesson is, paradoxically, 'beware of what you read, because it may be untrue', is one quite sophisticated way of using a negative aspect of the genre (its artificiality) as a positive. Most young society girls are brought up on the romantic model, imbibing Byron and Richardson amongst other romantic authors, leavened with sentimental texts and, at times, a few broadly idealistic philosophical ideas. The cynical lesson the society tale offers is of course that a view of love based on reading is artificial and bound to disappointment. This is one of the basics tenets of *Evgenii Onegin*, in the view of some critics the consummate society tale.[7] Literature and creativity are in general rather suspect, and 'sterile' (i.e. loveless) marriage is stronger. Even in a text such as Pavlova's *Dvoinaia zhizn'*, in which the heroine, Cecily, realises that marriage will probably mean the end of her creative life, the end to any chance, possibly, of becoming a poet (like her creator, Karolina Pavlova), marriage appears inevitable.[8] The rule of the crowd imposes its will, and this rule is that all women marry. Ergo, as is stated in the text, love will be '*vsegda neprava, / Vsegda bezvlastna*' ('ever untrue, / ever powerless') when pitted against the crowd; '*Ne sokrushish' tolpy ustava*' ('you will not smash the rule of the crowd'), says the narrator, addressing 'Love' directly.[9] Despite the fact that Pavlova's entire text, which has some moments of powerful expression, is a testament to the creative force, it appears that this creed is not seen as stronger than social mores and is even dangerous in its encouragement of anti-social daring in affairs of the heart.[10]

Pushkin parodies the literary influence on naive heroines in both *Evgenii Onegin* and *Pikovaia dama*. Tat'iana forms her ideas of life and

---

[7]See Ayers, op. cit., p. 107; she argues, however, that *Evgenii Onegin* is much broader than a standard society tale (pp. 10, 108).

[8]On Pavlova, see C. Kelly, *A History of Russian Women's Writing, 1820-1992*, Oxford, Clarendon Press, 1994, pp. 93-107; and D. Greene, 'Gender and Genre in Pavlova's A Double Life', *Slavic Review*, 54, 3, 1995, pp. 563-77.

[9]K. Pavlova, *Dvoinaia zhizn'*, in her *Polnoe sobranie stikhotvorenii*, Moscow-Leningrad, 1964, p. 295.

[10]The paradox of this lesson, however, is that, abandoning the artificial word of romantic patterns for the cynical world of society, heroines find themselves in an even more artificial world, one dominated by insincerity. One of the major tasks of the society tale is thought to be that of criticizing non-Russianness – i.e. the Western, artificial manners aped by the Russian aristocracy.

love from Richardson's tales of dashing and noble heroes, such as Sir
Charles Grandison or Lovelace;[11] Liza in *Pikovaia dama* opens her
heart to Germann (or Hermann) after reading his letters, which her
supposed suitor has copied from a German novel. It is no wonder that
women in the society tales, in some ways a broadly feminist genre
concerned with women's unhappy marital lot, tend to become the
ultimate cynics, able to perceive falsity under actual sincerity, and
suspicious of everyone. The best portrait of such a type is Odoevskii's
Kniazhnia Mimi, in the text of that name, an embittered spinster who
carries her spiteful suspicions of another society hostess, Baroness
Dauertal', to such an extreme that the Baroness dies from 'shame', and
her supposed lover, Granitskii (who in reality is pursing quite another
woman), dies in a duel. When Mimi and her companions are accused of
'having killed' the latter, Mimi argues; '*ubivaiut ne liudi, a bezakonnye
strasti*' ('it is not people who kill, but illicit passions'),[12] a neat way of
avoiding the responsibility she undoubtedly bears. Here one sees the
power available to women, once they renounce literary models of
behaviour; the power of scandal and spite.

Odoevskii arguably owes a debt to Pushkin, whose portrait of the
spiteful octogenarian Countess in *Pikovaia dama* had appeared the year
before. Pushkin's irony is clear in his depiction of the Countess as a
kind of social idol; she is the one to whom guests, arriving at social
occasions, first bow, '*kak po ustanovlennomu obriadu*' ('as in
accordance with an established rite').[13] An ugly, and now sexless (due
to her advanced years and despite her somewhat dashing youth) figure,
she encapsulates the real goal of society: not the admiration of beauty,
but of power, status and money. Pushkin appears to be allowing women
some power; however, it is not real. The Countess is powerful, but not
free. She has sold her soul to the devil for the secret of the cards, and
the devil comes to claim her in the form of Germann. In *Pikovaia
dama*, Pushkin brings to a climax his manipulation of *svetskie*
conventions and his concept of man's powerlessness. The Countess is
the ultimate symbol of heartlessness, constantly referred to in the text

---

[11]Tat'iana reads pre-Byronic works; she discovers Byron in depth later, in Onegin's
library: see J. Falen's annotations to *Eugene Onegin*, Oxford, OUP/World's Classics,
1995, p. 233.
[12]V.F. Odoesvkii, *Kniazhna Mimi*, in his *Povesti i rasskazy*, Moscow, 1959, p. 180.
[13]A.S. Pushkin, *Pikovaia dama*, edited by J. Forsyth, Oxford, Blackwell, 1986, p. 9.
Further quotations within the text are taken from this edition.

in terms of being 'barely alive', or 'outlived'; she is barely human, sunk in '*kholodnyi egoizm*' ('cold egoism', p. 9). Yet passion, which she has long since killed, enters her house, not in the guise of a lover, but in the form of a gross parody of the lover, for Germann lusts not for her but for her money, and ultimately for the power which riches will give him in society. Man may think he has risen, in society, above passion, into safety; but even in the bright world of the *bol'shoi svet* the darkness and danger of anarchic feeling can penetrate, and kill – or, at least, frighten to death. Society, in effect, unleashes the demons which destroy it.

The lesson the society tale heroine learns, therefore, is not merely one of disillusionment or suspicion. She learns the true nature of her state – one of captivity. Women such as Mimi or the Countess are indeed not merely keepers of social morals, as Mimi likes to think she is; they are, paradoxically, powerful jailers, ensuring that other women (such as the Countess's ward, Liza) feel the weight of their chains, the chains they themselves bear. Although society-tale writers often point this out rather unsubtly (particularly women writers such as Evdokiia Rostopchina, Elena Gan, and Mariia Zhukova), a more sophisticated form of the encoding of this theme can be found in the plot structures commonly used in the genre. Lack of freedom is the message conveyed clearly through three of the common plot types – the Cinderella variation, the chained lady and the cynical tale – while the fourth plot type, the 'death plot', used to significant effect in Pushkin's parodies of the genre, is the most sophisticated medium for this theme.

The Cinderella variation can be clearly seen in a text such as Evdokiia Rostopchina's *Chiny i den'gi* (*Ranks and Money*, 1837), in which young Svirskii (the Cinderella in this case) cannot marry his beloved Vera because as he is told with brutal frankness, '*Vy ne bogaty, vy ne v chinakh*' ('You are not wealthy, you are not of high rank').[14] The law of this society is '*Imeiushchemu dast'sia!*' ('To he who has, shall be given!', p. 302), and Vera marries someone else with more status and money; there is no fairytale ending. A variant of this appears in Nadezhda Durova's rather odd tale *Ugol* (*The Corner*, 1840), in which the hero is a rich count, and the object of his affections is a beautiful girl whose grandmother unfortunately was a freed serf.

---

[14]*Chiny i den'gi*, in E. Rostopchina, *Stikhotvoreniia. Proza. Pis'ma*, Moscow, 1986, p. 305. Further page references are taken from this edition.

Although the two lovers do manage to marry, the wife has to spend the next few years hiding herself and her children from the Medusa gaze of her dragon of a mother-in-law, the Countess Trevil'skaia. This Cinderella plot results in Fetin'ia's becoming, through marriage, a 'chained lady' (who even has to change her name, becoming 'Fanichka'). Although her marriage is relatively happy, unlike those of the heroines of many *svetskie povesti*, who are shown to be 'chained' by boring, and often cruel, older men of high social status, she is still rendered powerless, trapped inside her husband's suite of rooms in the family house, with a door always kept locked in case she and her children are discovered by the Countess. The fairytale element of the society-tale genre is strongly suggested in this story, with the figure of the Countess, as always, becoming some kind of an ogre or witch, who keeps a very tight grasp on the keys to happiness.

The cynical story is probably the most prevalent type of *svetskaia povest'*. It is often a variant of the Cinderella story, as in Durova's *Graf Mavritsii* (*Count Mavritsii*, 1838), which at first promises a happy ending;[15] a count marries a beautiful peasant girl; but even in this apparently truly Cinderella story happiness soon turns sour, for the count and his beautiful Iuzefa divorce. Love cannot last. In some tales the lesson is that it cannot really even begin, due, mainly, to the genre's focus on the society male, who is far too filled with *ennui* to have strength for much passionate feeling. Another of the paradoxes of this confused genre is that, although women are encouraged to be self-sacrificing and to learn that love is not worth social ruin, men are encouraged to be fickle and cold.[16] Society-tale heroes may have the rhetoric of love, the Byronic stance and the pleasing phrase, but Byronic romanticism conceals coldness. As the narrator of *Evgenii Onegin* remarks, [Byron] '*Oblek v unylyi romantizm / I beznadezhnyi*

---

[15]As noted by V. Uchenova, 'Zvezdy vtoroi velichiny', in her foreword to *Stepnaia baryshnia. Proza russkikh pisatel'nits XIX veka*, Moscow, 1989, p. 7.

[16]Self-sacrifice has little reward; in Elena Gan's *Teofaniia Abbiadzhio* (1841), the work by Gan which was apparently most admired by Belinskii, the hero, Antonio, agrees to marry Teofaniia in order to pay off a debt owed by his father to hers; she agrees in order to rescue her family from poverty, and renounces Antonio when she realises that he is in love with another (Teofaniia's 'friend' Ol'ga), marrying the 60-year old, but rich, Ertonio instead, presumably in order to secure her family's future. In both cases sacrifice (Teofania's and Antonio's) is shown to be uncrowned by happiness.

egoizm' ('He clothed his self-absorbed dispair / With a romantic, weary air').[17]

b) the paradoxically impotent yet predatory hero

Based on the foppish model, a dandy type, the hero is easily bored and rather passive. These men after all 'have no identity other than as a creation of society';[18] mere puppets, they demonstrate little energy, except for the conquest of women's hearts. One of Pushkin's society pieces, 'Gosti s"ezhalis' na dachu', an outline for a psychological novel,[19] describes this type of man, contrasting Minskii with the unconventional and passionate, Zinaida, of whom her fellow society ladies (who, in order to protect their own status in society, have to preserve the image of chaste womanhood at all costs) mutter darkly that *'strasti ee pogubiat'* ('passions will be the undoing of her').[20] Minskii does not suspect that Zinaida's passion for him is the 'real thing' and not merely a social flirtation which he smugly sees in terms of conquest, and the narrator warns:

> *Veroiatno, esli b on mog voobrazit' buri, ego ozhidaiushchie, to otkalzalsia by ot svoego torzhestva, ibo svetskii chelovek legko zhertvuet svoimi naslazhdeniiami i dazhe tshcheslaviem leni i blagoprilichiiiu.* (470-71)
> It is likely that if he had anticipated the storms awaiting him, he would have declined his victory, because a man of high society readily sacrifices his pleasures – and even his vanity – for convenience and seemliness.[21]

---

[17]A. S. Pushkin, *Evgenii Onegin,* London, Bristol Classical Press, 1993 (III: 12, lines 13-14); translations taken from *Yevgeny Onegin,* edited by A.D.P. Briggs, London, Everyman, 1995, p. 61.

[18]Tsvetkov, op. cit., p. 47.

[19]'Gosti s"ezhalis' na dachu' exists in three fragments, the first two of which appeared in 1828 and the third in 1830. This unfinished piece is believed to be one of the stimuli for Tolstoi's *Anna Karenina.*

[20]'Gosti s"ezhalis' na dachu', A.S. Pushkin, *Sobranie sochinenii,* vol. 5, Moscow, 1960, p. 468. Further quotations are taken from this edition.

[21]In 'Gosti s"ezhalis' na dachu' Pushkin constructs a dialogue in which two men discuss the weather and women. The Russian repeats a foreign view of St Petersburgites as being noted for the strictness and purity of their morals and adds not without irony that *'dlia liubovnykh prikliuchenii nashi zimnie nochi slishkom kholodny, a letnie slishkom svetly'* ('our winter night are too cold and our summer nights too bright for amorous adventures'), p. 467; translation taken from Paul Debreczeny's version: *Alexander Pushkin: Complete Prose Fiction,* Stanford, Stanford University Press, 1983, pp. 41-6.

Two other fragments which Pushkin produced between 1828 and
March 1831, at the time when he was finishing the last two published
cantos of *Evgenii Onegin*,[22] are 'Na uglu malen'koi ploshchadi', a
fragment produced during November 1830 and March 1831, and
'Roman v pis'makh', written in 1829. Both also have heroes unable to
sustain their passion; for example, in 'Na uglu malen'koi ploshchadi',[23]
the precipitant action of Zinaida (this appears to be quite a favoured
name for society-tale heroines) in separating herself from her husband
in order to permit greater access to her person on the part of her lover,
Volodskii, fills the latter with deep despair. The liaison to him, once all
is permitted, becomes as tedious as checking the monthly household
accounts.[24]

Pushkin was to take the dandy type to its amusing extreme when he
depicted Onegin as, paradoxically, both rather sexually predatory and
as womanish (a theory supported by critics who have argued that
Onegin's stabbing of Lenskii reveals homosexual inclinations).[25]
Onegin either refuses 'masculine' power (when he rejects Tat'iana), or
'perverts' it, as in the dream scene, when he attacks Lenskii (not
Tat'iana) with the 'iron phallus': i.e. a knife, which later becomes the
gun with which he finally kills Lenskii.[26] Onegin is actually rather an

---

[22]L.S. Sidiakov, '"Evgenii Onegin" i nezavershennaia proza Pushkina 1828-1830
godov', in *Problemy pushkinovedeniia: Sbornik nauchnykh trud*, Leningrad, 1975, pp.
28-39.
[23]See A. Akhmatova, 'Benjamin Constant's *Adolphe* in the work of Pushkin', *Russian
Literature Triquarterly*, 10, 1974, in which Akhmatova argues (pp. 163-7) that 'Na
uglu ...' shows the influence of Constant's novel, and also discusses its influence on
Evgenii Onegin.
[24]'Na uglu malen'koi ploshchadi', A.S. Pushkin, *Sobranie sochinenii*, vol. 5, Moscow,
1960, p. 494. This is the second of the Pushkin fragments which is believed to have
influenced the writing of Tolstoi's *Anna Karenina*.
[25]See D. Rancour-Laferrière, 'Pushkin's Still Unravished Bride: A Psychoanalytic
Study of Tat'iana's Dream', *Russian literature*, 25-2, 1989, pp. 215-49.
[26]Douglas Clayton comes to the interesting conclusion that the famous dream scene
encodes an image of Tat'iana masturbating; his argument contains some useful
references to woman taking power into her own hands, as it were. Clayton concludes
that Tat'iana eventually rejects Onegin due to his lacking the authority to deflower her
when they first meet; 'Onegin cannot offer her a phallus – which is to say that he does
not have the authority, or indeed the manhood, to make her happy': J. D. Clayton,
'Towards a Feminist Reading of *Evgenii Onegin*', *Canadian Slavonic Papers*, 29,
1987, pp. 255-65 (265).

emasculated figure, described in Chapter I as a flirt, a fop, able to squeeze out the required tear in moments of sentimentality (I: 10), and, as the narrator tells us with perhaps more than merely irony, '*podobnyi vetrene Venere*' ('Resembling Venus .../ (That giddy goddess)', I: 25). Evgenii's dashing to balls and country places looks very vigorous but in fact he is described in the initial chapter of the text as a traditionally passive, 'feminine' figure, called to dance attendance like a nurse or wife on a dying (i.e. impotent) man, his uncle, from whom he hopes to inherit a country estate. What he does find in the country is not so much material bliss as '*khandra*', or acidity, which runs after him like a shadow – or like a faithful wife ('*Kak ten' ili vernaia zhena*', I: 54). Onegin is the consort of powerful spleen, which saps his vigour and renders him bored and disillusioned. One may note that *khandra* 'overwhelms' Onegin ('*ovladela*', I: 38), as if possessing him, or perhaps, conquering him sexually. Small wonder that Onegin is not the most masculine of men, and indeed one who refers to himself as an 'invalid' in terms of love ('*v liubvi schitaias' invalidom*', II: 19), suggesting physical impairment (and an ironic prefiguring of the man Tat'iana does marry, her maimed general). Pushkin hints at the theme of impotence rather neatly in this way.

Another medium for conveying this theme is through the narrator, who, in *Evgenii Onegin*, for example, is fascinated by women's bodies; the famous pedal digression, for example, evokes the sensual image of water lapping a woman's legs, which the narrator wants to kiss, but such sensuality soon gives way to sighs and passion is deflated by nostalgia and irony. The narrator is unable to carry passion further, and he provides a typical titillating element, dwelling with pleasure on the flesh but always keeping it at textual arm's length. The narrator encapsulates the ambivalence typical of the society tale which appears to be iconoclastic, yet is in actual fact conventional.[27] He may state, as does the narrator of Odoevskii's *Kniazhna Mimi*, that he is 'immodest' (p. 146), and like to think that his banter is frequently subversive, yet often the narrator adopts an aphoristic style, suggesting possibly that conversational anarchy may at times yield to the impulse for control and categorization; the tendency towards the maxim may indeed be 'an inherently conservative impulse' and one which 'gives the speaker a

---

[27]Ayers, pp. 205-06. See also E.C. Shepard, 'The Society Tale and the Innovative Argument in Russian Prose Fiction of the 1830s', *Russian Literature*, 10-2, 1981.

measure of control over the situation'; also, often the narrator provides a wearily nostalgic framework suggestive of dampened passion.[28] The power of passion has been controlled, and social power reigns supreme; yet impotence is, unsurprisingly, and yet, paradioxcially, the result.

The hero is a mixture of *ennui* and sexual predator, encapsulating a paradox – although he may think he is civilised and socially accomplished, he is in fact the victim of his own baser instincts. Cynicism on the part of female characters in the society tale is the result of disillusionment, usually caused by the discrepancy between the appearance of the hero, who likes to show himself as romantic, and the reality of his sexuality. One good example of this gap occurs in Elena Gan's tale *Ideal* (*The Ideal*, 1837),[29] in which the hero is seen as romantic, poetic and ideal by the heroine; he is in fact a lustful and hypocritical cad. Gan suggest this rather amusingly when she describes her heroine, Ol'ga, declaiming frantically *'liubov' moia chista i bezgreshna..'* ('my love is pure and innocent'), while her would-be lover, apparently agreeing, demonstrates the following behaviour: *'No vzor poeta vpivalsia v vzvolnovannuiu grud' Ol'gi'* ('but the poet's gaze thirsted on Ol'ga's agitated breast': 467-8).

The weak heart – whether the heroine's, or, as at times, the loving hero's – is at risk in this predatory society world in which the naive heroine, such as Ol'ga, a 'chained lady' (i.e. married rather unhappily to an older man of some status), is easy prey. Pushkin parodies this briefly in his descriptions of Tat'iana as 'prey' in *Evgenii Onegin*: waiting for Onegin to reveal her fate to her in Chapter II, she is described as a butterfly or a hare, both in terror of death (III: 40). Even more satirically, Pushkin parodies the glittering revelries which in society tales are scenes of beauty, light and brilliance as well as cruelty

---

[28]Ayers, p. 38. If not the narrator, then the characters themselves appear always to be drawing back from the abyss of social indecorum. In Pavlov's *Maskarad*, there is one scene in which hero and heroine are left alone; the hero, Levin, begins to stare at the Countess intently. She becomes rather agitated: *'pripodnialas', tikho upala v kresla...ona vladela vsem ego sushchestvom...grafinia zadrozhala'* ('she raised herself, then silently fell back into the armchair ... she controlled his entire being ... the Countess began to tremble'), *Maskarad*, in *Russkaia svetskaia povest'*, p, 174. This suggestive scene is brought to a close when the Countess becomes rather frightened and Levin backs away.
[29]It has been argued that Gan demonstrates a nervousness towards the idea of 'narrative pleasure', or writing as 'sexual display' (Kelly, op. cit., p. 115).

(for here scandals begin, and malice and suspicion remain rampant) by exposing the more bestial side to them.

c) underneath the glitter...

Take, for example, the description of a typical society night out. Onegin and other young society bloods go to Talon's restaurant, where they drink wine, eat bloody roast-beef, truffles, Strasbourg (goose-liver) pie, Limburger cheese, golden pineapples and hot cutlets (I: 16-17) before rushing to the ballet, where they can lust after the dancers, traditionally easily beguiled from their short and hard lives into liaisons with the aristocracy. The emphasis in this scene is on sensual excess, rather than elegance (despite the good vintage and expensiveness of the food). This is suggested by the tactile, even slightly off-putting, details of the 'bloody' (*okrovavlennyi*, I: 16) roast beef, the goose-liver pie, which presumably smells rather strong and thus must be called 'fresh', and the cheese, which is a particularly strong-smelling kind. The red of the blood, the gold of the pineapples and harsh yellow of the Limburger, the greasy image of the cutlet in its hot fat (*goriachii zhir*, I: 17) and the detail of the dark, unattractive (albeit extremely tasty) truffles combine to create a visually rich scene with undertones of bestiality and of gorging.

The theme of eating or consuming is significant in the novel. Pushkin uses a common setting, that of the society dinner party (often combining it with another common setting, that of the ball or masquerade) to convey his message: this is a society which devours not merely good dinners, but itself. It is inherently self-destructive. The social scenes set on the Larins' estate appear peaceful and happy, but such domesticity hides a cruel truth; society trades its daughters, for Tat'iana will be sold off in marriage, and there are unpleasant references during the scene of her name-day party to the voracious guests – an odd collection of neighbours who gather to feast, jaws champing violently, upon meat and blancmange; '*usta zhuiut*' as Pushkin remarks (V: 29).

Chapter V of Pushkin's novel contains two opposed scenes of feasting: the feast of monsters glimpsed in Tat'iana's famous dream (V: 16-18), with its grotesque participants, with Tat'iana a frightened guest, and which culminates in a scene of violence; and Tat'iana's name-day feast, with its grotesquely described participants, with Tat'iana an embarrassed and confused focus of attention, and which will the next day culminate in the scene of the death of Lenskii at Onegin's hand.

Pushkin's scene of the dream feast presided over by Onegin, is mirrored by the name-day feast presided over by Tat'iana. The very presence of two parallel scenes indicates that there will be no harmony, joining of host and hostess, who are separated by that very divide between dream and social intercourse that the juxtaposition of the two feasting scenes suggests. Onegin and Tat'iana do appear on the edge of consummation during the dream feast; some critics have suggested that the dream has a clear sexual element when she dreams of Onegin – not only publicly claiming her as he does (shouting '*moe*', V: 19), but taking her into a corner, laying her upon a bench and placing his head upon her shoulder (V: 20). However, this sexual moment – if it is one – is short-lived, for instead of dreamlike consummation the dream ends with the intrusion of Ol'ga and Lenskii, the 'mirror' pair of the two lovers who are about to engage in intimacy, and who represent romantic and socially legitimized love; it has already been pointed out by the narrator that Lenskii is prepared to wait until after the marriage to bed Ol'ga (IV: 50). Passion and society are held in antithetical stasis, and it is small wonder that Onegin's feelings take the form of violence (warped sexual desire) in the revenge he exacts upon Lenskii, his 'social' alter ego: he stabs him with a 'long knife':

> *vdrug Evgenii / Khvataet dlinnyi nozh, i vmig / Poverzhen Lenskii* ...Yevgeny quickly / Grips a long knife – and straight he fells / Lensky (V: 21).

Society cannot deal with feeling except by ritualized feasting, marriage and duels, all of which allow passion to be destroyed and which demonstrate the power paradox of the society tale – that destroying passion does not lead to greater power and control, but merely to greater impotence. The fundamental message of the society tale is that man (and woman) is intrinsically powerless: thus the lack of happy ending, or of harmony between passion and society, and the use of the increasingly complex plot which merely underlines the lack of control society characters have over their own destinies, which conspire to thwart them. The best example of this is Pushkin's Germann, whom fate deals a most unkind blow by snatching away victory on the final fall of a card. Arguably, however, fate does nothing and Germann's failure to win and his subsequent madness are the result of his own behaviour, of his quashing of 'natural' passion for a woman for an 'unnatural' obsession with status.

The *svetskaia povest'* has to embroil hero and heroine in situations which ensure modesty and, when the plot gets out of hand, writers are forced to ever more inventive heights to render their passion chained and unable to find free expression. The cruelty of the society tale author, seen in *Evgenii Onegin* in which the hero and heroine come so close to freedom in love, yet are simply out of step with each other, is also clear in a text such as Odoevskii's *Kniazhna Zizi* (*Princess Zizi*, 1839). The *'nepozvolennaia strast''* ('unpermitted passion')[30] of Zizi for her brother-in-law must be resisted; but at the same time she cannot leave the household where she is forced to see him every day because of duty to her sister, for it was their mother's dying wish that Zizi look after her foolish sibling. Duty and passion combine in a titillating mixture that ensures that Zizi will constantly be before her lover's eyes, available to him for the squeeze of a hand or a smouldering look, but never *really* available. In this text it is quite amusing to note that Zizi is not only dressed in the chastity belt of sisterly devotion and daughterly duty, but also in the modest mantle of maternity; she takes on the care of her sister's child, and often shows herself to the gaze of her lover seated, like a madonna, babe sleeping in her lap. Odoevskii gives the reader all the feminine stereotypes of daughter, sister and mother in one tale, while Zizi is a real madonna, in that the child becomes hers sexlessly. Zizi encapsulates the paradox of the society tale heroine who exists at the nexus of two forces, infernal emotion and chastity. This suggests a dichotomy anticipating the Dostoevskian propensity for showing women as 'infernal' or 'madonnas' – the problem with which Tolstoi, too, grappled in his somewhat late (and arguably old-fashioned) society tale, *Anna Karenina* (1877).

When her brother-in-law is freed by the death of his wife, Odoevskii's heroine is still kept safe: the author quickly invents a sub-plot which reveals the lover to be concerned with his supposedly beloved sister-in-law's inheritance. Not only, therefore, does Odoevskii embed the first plot (of impotence) within another plot which thwarts passion, but he then removes the temptation by carrying the lover off

---

[30]V.F. Odoevskii, *Kniazhna Zizi,* in his *Povesti i rasskazy,* Moscow, 1959, p. 370.

(by means of an accident with horses: i.e. an '*equus ex machina*').[31] Odoevskii then uses another narrative stratagem to ensure that love will not have its day. A subsequent possible lover for Zizi quickly changes his mind, as she reminds him that she is forty years old. It is, in some ways, rather an unexpected ending to the text.[32]

One rather forced use of the death plot occurs in Nikolai Pavlov's *Maskarad* (*The Masquerade*, 1839), in which the heroine and hero are kept apart by the demise, from which he has not recovered, of the wife of the hero, Levin. However, the ending to the tale is rather abrupt and strange, as the heroine, who has been panting out her passion for Levin, says of him: '*u nego dolzhna byt' chakhotka*' ('he must be consumptive').[33] The story concludes with Levin going off somewhere to die. An even more bizarre example of a plot absurdly constructed to ensure that hero and heroine cannot unite, and with a strange ending, is A.F. Vel'tman's *Erotida* (1835).[34] The heroine, with the unlikely name of Erotida, meets the hero while still a naive girl; they pledge undying love and exchange rings, but she refuses to elope with him. They meet again some years later, and the hero somehow fails to recognise his now long-forgotten and betrayed love Erotida in the fashionable Emiliia, taking the waters at Karlsbad. He demonstrates this remarkable lack of perspicacity not once, but twice. He encounters a young officer who decides to champion Emiliia's cause, on the basis that the 'hero' is rather a cad and a bounder, and who challenges him to a duel. Rather unfortunately, it is not the cad who dies, but the young challenger, who is, as he lies dying, revealed to be Emiliia/Erotida. The image that Velt'man's story provides is quite significant. Erotida is passion personified: so what does the society tale do, but shoot her. The hero then throws her body in the river and continues his philandering existence.

---

[31] Neil Cornwell's phrase, see his essay in this volume.

[32] As noted by Cornwell, in his essay in this volume.

[33] N. Pavlov, *Maskarad*, in *Russkaia svetskaia povest'*, p. 206.

[34] See John Mersereau's brief discussion of this tale in *The Cambridge History of Russian Literature*, edited by C. Moser, Cambridge, Cambridge University Press, 1992, p. 164. This must qualify for the award of 'most unlikely society-tale plot', though perhaps there is actual precedent, for another society-tale writer, Nadezhda Durova, did dress up as a soldier and, calling herself Aleksandrov, went off to fight Napoleon in 1806. She was actually decorated for bravery and became an officer during the course of a ten-year army career. After a successful writing career she ended up as governor of the town of Elaburg.

In yet another variation, Elena Gan's *Sud sveta* (*Society's Judgement*, 1841), the death plot assumes almost operatic proportions as everyone dies. Vlodinskii's passion for a certain sultry Zenaida is thwarted by the fact that she has, it is rumoured, a lover. Having disposed of the latter by means of a duel, Vlodinskii is, of course, horrified to discover that he has killed the wrong man and has in fact disposed of Zenadia's brother, who just happened to be rather like the alleged lover in height and appearance.[35] Zenaida's father dies of grief, on hearing of his son's demise, and Zenaida then dies as well.

In Pushkin's *Evgenii Onegin*, the duel scene, in which Onegin realises that he has committed a dreadful deed for no very good reason, indicates the price to be paid for trying to kill passion.[36] Arguably, Onegin agrees to the duel out of vanity (he fears that his reputation may suffer if he backs down) and because he wishes to kill feeling: as if by murder he can turn himself to the ice he likes to think he is. It is a superman ploy which sadly reveals his impotence; or, paradoxically, it is an action taken out of an impotent denial of passion which reveals itself in destruction. It encapsulates the paradox of the society-tale genre: man shoots his own better nature, the romantic side of himself. Another Pushkinian example of a duel text is *Vystrel*, in which the hero, Silvio, is unable to conform to the society-tale convention of a duel; he needs it to have meaning and is dismayed by the insouciance of his opponent. And yet when, after some years, his opponent does finally show fear, it is Silvio who cannot bring himself to kill. The duel scene is another example of the power paradox of the society-tale genre; it shows both the force of the passions, yet it is in fact directed against meaningless passion, operating either to destroy passion or as an example of a passionless action.

---

[35]E. Gan, *Sud sveta*, in *Russkaia svetskaia povest'*, p. 225. Further quotations are taken from this edition. See J. Andrew's discussion of this tale, 'Resurrection and Rebirth: Elena Gan's *Society's Judgement*', in *Literary Tradition and Practice in Russian Culture*, edited by V. Polukhina, J. Andrew and R. Reid, Keele, Keele University, 1993, pp. 264-77.

[36]The death plot was one taken up by Pushkin in his unfinished *Egipetskie nochi* (1835), in which the Cleopatra theme is explored briefly (Pushkin had looked at the Cleopatra theme before, in his 1824 poem 'Kleopatra'). See also his 1835 fragment 'My provodili vecher na dache' ('We were spending the evening at Princess D.'s dacha').

In *Pikovaia dama*, passion becomes something rather comic and unpleasant, as in the perverted love scene in which, instead of laying himself at the feet of the beautiful and unhappily circumstanced Liza, German stays downstairs paying court – phallic pistol at the ready in his pocket – to her benefactress, the wrinkled octogenarian countess and the goddess of this society: one to whom the young people all pay homage on entering that temple of social delights, the ballroom. When Germann produces his pistol, death is the result – another indication of how the tale seems unable to deal with such naked passion, whether for money or sex, without frightening itself into annihilation. Pushkin's story plays with society-tale conventions in order to reveal the absurdity of matching a love story with what is in effect a tale of calculation, for it is clear from the beginning that there is no love, only a lust for money. Germann is using Liza as his means of introduction to the Countess's house, where he hopes to frighten out of her the secret of her money-winning cardplay. Liza, too, is not entirely the usual chaste young girl of the society tale, one who is meekly angelic, accustomed to living life out of novels, and self-sacrificial. Her bold step in inviting Germann to her room late at night is an action which contradicts all rules of social decorum. The story is not only a parody of the society tale and its paradoxes, however. Pushkin plays with the very idea of genre itself. A genre, involving a set of expectations on the part of a reader who understand the rules of the generic game and expects no surprises, has a much closer linkage to theme when the text itself places expectation at its very centre. This is the central idea of *Pikovaia dama* – the expectation of Liza that Germann will offer her his heart, and the expectation of Germann that through Liza and the Countess he will gain riches and thereby social status. Disappointed expectations leave both reader and characters disempowered, in a society tale in which nobody wins.

As the reader knows, the story represents a rather strong thwarting of any such expectations; even the Countess's apparent belief in her own immortality (to which her attempts to dress and behave like a young woman instead of an octogenarian attest) is revealed to be erroneous. Pushkin goes further than most society writers by making the card game, often a conventional part of the society-tale setting, a central issue. Germann attempts to control the random fall of cards by using a demonic secret; selling his soul for this knowledge, he loses his mind and ends up in the eternal limbo of the mad. The fantastic element which appears in *Pikovaia dama* (and which is occasionally introduced into the society tale) acts as a subversive force which, of its very nature, undermines society's belief in the power of cold – i.e. rational, – behaviour.[37]

Pushkin's gambling metaphor in *Pikovaia dama*, although primarily a metaphor which reveals a profound truth about man's destiny, is also a very relevant comment on the society-tale genre. The denial of love, as in the case of Germann, in favour of social advancement is not an indication of man's Napoleonic superiority. Rather, the society tale offers the reader men who show themselves as weak, or bestial, or casually destructive beings, killing that which they did not intend to, or (as in the case of Silvio) unable to carry the deed through. Women end up with second-best, marrying whom they can get, once their ideal suitors are shown to be calculating cads. The eventual fate, even of those who do survive in this society and have power, as the Countess does (her husband feared her: she was rich, titled, and the queen of the ballroom), is to be frightened to death. Even in the grave she is forced 'against her will' to play a game with Germann. Power in the society tale, after all, remains a myth.

---

[37]The Gothic and fantastic are often elements in the society tale; ostensibly filled with rather lowbrow romantic tropes, in terms of its love intrigues, it is at the same time realistic in its depiction of the loving heroine's doomed idealism. Arguably, the move towards greater realism in the 1850s sounded its death knell, for the text can only work (even if rather inefficiently) as long as it leans heavily on the romantic tradition, which it in fact criticises.

PRINCESS LIGOVSKAIA AND *PRINCESS MARY*: THE SOCIETY TALE GOES TO THE CAUCASUS

ROBERT REID

Lermontov's contribution to the society tale proper is as modest as it is crucial to any discussion of the nature and significance of that genre in the 1830s and 40s. *Kniaginia Ligovskaia* (*Princess Ligovskaia*), for all its imperfections and incompleteness has long been held up as exemplifying the society tale, though it is also some measure of the relative neglect of typological approaches to the genre that it is still, on the whole, easier to exemplify than to define it. The relationship between *Kniaginia Ligovskaia* and Lermontov's other society tale, 'Kniazhna Meri' ('Princess Mary'), is also well known, though the affinities between the two works, beyond the strikingly onomastic, are not as great as is sometimes assumed. The study which follows has several aims. The first will be to make some tentative suggestions towards a theoretical approach to the society tale. This, briefly, entails laying greater stress on the society than on the tale and developing, in particular, a topological perspective. The second aim is to consider the differentiating features of 'Kniazhna Meri', not only in relation to its predecessor *Kniaginia Ligovskaia* but also in terms of its incorporation into a larger text, *Geroi nashego vremeni* (*A Hero of Our Time*), and its Caucasian setting. A third and concluding consideration is that some of the more generalized features of the society tale, particularly those concerning the relationship between individual and collective, were, in a broad sense, always central to Lermontov's work, so that the strict proposition that only *Kniaginia Ligovskaia* and 'Kniazhna Meri' are germane to the present theme will need to be somewhat modified.

While the typology of the society tale awaits full elaboration, it remains, nonetheless, possible to isolate certain structural and thematic features which are generally held to be fundamental to it:

1) the society tale deals with the manners and mores of the upper classes of Russian society in the first half of the nineteenth century.
2) this society manifests itself collectively at formal social gatherings

which frequently underpin key structural moments in individual works.
3) the style of depiction and narration is broadly realistic; in particular there is a strong emphasis on the description of social realia.
4) the *tale* was not the only literary medium in which these features of high society were depicted (we find them also in novels, plays and poetry of the time).
5) the rise in popularity of the society tale coincides with aristocratic insecurity about its position in the post-Decembrist status quo.[1]

These latter anxieties were reflected in upper class élitism (the specific manifestations of which were dandyism and officerism) as well as concerns surrounding marriageability and advantageous match-making. In the society tale such uncertainty is detectable in an oscillation of point of view between that of high society, or its representatives, and that of relative parvenus and bourgeois interlopers like Hermann in Pushkin's *Pikovaia dama* (*The Queen of Spades*). There are, of course, also distinguishing formal features of the society tale, but in the present context I am not going to dwell on these in any detail. However, Helena Goscilo's contrast between the biographical comprehensiveness of the picaresque and the society tale's restriction 'to a single central episode, the circumstances leading up to it and its consequences', (with the corresponding inclusion of only the most essential material relating to past events) does have some relevance to the structure and narrative technique of 'Kniazhna Meri'.[2] In particular, the structural circumscriptions alluded to here suggest the possibility of defining the society tale by means of a sharply focused chronotope: the depiction of a clearly demarcated *kairos* in a specific social *topos*. But of this more later.

A relaxation of the formal *genus* of the term society tale in favour of the social *differentia* allows us to broaden our consideration of social thematics to embrace such defining works as *Gore ot uma* (*Woe from Wit*) and *Evgenii Onegin*, which helped to lay down the parameters of sociality in which subsequent writers, including

---

[1] I base these categories partly on 'The Society Tale' in Victor Terras (ed.), *A Handbook of Russian Literature*, New Haven and London, Yale University press, 1985, p. 431.
[2] Helena Goscilo, 'The First Pechorin en Route to *A Hero*: Lermontov's *Princess Ligovskaja*,' *Russian Literature*, 11, 1982, pp. 129-62 (131-2).

exponents of the society tale proper, operated. Both of these influential works identify society with the metropolis, with Moscow and St Petersburg respectively. The society setting is, however, reflected in literature in a complex and inevitably hierarchized way. Leaving aside the social apex of the imperial family, which censorship rendered out of bounds as a literary theme,[3] it is those works set at the highest level of St Petersburg society which most completely depict the *svet* of the *svetskaia povest'*. Although the Moscow setting of *Gore ot uma* might be thought interchangeable with that of St Petersburg, in terms of the preoccupations of its characters, their cultural status, the social environment, and so on, it is clear that, already in the 1830s, the Moscow setting was being made to engage polemically with St Petersburg, as the representative of something older and more genuinely Russian and thus subversive of the St Petersburg *svet*'s self-definition. In *Kniaginia Ligovskaia*, for instance, the representatives of the Moscow aristocracy are depicted as more informal and easy-going than their St Petersburg counterparts; in particular, it is a Muscovite visitor who relieves the embarrassment of Krasinskii, a *chinovnik* socially out of his depth at a high society *soirée*. As well as contrasting with the artificiality of the St Petersburg social structure as a primaeval *communitas*, Moscow is the happy childhood home of the aristocratic Pechorin (in *Kniaginia Ligovskaia*), and thus a symbolic matrix of true emotions lost under the patina of cold formality imposed by the St Petersburg *svet* (Lermontov would use this same model of psychic alienation, shorn of its geographical specificity, in his characterization of the later Pechorin in *Geroi nashego vremeni*).[4] *Kniaginia Ligovskaia* abounds, moreover, not merely in descriptions of the St Petersburg *svet*, but with quasi-philosophical reflections on the nature of it. This hyper-sensitivity to the contradictions of a social milieu is something it shares with Gogol''s works set in the capital and also those of the early Dostoevskii. Furthermore, the social meditations which punctuate the society tale narrative, in the form of socially-aware asides about St

---

[3]It is true that works such as *The Negro of Peter the Great, The Bronze Horseman, War and Peace, Levsha* etc. demonstrate that the thematic taboo was by no means universal. However, in the case of the society tale, we are dealing by definition with texts with immediate social and ideological impact rather than (as in the case of those cited above) works whose ideology is refracted obliquely through a historical medium.

[4]For an exploration of the *communitas*/structure relationship see Victor W. Turner, *The Ritual Process: Structure and Anti-Structure*, Chicago, Aldine, 1969, pp. 128-9.

Petersburg life, cannot be divorced from the wider discourse taking place in the 1830s (encompassing both the history of the capital and the nature of Russia's historical destiny), the most celebrated expressions of which are to be found in the writings of Chaadaev and in Pushkin's *Mednyi vsadnik* (*The Bronze Horseman*).

Although the élitist thematics of the society tale may seem to demand the depiction of social exclusivity, contradictions in the social reality depicted mean that this is rarely attained in unalloyed form. If we accept that the genre itself articulates the anxieties and insecurities of the *svet* of the 1830s then it is not surprising that this élite is rarely represented as a perfectly closed social system with its own preoccupations, but rather as one only imperfectly fortified against assaults from the extra-systemic Other. For the metropolitan *svet* this Other is most frequently manifested by the omnipresence of fellow citizens of inferior class, but it may equally present itself in the form of the geographical Other, like those provincials who, at the beginning of Zagoskin's *Kontsert Besov* (*Devils' Concert*), descend on Moscow 'in endless caravans of kibitkas and carts' as winter approaches looking for social excitement.[5] The degree of otherness intensifies as we approach (to use a perspective of Edward Said) the peripheries, whether these are located in some benighted provincial town in the Russian hinterland or are pushed as far as the war-torn asiatic outposts of empire. The Other may also be represented by anything which challenges the rational coherence, predictability and social identity of the *svet*, hence the readiness of society-tale writers to incorporate fantastic or supernatural elements into the narrative dynamic of their plots: *Pikovaia dama*, Odoevskii's *Zhivoi mertvets* (*The Live Corpse*), Melgunov's *Kto zhe on?* (*Who Is He?*), Titov's *Uedinennyi domik na Vasil'evskom* (*The Lonely House on Vasil'evskii Island*). In all of these works mysterious agencies intervene to deconstruct, estrange or alienate key settings of the society tale: the gambling house, the salon, the social card game, the dramatic performance, or even the high-society auction.

As a way of further exploring the topological dimension of this subject, it may be helpful to apply a fourfold model which formalizes some of the foregoing observations about the society tale. This model

[5]M.N. Zagoskin, *Kontsert besov*, in *Russkaia romanticheskaia novella*, Moscow, 1989, pp. 214-28 (214).

bases itself on the concept of 'sociotope': the relationship between a given social group and its *topos*, or the environment it inhabits.[6] This relationship is essentially attributive in that, in its simplest form, it defines a given social group in terms of the place it finds itself in (the peasant in his village, for instance). In most instances of this relationship, but not all, there is a normative sociotope which, as in the case of the peasant in the village, expresses the usual, traditional or expected location for that social group.[7] Clearly, however, social mobility or dislocation will produce a variety of sociotopes (e.g. the peasant in the town) which contrast with the normative under the general formula (to conclude or continue the present example) of 'the peasant not in the village'.

The normative sociotope of the society tale is the *svet* (as a social class) in its own *topos* (the metropolis). This basic sociotope yields three others as corollaries to it:

1) the non-*svet* (other social classes) in the metropolis
2) the *svet*, or its bearers or representatives, in the non-metropolis
3) the non-*svet* (defined either in social or ethnic [or a combination of the two] terms) in the
non-metropolis

The *topos* 'non-metropolis' needs some elucidation: it is not merely a generalized privative designating any location beyond the capital (or

---

[6]This is a refinement of 'ethnotope', which I used to explore the relationship between *ethnos* (nationality) and *topos* (place) in relation to Lermontov's Caucasian poems. As the components suggest the term itself is derived from the Bakhtinian 'chronotope' by replacing the temporal with an anthropological (in the broadest sense) co-ordinate. However, for critical purposes, ethnotope (or 'sociotope') and chronotope are complementary, addressing between them the three structural fundamentals of plot: setting; human actants within the setting; time as a function of human activity within the setting. See Robert Reid, 'Ethnotope in Lermontov's Caucasian Poemy', *Russian Literature*, 31, 1992, 555-73.

[7]There are clearly some social, or ethno-social groups, for which the normative *topos* is difficult to define: gipsies would be an obvious example, although it is interesting that Pushkin, in opening his eponymous poem, takes care to restrict their peregrinations within a specific (and romantically evocative) southern *topos*. For quite different reasons, the nineteenth-century Russian intelligentsia, though arguably a discrete social group with certain common features, is equally difficult to 'locate', something borne out by the diverse settings of Chekhov's *intelligent*-based stories.

capitals). Non-metropolis inevitably implies regions with their own distinctive non-metropolitan culture, and thus with the real potential to act as polemical alternatives to metropolitan orthodoxy. The provincial towns and micro-autocracies in *Revizor* (*The Government Inspector*) and *Mertvye dushi* (*Dead Souls*) fall into this category, as does the provincial society described in *Evgenii Onegin*. In such an environment the perceived bearer of metropolitan culture, however unworthy, becomes the representative of *svet* within a comparatively alien environment. In quite different ways, and in different contexts of social gullibility, Onegin and Khlestakov come to represent the metropolitan *svet* for those they find themselves among. This corollary of the normative society tale sociotope ('*svet* in the metropolis') has been immensely influential in the development of Russian literature. It might be figuratively termed '*svet v t'me*' if by *t'ma* one means that menacing undifferentiated social Other which constantly threatens to snuff out the metaphorical light: Turgenev's Rudin arriving in the provincial salon; the metropolitan Ivan Karamazov and Stavrogin among uncomprehending provincials; Boris Dikoi surrounded by savage samodurs; Serebriakov marooned on the country estate. The most satisfying expression of this symbolic *lux in tenebris* is found in Zamiatin's *Sever* (*The North*), admittedly well beyond our nineteenth-century parameters, the naive hero of which, beguiled by a Russian trader into believing that St Petersburg is lit in winter by huge artificial lamps, unsuccessfully attempts to construct a gigantic lantern which will do the same for the northern wilderness inhabited by Lapps and fishermen: the kind of primaeval, pre-Petrine chaos which Pushkin briefly conjures up at the beginning of *Mednyi vsadnik* (the diachronic Other of the future metropolis).

As in much else, *Evgenii Onegin* is a crucial paradigm, because its action is so elegantly balanced between two contrasting sociotopes: the *svet* in the metropolis and the representative of *svet* (Onegin) in the non-metropolis (the provinces). It is important to stress that *Evgenii Onegin* is no less a society text (if not a tale in the formal sense) for sandwiching this generous portion of provincial sociotope between the two slabs of normative *svet*-sociotopes which contain the prologue and the dénouement of the work. For, despite its thematic and structural essentiality, the sociotope represented by Onegin in the country is embedded in a dominant metropolitan sociotope: the metropolis draws

Onegin back to itself and assimilates, though with reservations, Tat'iana into the role of society heroine. The interaction between these two sociotopes we may call inter-topological: the *svet*, as incarnated by Onegin, remains constant. It is the *topos* which changes through the several chapters of the novel: first the metropolis; then the provinces; then the metropolis again.

In other society works, by contrast, the intra-topological situation is more important: the interaction between the normative high-society sociotope (*svet* in the metropolis) with its corollary on the same ground, as it were – the non-*svet* in the metropolis. It has often been observed that the 'little man' story is the antithesis of the society tale.[8] In our terms, however, it is better to say that it is the inevitable complement to it. Typically, the society tale is full of an awareness of the flaws of the social milieu it describes, but restricting itself to such *topoi* (ballrooms, gambling houses, salons, theatres and the like) as are its exclusive social preserve, it is immune from significant interaction with other non-*svet* social groups. Outside these often enclosed *topoi*, the likelihood of exposure to the Other increases. Commenting on the scene which confronts Pechorin on leaving the theatre in *Kniaginia Ligovskaia*, Lermontov observes that the crowd gathered around the doors was 'a picture in miniature of the whole of St Petersburg society'.[9] However, Pechorin is only exposed to it during the time it takes him to reach his carriage. The society tale allows its reader the restricted view of the social Other which was available to its protagonists.

The role of Krasinskii, as representative of this social Other in *Kniaginia Ligovskaia* is instructive in this respect. Our first encounter with him is as a pedestrian knocked down, but not seriously injured (physically, at least), by Pechorin's carriage: lowly civil servants on foot being fair game for young aristocrats in a hurry. This is an acceptable degree of tangentiality between the two sociotopes within the grand plot of the society tale. *Kniaginia Ligovskaia*, however, takes the contact further, arguably to the point at which it cannot fail to

---

[8]For instance Goscilo, op. cit., p. 147.
[9]M.Iu. Lermontov, *Sobranie sochinenii v chetyrekh tomakh,* vol. 4, Moscow, 1965, p. 259 (translation mine). Subsequent primary source quotations are from this edition, unless stated otherwise.

compromise the society tale's integrity of theme. For Krasinskii seeks Pechorin out in the tavern he frequents with fellow aristocrats and army officers and insults him by upsetting a glass on his table. When Pechorin challenges him to a duel, Krasinskii declines because his death would leave his mother without financial support or protection. The different attitudes to duelling displayed by the two protagonists underlines their different sociotopes: duelling being a defining behavioural norm in the society tale. It is the introduction of Krasinskii which causes the thematic integrity of *Kniaginia Ligovskaia* to falter. To a story which has so far faithfully adhered to the grand plot, with its bored society hero engaged in competing love intrigues with society women, Lermontov introduces strong competitive elements from the opposite sociotope. Pechorin is subsequently depicted seeking Krasinskii out in a squalid neighbourhood and talking to his mother. Krasinskii himself is characterized in scenes, involving only his mother and himself, in which they bitterly reflect upon their humble social condition.

In *Kniaginia Ligovskaia,* unlike *Evgenii Onegin,* the induction of a competing sociotope does not result in complete incorporation and ultimate restatement of the grand plot but in a faltering of the story, as its dominant point of view is progressively appropriated by a representative of the non-*svet* and the work as a whole draws perilously close to the little man genre. These competing sociotopes could only have been reintegrated within the much larger compass of a genuinely polyphonic work in which the conflicting sociotopes could have related to one another via collocation and juxtaposition, rather than by subordinate emplotment one to another. It is clear, however, from what appears to be a serious structuro-thematic flaw in *Kniaginia Ligovskaia,* that Lermontov wished his critique of the *svet* sociotope to go much further than an ironization of social mores of the kind conventional in society tales. He appears to have found it impossible to take the 'democratic' route to this goal followed by Gogol' and Dostoevskii. Krasinskii's psychology, his shame and his resentment in response to social humiliation are exactly like those of Dostoevskii's early heroes – and perhaps influenced their characterization. Lermontov never elaborated this disempowered urban resentment into a plausible point of view. As an essentially romantic writer, one for whom exile and army life were vivid formative experiences,

Lermontov pursued his critique of the *svet* by inter- (rather than intra-) topological means.

The two most obvious modifications made by 'Kniazhna Meri' in relation to *Kniaginia Ligovskaia* are the change of *topos* from the metropolis to the spa and the change of the narrative medium from omniscient third person narrative to first person diary form. There is, of course, much more to these changes than what is baldly stated here: not least, the transformation of the hero from a passively superfluous Pechorin in *Kniaginia Ligovskaia* to his cunning and disruptive successor in 'Kniazhna Meri'. This change too, however, is in great measure facilitated by the aforementioned modifications in setting and narratorial medium.

There are certain problems in incorporating the spa into the sociotopic model we have adopted thus far. Superficially it appears that the spa, as a sociotope, relates, like the provinces, inter-topologically to the metropolis – spa society being expressible as 'the *svet* in the non-metropolis'. However one important defining feature of the sociotope '*svet* in the non-metropolis' is the disempowerment experienced by the representative of *svet* in an alien *topos*. In the case of the spa there is no such disempowerment. Quite the contrary: the spa seems to intensify many of the defining characteristics of the *svet* sociotope. Relative to the capital, for instance, where there is inevitably intra-topological friction with the opposing sociotope (with the lower class Other), the spa displays a kind of social *beskonfliktnost'* (or 'conflictlessness'). Though Pechorin in Piatigorsk is able ironically to typologize the social strata which constitute the spa society surrounding him, the social types he distinguishes are all, if not *svet* in the purest sense, then close enough to it not to provide material for the sort of painful class confrontations which engulf Pechorin and Krasinskii in *Kniaginia Ligovskaia*. That the spa is a specific instance of, rather than something opposed, to the normative metropolitan *svet* sociotope, is supported by the following observation from *Kniaginia Ligovskaia*: Lizaveta Nikolaevna is described as 'born in St Petersburg and never having left it. True she once spent two months taking the waters in Revel, but you are well aware that Revel is not Russia and so the direction of her Petersburg education underwent no modification' (262). The implication here is that exposure to non-Petersburg Russia would have challenged her metropolitan outlook, whereas Revel, though situated outside Russia would simply reinforce it. In this sense the geographical location of the spa may not be important, although, in the case of 'Kniazhna Meri', the geographical transgredients of the Caucasus do manage to make themselves felt in a significant way.

The spa is best thought of as a microcosm or quintessence of the metropolitan sociotope.[10] It cannot simply be reduced to the status of a constituent metropolitan *topos* as is the case with the gambling house, the salon, the ballroom etc; for essential to the spa is the notion of an overarching 'spa society', whereas we cannot speak in the same way of ballroom society or gambling house society.[11] Moreover the nature of spa life naturally foregrounds certain aspects of metropolitan culture and backgrounds certain others. Open spaces become more important than closed; balls and *soirées* than theatres or operas. Promenading and walking, gathering near water fountains, as well as vacational or holiday pursuits (outings, even souvenir hunting), motivate enhanced possibilities for chance meetings and easy acquaintanceships. Accommodation is temporary and informal, and access to it by outsiders is accordingly more relaxed. Above all the spa is a chronotope in the full sense of the word: unlike the metropolitan *svet*, with its associations of luxurious, but often tedious, permanence, repetitiousness and predictability, the spa is by definition an ephemeral experience for those who go there. Temporal conditionality is built into it. Descriptions of spas in literature tend to be descriptions of sojourns

---

[10]It is certainly the case that the spa can, on one level, be contrasted with its barabarous highland surroundings in the binary terms of metropolitan/primitive. Yet, on another level, an expedition to the Caucasus, even to a spa, represents a journey – as Peter France puts it – in search of primitive things which 'offer refreshment to the jaded city dweller': Peter France, 'Western European Civilisation and Its Mountain Frontiers (1750-1850)', *History of European Ideas*, 6, 3, 1985, pp. 297-310 (309).

[11]Elizabeth Shepard regards the ballroom as the central *topos* of the society tale, because of its heightened potential for unmasking social pretensions (of itself a prime theme of the genre). See Elizabeth Shepard, 'The Society Tale and the Innovative Argument in Russian Prose Fiction in the 1830s', *Russian Literature*, 10, 1981, 111-162 (136). However, Shepard also accepts that there may be close equivalents to this *topos* which perform much the same critical and structural functions. Clearly, the precise nature of these social gatherings is thematically less important than their carnivalizing potential. Thus in the 'society play' *Woe from Wit* it seems to matter little (except for the purposes of social verisimilitude) that the social gathering at which Chatskii is scapegoated is not a ball (since the Famusovs are in mourning), but rather a *soirée*.

at a spa. This temporal circumscription, as we shall see, has profound implications for the narrative structure of 'Kniazhna Meri'.

Spa life is also steeped in teleological and motivational ambiguities absent in the capital. Those who visit the spa may be physically or emotionally disabled; or they may be companions of the disabled, or else simply resting or vacationing: *eros* and *thanatos*, pleasure and pain, hypochondria and true illness, with all the intervening shades, are readily accommodated in the lax house-rules of the spa. The Piatigorsk spa has transgredient features peculiar to the Caucasus. The men who arrive there may be pausing on their way to active service. Or they may be recuperating from wounds or fatigue. Male society in Piatigorsk is not typical of spa society in this respect. The military presence sharply defines the masculine ethos in 'Kniazhna Meri' and inevitably serves to enhance distinctions between the sexes along stereotypical lines.[12] The women, too, are not just society women; their presence at the spa suggests a potentially disempowering social or physical inadequacy: a need to search for a husband outside the capital, or to take 'the cure' for an ill-defined bodily or spiritual malaise (both Vera and Princess Mary herself betray these characteristics). A particular perception of women as weak in the broadest sense is enforced or reinforced by their presence in the spa. If the women are neurasthenic, prone to mysterious complaints and emotionally vulnerable, the soldiers are as predictably macho. The military ethos intensifies the duelling, gambling and womanizing found in the metropolitan *svet*; however, in the male society of Piatigorsk, challenges to a duel will not be declined, as in *Kniaginia Ligovskaia*, for fear of upsetting one's mother.

A strong argument can be made for regarding the army as a distinct sociotope from the metropolitan *svet*, and one moreover sharply contrastive to it in terms of ethos and gender value. One might say that the army sociotope could be formulated as 'the army in its barracks'. This separate quartering, or topological segregation of the army,

---

[12]The androcentric structure of the majority of the stories in *A Hero of Our Time* (*'*Maksim Maksimych', 'The Fatalist' and, despite the title, 'Bela') serves to highlight the more equable gender distribution in 'Princess Mary' and thus to set it off more clearly as a society tale in the true sense. This is because, even in its earliest critical definitions, the society tale was regarded as a narrative form 'in which the figure of the female protagonist is frequently as persuasively realised as is that of the hero', so that 'it is in the society tale that the woman question enters Russian prose fiction' (Shepard, op. cit., p. 112).

enhances its otherness as an autonomous male community opposed to the civilian *svet* with its female-oriented culture. Many different works of Russian classical literature confirm this opposition: Pushkin's *Vystrel* (*The Shot*), for instance, with its contrasting military and civilian *topoi* and the implied difference in the significance of duelling in these *topoi*; or, much later, Chekhov's *Tri sestry* (*The Three Sisters*), with its strong opposition between idolized metropolitan culture and life in a garrison town. On the whole, however, it would seem that the military sociotope serves to gender the *svet* sociotope in a particularly stark way. These male and female roles are heightened to the point of caricature or, indeed, as Pechorin constructs them in 'Kniazhna Meri', to the point of melodrama.

That the spa is a chronotope, that is a place, the notion of which is necessarily associated with a finite time-span or *kairos*, is underlined by the use of diary, that most chronologically self-conscious of discourses, as the narrative medium of 'Kniazhna Meri'. The diary has far-reaching implications, both for telling and for characterization. The distinction between mimesis and diagesis, fairly distinct in *Kniaginia Ligovskaia*, · becomes inevitably blurred in the later work. Where Pushkin, in his novel in verse, successfully managed to keep the authorial voice distinct from that of the work's protagonist, Lermontov willingly allows them to melt into one another. Under these conditions all actions and utterances by the hero become intensely self-aware, and hence ironic in the transcendent sense of that word. There is a move, too, from sociolect to idiolect, from the desire to describe social mores faithfully and observantly in *Kniaginia Ligovskaia* (a feature of much society tale writing), to a desire to describe only the individual psyche, to explicate the self even at the risk of tautology. The diary itself, of course, along with letters, epigrams and album entries, may be considered part of the scriptive paraphernalia of the *svet topos*. Certainly, the decidedly non-*svet* Maksim Maksimych appears to have taken no steps to explore the private writings Pechorin has entrusted him with – less out of delicacy than because it never occurs to one of his background that 'some notes or other' could tell him anything interesting about a man who otherwise fascinated him.[13] Also

---

[13]This would seem to be the most obvious explanation. It is always possible, however, that Maksim Maksimych, in his chagrin at Pechorin's treatment of him, is deliberately feigning disinterest in the notes. Though he himself threatens to 'have them made into

interesting is the exotopic disengagement from the diary which Pechorin effects once he has returned to the fort after the death of Grushnitskii. Pechorin is capable of forms of discourse other than the journalistic, and the collapse of the diary form into pure narrative in order to describe the duel and its consequences acts as a kind of narrative buffer between the journalistic discourse of the spa and the more orthodox narrative discourse of the rest of the journal, while further helping to underline the status of the spa as a distinct chronotope in the novel.

Only while Pechorin is scripting or controlling the plot does he use the diary form. Nevertheless the plot which he scripts is in all senses a true society tale, so that 'Kniazhna Meri' in effect represents Pechorin's attempt to write a society tale. It is an Oneginesque drama with all the characteristic society ingredients: the double of the society hero; the innocent young heroine, the tempted adulteress (all these figures appear too in one form or another in *Kniaginia Ligovskaia*). This grand plot is presented to us by Pechorin as a kind of anthropological inevitability, given the strict and predictable social conditions prevalent in the spa. In accurately reading and anticipating the milieu around him, according to a keen understanding of its interpersonal code, Pechorin acts, in a narrative functional sense, as his own Greimas or Propp, and we could formalize what unfolds according to either of their paradigms: the hero > the quest (seduction) > the rival > the facilitator (Werner) etc. Pechorin emplots for his diary something already pre-existing, both in that society and in literature written on and for that society. This highlighting of the programmatic nature of high society life, present to a lesser extent in *Kniaginia Ligovskaia*, feeds directly into the wider philosophical task of the novel: to investigate the role of fate and free will in human activity. Lermontov has appropriated the formalized and ritualized nature of high society as described in the society tale and drawn it into a more general meditation on the predictable nature of human activity in general.

The kind of thematic polyphony which Lermontov sought and failed

---

cartridges', an extreme act of philistinism, he also gives the Narrator of 'Maksim Maksimych' *carte blanche* to 'Print them in the papers if you like...', suggesting that he has at least a general opinion of their literary or journalistic value. Quotations are from Mikhail Lermontov, *A Hero of Our Time*, revised and edited by Neil Cornwell, translated by Martin Parker, London, Everyman (Dent), 1995, p. 46.

to achieve in *Kniaginia Ligovskaia* was realised in 'Kniazhna Meri' by collocating the society tale within an ingenious macrostructure, together with other stories based on different and contrasting sociotopes and ethnotopes. This allows 'Kniazhna Meri' to function unambiguously as a society tale, which is not the case with *Kniaginia Ligovskaia*. 'Kniazhna Meri' exemplifies the paradox which we find in Tolstoi's *Kazaki* (*The Cossacks*): a work set in the non-Russian (Muslim) Caucasus, but devoted nonetheless wholeheartedly to the pursuit of a largely Russian moral theme.[14] The Caucasus, however, does interact with 'Kniazhna Meri' as a transgredient, both via the other constituent stories of *Geroi nashego vremeni* and, though to a lesser extent, by means of Caucasian motifs in 'Kniazhna Meri' itself. The most obtrusive of these is Pechorin's full Caucasian dress and riding gear with which he terrifies a Princess Mary already aware that Circassians make occasional incursions into the environs of the spa town.[15] The wounded Grushnitskii is also a reminder of the war with Muslim tribesmen not far away. The capital, too, is equally an inferred though distant presence. The arrival of Vera reminds Pechorin of his past liaison with her in St Petersburg. The Caucasian presence is, of course, reinforced in the story by the narrative hiatus brought about after the description of the duel with Grushnitskii. The conclusion, unlike the bulk of the tale, is written weeks later when Pechorin is at the border fort along with Maksim Maksimych. In closing 'Kniazhna Meri' with the epilogic 'now' of the fort, Lermontov concedes that he has to find some way of inducting this society narrative into the wider setting of a novel, the thematic and locational preoccupations of which are far from 'societal'.[16]

---

[14]For a full history of the evolution of the Caucasian theme in Russian nineteenth-century literature, see Susan Layton, *Russian Literature and Empire: Conquest of the Caucasus from Pushkin to Tolstoy*, Cambridge, Cambridge University Press, 1994.
[15]This is nonetheless an ambiguous cultural manifestation. As Peter France has noted, of urbanites who are drawn to the mountains: 'Many modern city dwellers go to the mountains because they want a solitude to play savages in, now that the savages have been civilised or destroyed' (France, op. cit. p. 309). Although the 'savages' are still there, Russian military might and the treachery, cynicism and weakness of its representatives (Pechorin, Maksim Maksimych) in dealing with the native inhabitants of the Caucasus will ensure that the latter ultimately succumb. Meanwhile, Pechorin – in Circassian garb – is to this extent ahead of his time: a genuine metropolitan 'playing savages'.
[16]This raises the possibility that the wild Caucasus functions as a basic existential

We have stressed in this paper that the normative *svet* sociotope (*'svet* in the metropolis') implies a corollary (*'svet* in the non metropolis') and that this displacement, as in *Evgenii Onegin*, commonly results in the real or symbolic disempowerment of the representative of *svet*. In the context of *Geroi nashego vremeni* as a whole it is 'Taman'' which illustrates this effect. Indeed, 'Taman'' is quite an extreme instance of metropolitan disempowerment by the provincial, the centre by the periphery. The hero, identifiable as Pechorin only because the story forms part of his Journal, is a travelling officer on government business; his opponents are smugglers of vague affiliation and provenance. The disempowerment of the representative of imperial authority, of the centre, is realised in part by a skilled management of the fantastic by his opponents, in which fantasy, as suggested earlier, is clearly in opposition to the rationale of the dominant or ruling world view. In 'Bela', too, we find Pechorin functioning as the bearer of St Petersburg culture simultaneously in both ethnotope and sociotope: in the first instance in his relations with the Circassians (Kazbich, Azamat and Bela); in the second with respect to Maksim Maksimych, who himself serves in the novel as a one-man representative of the provincial point of view from which the metropolitan hero is incomprehensible. (Equally, such prolonged exposure to Maksim Maksimych's provincial companionship induces the inevitable *tedium vitae* in the sophisticated Pechorin.)

Thus *Geroi nashego vremeni*, as a whole, provides several competing sociotopes for 'Kniazhna Meri'. Moreover, these sociotopes are encountered by the reader in advance of 'Kniazhna Meri'. In receptional terms, the reader will already have concretized the character of Pechorin before reading 'Kniazhna Meri': Pechorin's characterization has already been largely accomplished by the time he appears in this society tale. The hero in this case is much more than his mere participation in the spa sociotope might imply. Equally important is the fact that 'Kniazhna Meri' is not the last story in the novel. In its

reality in the midst of which the spa sets up its surrealistic imitation of metropolitan high society. Romantic features notwithstanding, the Caucasus of *A Hero of Our Time* must be seen as contributing to 'the steady growth of factual knowledge' about the region, which Layton sees as competing with the more traditional romanticized depictions as the century proceeds: Susan Layton, 'The Creation of an Imaginative Caucasian Geography', *The Slavic Review*, 45, 3, 1986, pp. 470-86 (484).

early drafts, of course, 'Kniazhna Meri' was all there was of Pechorin's Journal. Not only is this the case, but, unlike all the other stories except 'Maksim Maksimych', it was not published separately and was presumably written for incorporation in the organic structure of the novel. In the next draft 'Fatalist' ('The Fatalist') was introduced, but in the position now occupied by 'Taman''. Only in the final version was 'Taman'' introduced, forcing the relocation of 'Fatalist' to the end of the novel. This clearly had important implications for the receptional impact of 'Kniazhna Meri'. Although it is often said that 'Fatalist' serves as the philosophical conclusion of the work as a whole (its key, as has sometimes been claimed), it is equally significant in a thematic sense for explicitly reinstating the military or martial theme with which the novel begins and which is gradually attenuated via the rather different concerns of 'Maksim Maksimych', through 'Taman'', to 'Kniazhna Meri'. Where a conclusion of the novel with 'Kniazhna Meri' would suggest a movement from the barbarous periphery to the civilised centre, the quasi-metropolis of the spa, the conclusion with 'Fatalist' takes us back to the embattled periphery again Moreover, the ingredient of philosophical speculation around the question of fate adds a certain grandeur and finality to this movement. *Geroi nashego vremeni* ends as the tale of a soldier, and an exiled one at that. Where Onegin moves from the centre towards the periphery and back to the centre, Pechorin makes the opposite journey, so that his surrogate metropolis, the spa, is merely a stopping-off place which, having disrupted and exposed, he leaves.

As I suggested at the beginning of this paper, we do not do full justice to Lermontov's contribution to the society *theme* if we confine ourselves to the two stories of his which address it within the strict confines of the specified *genre*. A society defines itself as much through those it alienates or exiles as through those whose wholehearted participation contributes to its constitution. To this extent Lermontov defies the literary trend of the first three decades of the nineteenth century, when, according to Goscilo, 'the romantic faith in the ability of the imagination to transcend environment had gradually dwindled',[17] and a realist account of social interaction began to supplant the romantic. Lermontov's poetry, like many romantic works,

---

[17]Goscilo, op. cit., p. 130.

abounds in images of exile from society and his narrative poems are mostly studies of the effect of social estrangement on the individual. Both *Mtsyri* (*The Novice*) and *Demon* (*The Demon*) evoke religious archetypes of the ideal society (the monastery, God and his angels) to emphasise the despair consequent upon social exclusion or ostracism. *Demon* in particular suggests the sort of dissociation which is the shadow inevitably cast by an élite sociotope, but the social stakes are in this case raised to the highest metaphysical level: representatives of the *svet* to which the damned hero wishes to return really do shine blindingly as they repel him with flaming sword, while the Demon himself is an unwilling sojourner in the *t'ma* into which his rebellion against the omnipotent *svet* has forced him.

V.A. SOLLOGUB AND *HIGH SOCIETY*

MICHAEL PURSGLOVE

If it is a prerequisite for the writer of society tales to be a member of high society, Vladimir Aleksandrovich Sollogub[1] was eminently well qualified. Born in 1813, he was the son of Aleksandr Ivanovich Sollogub, an extremely rich patron of the arts, especially the theatre, and a luminary of Petersburg high society, who makes a brief appearance in a draft of Chapter One of *Evgenii Onegin.* The mother of Vladimir Aleksandrovich was a friend both of Alexander I and of Aleksandr Pushkin. His paternal grandfather was a Polish aristocrat who had settled in Russia at the time of Catherine II and on his mother's side he was a descendant of the eighteenth-century court favourite, Biron. Among the relatives of the Sollogub family was the Olenin family, one of whose members, Aleksei Nikolaevich, was President of the Academy of Arts and introduced Sollogub to many of the leading artistic figures of the day, including Pushkin, Krylov, Gnedich and the painter Briullov. Always referred to by his title of Count (*Graf*), in 1840 Sollogub married the equally well-bred Sofiia Mikhailovna Viel'gorskaia, whose father, the musician and patron of the arts Mikhail Iur'evich Viel'gorskii, had close connections at court. Vladimir Aleksandrovich's aristocratic manners and bearing were repeatedly remarked upon by his contemporaries. Ivan Panaev, in whose journal *Sovremennik* Sollogub published two early stories, is a case in point:

> Encouraged by the dazzling success [of *Istoriia dvukh kalosh* (*The History of Two Galoshes*)], Sollogub enthusiastically set about writing a new story. From time to time he began to appear among *literati*, but he did not feel quite at ease in this company, which was new to him. Among them he played the rôle of High Society Man [*velikosvetskii chelovek*] and seemed to be somewhat embarrassed [*neskol'ko zhenirovalsia*] by the profession of *littérateur* [...] At first Count Sollogub had an irresistible penchant for literature, but his high

---

[1]Descendants of the family in England use the form 'Sollohub'.

society views and habits prevented the development of this penchant and he
subsequently took only a dilettante interest in literature.[2]

In her memoirs, Panaev's wife Avdot'ia confirms the picture, noting
incidentally that neither Sollogub's father nor his brother Lev exhibited
the same extreme aristocratism as the writer:

> If Sollogub had not put on airs so much, he would have been a pleasant
> companion. But he was often insufferable, for ever posing either as a student
> from Dorpat or as an aristocrat. In high society he prided himself on being a
> *littérateur*; in literary society he prided himself on being an aristocrat.[3]

Panaeva numbered Sollogub among the 'society literati' (*svetskie
literatory*) who attended her *soirées* (the others were V.F. Odoevskii,
A. Bashutskii and S. Sobolevskii). Even in this company, Sollogub
stood out 'for his insouciant manners, drawling speech and distracted
air'.[4]

Dmitrii Grigorovich, whose father had worked on the Sollogub
estate near Simbirsk, has left us a portrait of the man:

> Another leading light in the house of Count Mikhail Iur'evich [Viel'gorskii] was
> his son-in-law Count V.A. Sollogub, the well-known *littérateur*, a man who
> was also remarkably gifted but who, given his brilliant ability, achieved less
> than might have been expected. Count Sollogub was not liked in literary circles.
> The reason for this lay in his character, which was distinguished by extreme
> vicissitudes of behaviour: one day he would be hail-fellow-well-met, the next
> he would suddenly not know you and barely extend his hand. One can be more
> kindly disposed towards him for his ardent love of Russian literature. In his
> father-in-law's house he was useful for the fact that he introduced into it a
> Russian spirit, Russian speech and an interest in Russian literature. Such
> interest was often lacking owing to the influx of foreigners. A talented writer
> had only to appear for Sollogub to know no rest until he had brought him to
> Count Viel'gorskii's salon. If an outstanding new work appeared, Count
> Sollogub hastened to acquaint society with it. With this aim in view, he would
> gather a select audience at his father-in-law's house. He was a magnificent
> reader; rare was the author who, in reading his work, could express all the
> nuances or underline all the apt passages with the same skill as Count
> Sollogub.[5]

---

[2]I.I. Panaev, *Literaturnye vospominaniia,* Moscow, 1988, p. 161.
[3]A.Ia. Panaeva, *Vospominaniia*, Moscow, 1972, p. 90.
[4]Ibid., p. 93.
[5]D.V. Grigorovich, *Literaturnye vospominaniia*, Moscow, 1961, pp. 113-14.

Many people detected in Sollogub a tension between the aristocrat and the would-be writer. His literary connections began very early. One of his tutors was Ernest Charrière, later the first translator of Turgenev's *Zapiski okhotnika* (*A Huntsman's Sketches*) into French. Another was Petr Pletnev, who taught him Russian literature and dedicated a scholarly work on that subject to Sollogub's mother, Sofiia Ivanovna. Among his fellow-students at Dorpat University between 1829 and 1834 were the two sons of Karamzin, Andrei and Aleksandr. Panaev comments:

> In Sollogub, after he left university, one was keenly aware of a mixture of German student manners, Russian aristocratic manners and pretentiousness, a strange mixture which always put him awkwardly at odds with himself.[6]

After university Sollogub became an official in the Ministry of the Interior but soon found himself moving in literary circles, so much so that in the course of a single year, 1836, he managed narrowly to avoid fighting a duel with Pushkin and to have himself nominated as Pushkin's second in a duel which never took place.

Today Sollogub is best remembered for *Tarantas* (*The Tarantas*, published in part in 1840 and in full in 1845), a kind of fictionalized travelogue which brought the Slavophile-Westernizer debate into sharp focus. The influence of Gogol"s *Mertvye dushi* (*Dead Souls*) can be seen throughout *Tarantas* and, indeed, Nicholas I is said to have assumed that Sollogub was the author of the celebrated *poema*. However, Sollogub wrote much more besides *Tarantas*. Indeed, there is hardly a genre of literature to which he did not turn his hand. Having become known primarily as a writer of *povesti*, Sollogub abandoned this genre altogether in 1850, turning instead to light verse, narrative poems, history, and the theatre. He was named Court Historiographer in 1856 and two years later was sent abroad to study European theatre. At the end of his life he resurrected his somewhat flagging reputation with the publication of his witty and informative memoirs. He died in Hamburg in 1882.

Sollogub was at the height of his fame between 1839, when his story *Istoriia dvukh kalosh* was published, and 1845 when *Tarantas* appeared in full. By the time his *Collected Works* were published in

---

[6]Panaev, op.cit., p. 307.

five volumes in 1855, Sollogub was something of a back number, at any rate if we are to believe Dobroliubov, who wrote a scathing review of them in 1857.[7] All his society tales belong to this six-year period. They are *Bol'shoi svet* (*High Society*, 1840), *Medved'* (*The Bear*, 1841), *Lev* (*The Lion*, 1841), *Bal* (*The Ball*, 1845).[8] A number of other stories contain 'society' characters, notably *Serezha* (1838), *Aptekarsha* (*The Apothecary's Wife*, 1841), *Metel'* (*The Snowstorm*, 1849) and *Starushka* (*The Old Woman*, 1850), but, since none of them are set in the *beau monde*, they fall outside our present study.

The most famous of Sollogub's society tales is the first, *Bol'shoi svet*. It has been reprinted in all three selections of Sollogub's prose which have appeared since 1962[9] and is the story by which he is represented in the volume *Russkaia svetskaia povest'* (*The Russian Society Tale*, 1990). The story appeared in number three of *Otechestvennye zapiski* in 1840. According to Panaev, the choice of this liberal journal owed less to Sollogub's views than to his friendship with its editor, Andrei Kraevskii; and, in a wry aside, Panaev comments that the commercial success of Kraevskii's journal weighed heavily with Sollogub because 'it is well known that young people generally, and fashionable (*svetskie*) young people in particular, are always carried away by success, even if they do not sympathize with the cause of it'.[10]

The story was written in circumstances redolent of the genre itself. Sollogub's intended wife Sofiia Mikhailovna was a lady-in-waiting to the Tsar's daughter, Grand Duchess Mariia Nikolaevna. Her engagement to Sollogub was announced on 19 April 1840, just one month after the publication of *Bol'shoi svet*. According to Sollogub's memoirs, the Grand Duchess herself had commissioned the story from

---

[7]'Sochineniia grafa V.A.Solloguba' in N.A. Dobroliubov, *Sobranie sochinenii v deviati tomakh*, Moscow-Leningrad, vol. 1, 1961, pp. 520-43.

[8]In Sollogub's *Sobranie sochinenii*, *Bal* (*The Ball*) was amalgamated with two other stories, *Kniaginia* (*The Princess*) and *Dve minuty* (*Two minutes*), under the title *Zhizn' svetskoi zhenshchiny* (*The Life of a Society Woman*).

[9]V.A. Sollogub, *Povesti i rasskazy*, Moscow-Leningrad, 1962 (introduction by E.I. Kiiko); V.A. Sollogub, *Tri povesti*, Moscow, 1978; V.A. Sollogub, *Povesti i rasskazy*, Moscow, 1988 (introduction by A.S. Nemzer. Quotations from *Bol'shoi svet* (High Society) are taken from the 1978 edition. Translations are my own.

[10]Panaev, op.cit., p. 306.

him.[11] The suggestion has been made that his reward for writing it was the hand of Sofiia Mikhailovna. Certainly Sollogub's verse introduction to the story, beginning 'Three stars in the sky' (*Tri zvezdy na nebe*) seems designed to curry favour with the Royal Family, since the three stars in question are the Empress Aleksandra Fedorovna ('The Star of Russia'), Mariia Nikolaevna ('The Star of Poetry') and her sister Ol'ga Nikolaevna ('The Star of Beauty'). Sollogub married Sofiia Mikhailovna in November 1840 and he and his wife established one of the most brilliant literary salons in the capital, to which men like Gogol', Grigorovich, Lermontov, Nekrasov, Pisemskii, Turgenev and Lev Tolstoi were regular visitors.

The fame of *Bol'shoi svet* rests not so much on its intrinsic literary merits as on its connection with Lermontov. He is depicted in the person of the young protagonist of the story, Leonin, a name which suggests a society 'lion'. Leonin unsuccessfully pays court to three women: Armidina, the foremost beauty of the distinctly unfashionable Kolomna district of Petersburg, who is referred to as the 'Kolomna Sylphide' (*kolomenskaia Sil'fida*)[12] and who eventually marries a senior *chinovnik* and acquires the distinctly unromantic name of Krivukhina; Countess Vorotynskaia, over whom Leonin almost fights a duel with an older, more worldly rival Shchetinin; and her younger sister Naden'ka, or Nadine, who eventually marries Shchetinin. To identify Leonin with Lermontov is not difficult. His christian name is Mikhail; he was brought up by his grandmother in rural Russia; he enters the story in 1838, the year Sollogub first met Lermontov; his attempts to become a Petersburg 'lion' are unsuccessful; he is a military man who has occasional brushes with his superior officers over disciplinary matters; at the end of the story he departs for the Caucasus, a disappointed man.

Lermontov himself, like all Sollogub's contemporary readers, recognized his portrait and was, apparently, unfazed by it and continued to visit the Sollogubs' house. Sollogub attempted to

---

[11]According to the entry on Sollogub in *Lermontovskaia entsiklopedia*, edited by V.A. Manuilov, Moscow, 1981, he read the story to the Imperial Family in spring 1839. If this is so, it can only have been the first part.
[12]This is also a reference to *La Sylphide*, the ballet created by Filippo Taglioni in 1832 for his daughter Marie. She is referred to twice in the story.

obfuscate the issue by claiming in his memoirs that the story was not a portrayal of Lermontov himself but rather of his 'significance in society' (*svetskoe znachenie*).[13] This seems disingenuous since, quite apart from the evidence cited above, the name of Lermontov, thinly disguised under the initial 'L', occurs in the story when Shchetinin is talking to Countess Vorontynskaia and saying he will do anything for her, even to the extent of reading the verse of 'L' or the stories of 'S...b'.[14] Furthermore, as Emma Gershtein has demonstrated in her book *Sud'ba Lermontova* (1964), there are in the story oblique references to several of Lermontov's poems, including *Est' rechi*...('There are speeches...'), *Molitva* (*The Prayer*) and *Pervoe ianvaria* (*The First of January*), and to his prose piece *Shtoss.* This evidence was sufficient for Apollon Grigor'ev, who agreed with what he called 'literary traditions which were no longer a secret from anybody',[15] adding that in the character of Leonin Sollogub was making fun of Lermontov's social aspirations.

Why, however, should Sollogub choose to present, in the character of Leonin, a portrait of Lermontov which is, at best, unflattering? Why should he choose Lermontov at all? Gershtein appears to have found the answer to both these questions. Sollogub had become friends with Lermontov in the course of 1838 and 1839, mainly on account of their being *habitués* of the same salons. Sollogub translated some of Lermontov's poetry into French and the two men wrote a poem together. Their cordiality, however, may have been no more than superficial, since it seems that Lermontov took a keen interest in Sofiia Mikhailovna Viel'gorskaia, whose interest in Sollogub was at this stage no more than lukewarm. The story *Bol'shoi svet* is Sollogub's revenge for this humiliation. In it Leonin is unsuccessful in his pursuit of Naden'ka, a character based on Sofiia Mikhailovna herself.[16] The successful suitor for her hand is Shchetinin, a self-portrait of Sollogub himself. Leonin is equally unsuccessful in his pursuit of Armidina, based on Elizaveta Sushkova, the object of Lermontov's affections between 1830 and 1835. The third woman pursued unavailingly by

[13]V.A. Sollogub, *Vospominaniia*, Moscow-Leningrad, 1931, p. 376.
[14]V.A. Sollogub, *Tri povesti*, p. 80.
[15]Quoted in E.G. Gershtein, *Sud'ba Lermontova*, Moscow, 1964, p. 215.
[16]Gershtein suggests that Leonin's relationship with Naden'ka also recalls Lermontov's relationship with Varvara Lopukhina (op. cit. , p. 240).

Leonin, Countess Vorotynskaia, cannot however be linked to a woman in Lermontov's life. The character is based on Countess Aleksandra Vorontsova-Dashkova, Sofiia Mikhailovna's cousin and one of the most dazzling society hostesses of the age. Her portrait would have been instantly recognized in the high-society literary circles in which Sollogub moved, as would that of Pushkin's friend, the minor poet Sergei Sobolevskii, who in the story becomes the sardonic Saf'ev and whose habit of standing with his finger tucked into his waistcoat is faithfully reproduced.

Although the connection with Lermontov has generated a good deal of interest, *Bol'shoi svet* was well received in its day for quite other reasons. Belinskii, for instance, who had commented favourably on *Istoriia dvukh kalosh*, noted that *Bol'shoi svet* was not as well plotted. However, he praised the wit and eloquence of Sollogub's language in *Bol'shoi svet*, noted that that there was 'page after page shining with genuine unforced wit, the like of which we do not see in our novelists'; he also spoke of 'other pages which are distinguished by their true lofty eloquence' and 'whole scenes inspired by deep feeling and true observation'. He then recommends seven such scenes from the story for his readers' delectation. His only reservation concerned some grammatical solecisms and the character of Saf'ev, which he described as 'remarkable and original but [...] too exaggerated, although, overall, he found the story 'extremely interesting for its careful, decisive characterization'.[17] In private he was even more effusive. Writing to Botkin in March 1840 he says: 'In *Notes of the Fatherland* No. 3 there's a splendid story by Sollogub. His is a marvellous literary talent. He is more profound than all your Balzacs and Victor Hugos, although the essence of his talent is akin to theirs'.[18] The crux of the matter for most critics seems to have been Sollogub's language. Viazemskii, for example, who appears to take *Bol'shoi svet* as a piece of realism, commented:

Sollogub has written a story in which there are many Petersburg allusions and pieces of *actualité* [*mnogo peterburgskikh namekov i aktualitetov*]. But I don't

---

[17]V.G. Belinskii (review of V.A. Sollogub, *Na son griadushchii*), *Polnoe sobranie sochinenii,* vol. 5, Moscow, 1954, pp. 153-58.
[18]V.G. Belinskii, *Polnoe sobranie sochinenii,* vol. 11, Moscow, 1956, p. 496.

> like the conversational language: the scene in the fashionable salon is [...]
> realistic [...] but the conversation comes from Kostroma.[19]

while even Dobroliubov had to concede Sollogub's expertise as a creator of puns.[20]

Those readers who focused on things other than Sollogub's language found little to interest in them. One correspondent of Belinskii's, for instance, reported that the story 'had a completely repellent effect on him' and added: 'In Sollogub's story I found not a single genuine feeling and therefore put it aside without any compunction'.[21] Botkin, too, did not care for the story, or so we can deduce from another letter to him from Belinskii. Belinskii defends his own admiration for the story, but then concedes that in it 'there is no depth, little feeling, much sensibility, and even more dazzle'.[22]

Bol'shoi svet must have some claims to being the archetype of the *svetskaia povest'*. The word *svet* and derivatives occur at least 120 times in a story which runs to 68 pages in the most recent edition. Mostly the word is used, as in the title, in the sense of 'high society', a meaning first attested in 1731.[23] However, Sollogub does ring the changes and make some play with the original meaning of the word – 'light'. It is almost a cliché of Sollogub's writing that light, or perhaps bright lights, is a defining feature of high society. This can be seen in his description of the balls which constitute the crucial scene in each of the two parts of the story. For example, the description of the ball in the final chapter of Part One begins: 'The ball gleamed with dazzling light' (*Bal gorel oslepitel'nym svetom*).[24] The inhabitants of the *beau monde* live in a world of illuminated entrance porches (another cliché, which is to be found, for instance, in Gogol''s *Nevskii Prospekt*) and glittering diamonds – references to *bril'ianty* being almost obligatory in Sollogub's descriptions. This suggests a writer preoccupied with

---

[19] Quoted in Gershtein, op.cit., p. 215.

[20] N.A. Dobroliubov, op.cit., p. 530.

[21] Quoted in Gershtein, op.cit., p. 213.

[22] V.G. Belinskii, *Polnoe sobranie sochinenii*, Moscow, vol. 11, 1956, p. 510.

[23] The term *svetskaia povest'* is used in *Bol'shoi svet* (p. 24), when Leonin is dismissed by Saf'ev as being suitable 'neither for the Countess, nor for Shchetinin nor for society tales' ('*ni dlia povestei svetskikh'*).

[24] V.A. Sollogub, *Tri povesti*, p. 89.

externals and, indeed, this is one of the main flaws found in Sollogub's writing by Dobroliubov, who also quotes with approval a celebrated review article by N.F. Pavlov which makes the same charge.

Sollogub's use of the word *svetlyi* is interesting. Unlike its close relative *svetskii,* which in Sollogub is a negative or, at best, neutral word, *svetlyi* has positive connotations.[25] It is associated with pleasant memories, with Nature and, above all, with true love. Both Leonin and his rival Shchetinin use the word in association with Naden'ka. Thus, in a flashback scene set, significantly, not in Petersburg but in a country dacha, the worldly Shchetinin spends an evening carousing with his fashionable friends. In the morning he catches a glimpse of Naden'ka, then still a child, and we read: 'The little girl who appeared to him on this bright morning (*svetloe utro*) was the sister of the countess'.[26] In the very next sentence Sollogub reverts to using *svet* in the sense of 'high society' and, incidentally, uses one of his favourite epithets for it, 'noisy' (*shumnyi*). Leonin, too, speaks of Naden'ka in similar terms in a letter which he sends to her before the ultimately aborted duel with Shchetinin. The language is so clichéd and stilted as to constitute a parody of Lermontov's own speech and writing. Of his childhood he writes: 'In my whole childhood there was not a single bright moment [*ni odnoi svetloi minuty*]'[27] and of Naden'ka's effect on him he effuses: 'I felt that you penetrated the gloom of my life like a bright ray [*pronikli svetlym luchom v mrak moei zhizni*]'.[28]

Bol'shoi svet can be viewed as a struggle between brightness (*svetlost'*) and fashion (*svetskost'*). It is an unequal struggle; Leonin's undue preoccupation with the latter proves disastrous, his attempt to become a member of the *svet* ending in Lermontovian gloom (*mrak*): 'Nature was gloomy, the officer's soul was gloomy'.[29] As Leonin heads for the Caucasus, the last paragraph of the story takes us to his Petersburg flat, where a flickering light (*drozhashchii svet*) dimly illuminates his old grandmother as she prays for his well-being.

We should not perhaps take the Lermontovian dimension of *Bol'shoi svet* too seriously. Sollogub recycled the character of Leonin

---

[25]The same play on derivatives of *svet* can be found in Sollogub's story *Metel'.*
[26]V.A. Sollogub, *Tri povesti*, p. 71.
[27]Ibid., p.115.
[28]Ibid., p.116.
[29]Ibid., p.126.

in *Bal*, which bears the subtitle 'From Leonin's diary'. Here Leonin is simply a conventional first-person narrator and bears no particular resemblance to Lermontov.[30] In *Bal*, as in all Sollogub's society tales, the characters are two-dimensional and more or less interchangeable. For example, Countess Vorotynskaia from *Bol'shoi svet* is indistinguishable from the Countess in the earlier story *Serezha*. Indeed the eponymous hero of that story might be taken as an exemplar of all Sollogub's characters in that his chief characteristic is his lack of character. Dobroliubov ascribed this to Sollogub's total immersion in the empty, lifeless world of high society, which led to his regarding other groups in society as being similarly lacking in life and character.[31] Nor is this lack of characterization compensated by variety of action. The only action in *Bol'shoi svet* is utterly predictable: a masquerade, two balls, a duel, and endless conversations. Sollogub readily owns up to the charge of what the critic A.S. Nemzer calls 'uneventfulness' (*bessobytiinost'*):

> It is probable that you, my severe critic, reading my defenceless story in the line of duty, have already reproached it more than once for being uninteresting, for not containing any startlingly unexpected occurrences, for not swarming with events or trembling with impressions.[32]

In the course of the next page Sollogub offers a defence of realism against this charge, a defence which can be summarized by its final paragraph:

> And so, o critic, my stern judge, be magnanimous and forgive me if, in my story, which, according to its title, ought to be nothing more than a poor copy of a poor picture of high society [*bednyi snimok s bednoi kartiny bol'shogo sveta*], if in my story you find nothing but the ordinary and the run-of-the-mill.[33]

This is a defence Sollogub has already used, as early as the second chapter of the story, where he claims that for choice he would have

---

[30]The character of Shchetinin was also recycled, reappearing in *Medved'*.
[31]N.A. Dobroliubov, op.cit., p. 535. Belinskii, on the other hand, also acknowledged the breadth of Sollogub's social canvas, but made no such criticism (*Polnoe sobranie sochinenii*, vol. 5, p. 157).
[32]V.A.Sollogub, *Tri povesti*, p. 99.
[33]Ibid., p. 100.

written about 'a man with heroic qualities, with a strong, rock-hard will, but possessed of a terrible, mysterious passion'. However, like the narrator of *Mertvye dushi*, he is saddled with the banal and mundane characters of everyday reality:

> But alas! I must choose the characters of my story not from a world of the imagination, not from among unusual people, but from among you, my friends, whom I see and meet everyday, one day in the Mikhailovskii Theatre, the next at the railway station, and always on Nevskii Prospekt.[34]

Here, as often in Sollogub, there is a considerable tongue-in-cheek element, with the substance of what is said being less important than the tone. Here, and indeed throughout the story, the narrator adopts a conspiratorial tone with his readers which suggests that both he and they know more than is set out on the page. He is a *svetskii chelovek* and so are they. Here, too, Sollogub deploys one of the large number of antitheses which characterize his style in *Bol'shoi svet* and which echo the underlying duality of the *beau monde*. In an authorial comment at the beginning of Part 2 the image of a theatrical stage seen from the back is used to illustrate the downside of high society:

> I think that it is funny and frightening to see high society inside out! So many intrigues, so many unknown presents! So much kith and kin! So much dandyfied poverty! So much happy envy...[35]

Shchetinin, the sardonic participant in and observer of this society, feels the same duality within himself when he continues to live the life of a *svetskii chelovek* while at the same time concealing his love for Naden'ka:

> So he spent two years in this dual existence [*dvoistvennaia zhizn'*]. None suspected, and no-one thought to suspect, his secret. Moreover, he continued his former mode of life: he went into society and did not neglect his friends.[36]

Chief among the antitheses iin *Bol'shoi svet* is the contrast between town and country, familiar to any reader of Russian literature. Apart from the flashback scene at the dacha cited above, the whole of the

---

[34]Ibid., p. 62.
[35]Ibid., p. 92.
[36]Ibid., p. 71.

story is set in St Petersburg. The countryside is represented by Leonin's grandmother, who sends him letters (to which he does not reply) describing her tranquil rural existence, and who eventually comes to the city to rescue her errant grandson from a duel. The countryside is also represented by Naden'ka, and her nanny Savshina, who retain their rural values even after moving to the city. There are, however, many other antitheses: military/civilian and (within the military) guards officers/other military men; young/old; Good/Evil; religious belief/atheism; inexperience/ experience; noise/ silence; French/ Russian; Moscow/ Petersburg.[37] There is also an important stylistic antithesis between third-person narrative and dialogue. There is a great deal of dialogue in all Sollogub's society tales – especially *Lev*, so much so that Dobroliubov was moved to exclaim: 'Good Lord! How they talk! How eloquently and at what length.'[38]

In Sollogub high society and Petersburg society are synonymous. Although other writers set their society tales in Moscow, Piatigorsk and Karlsbad, Sollogub confined himself to St Petersburg. Yet Sollogub's attitude to the Imperial capital is ambiguous, compounded of mockery and admiration in equal proportion. Such was Sollogub's attitude to most things, an attitude which Nemzer characterizes as 'pessimistic' and which the author makes clear by frequently stepping outside the narrative to indulge in *Onegin*-like digressions.[39] For him wit was more important than commitment. The *beau monde* may be brilliant and glamorous but it is also trivial, empty, superficial and cynical. The countryside may be the home of virtue and decency but it is also extremely tedious, full, it seems, of half-educated minor nobility with comic surnames and very few serfs. Love may be found only in idyllic country settings, but it often appears to be largely the invention of dreamy romantic poets and to be as risible as the eternal *ronde* of High Society salons and ballrooms. The major metaphor for this in *Bol'shoi svet* is the dance: the subtitle of the story is 'A tale in two dances' and each of the two parts of the story carries the name of a dance as its title: '*Pot-pourri*' (a dance medley) and 'Mazurka'. The

---

[37]One of Sollogub's earliest stories, *Dva studenta* (*Two Students*, 1837), is entirely based on antithesis. One of the two students chooses the tranquillity of provincial life; the other sacrifices everything for the lure of *svetskaia zhizn'*. *Tarantas* is also structured upon a pair of contrasting portraits.
[38]Dobroliubov, op.cit., p. 527.
[39]The digression on 'northern beauties' in Chapter 7 is an excellent example.

balls in each of the two parts (Chapters 7 and 11) form structural pivots for the narrative and in each of the two parts the ballerina Taglioni dances (Chapters 5 and 15).[40] Nowhere is ambiguity better seen than in *Bol'shoi svet*, where in Chapter 3, Shchetinin (Sollogub's *alter ego*) is characterized thus:

> From childhood he had been part of the element of high society, had been educated abroad and had then arrived in Petersburg. From the start he had taken his place among the foremost of high-society young men. For him society [*svet*] was something ordinary, to which he was accustomed; for him society was neither disagreeable nor unattractive. It did not surprise him; it was merely that frequently he did not find much in it and for a long time did not understand what he did find in it.[41]

Lev, too, provides some excellent examples of Sollogub's sardonic attitude towards High Society, nowhere more so than in the opening lines:

> In Petersburg, as you and I know, the fashionable world [*modnyi svet*] imitates Paris and London. Because of this, many people think, thank God erroneously, that a desire to imitate is one of the characteristics of the Russian character. This is not the place to expatiate on such a lamentable accusation and the reasons which give rise to it. But is it not strange, is it not laughable to draw conclusions about an entire state on the basis of a small handful of people of a certain class, who are more or less the same everywhere? Petersburg is a dot on the map of Russia; the fashionable world is a dot on the map of Petersburg.[42]

The *bol'shoi svet* is not so big after all nor, for all its glitter, does it illuminate the soul.[43]

One might add that Sollogub himself was but a dot in the *modnyi svet*, but he was an important dot who made the most of his impeccably aristocratic social connections, and a modest literary talent, to hold centre-stage in high society and to play a significant role in the development of Russian literature between 1839 and 1845. By 1846 his

---

[40]In Chapter 1 the dance metaphor is extended to include the masquerade when the Countess speaks of the need to wear another 'mask' after the masquerade in order to disguise her true feelings.

[41]V.A. Sollogub, *Tri povesti*, p. 68.

[42]V.A. Sollogub, *Sobranie sochinenii*, St Petersburg, vol. 1, 1855, p. 345.

[43]Sollogub indeed stresses the narrow confines of high society, speaking of the 'narrow circle' (*tesnyi krug*) within which a society beauty shines (V.A. Sollogub, *Tri povesti*, p. 80).

star had dimmed and Aleksandr Herzen was able, in October of that year, to make the caustic comment: 'He had a great deal of wit but finally he drowned in champagne'.[44]

---

[44]A.I. Gertsen [Herzen], *Polnoe sobranie sochinenii v tridtsati tomakh*, Moscow, vol. 1, 1954, p. 298.

I. I. PANAEV'S 'THE ONAGER' – A HYBRID BETWEEN SOCIETY TALE AND PHYSIOLOGICAL SKETCH

RUTH SOBEL

The genre of 'society tale' enjoyed a brief flowering in Russia in the decade between 1830 and 1840 when many famous writers of the day, including Lermontov, tried their hand at depicting and probing the life of the Russian *beau monde*. This genre opened new directions in the development of Russian prose fiction, bringing about a retreat from the broad historical panorama of earlier novels, leading it away from improbable and fantastic adventures, and directing it towards everyday life and ordinary, uneventful existence. Russian writers abandoned past ages, battlefields, castles, witches and the rugged romantic scenery of the historical and the adventure novel and entered the high society salon, the boudoir and even the bedroom (especially that of the society lady).

Although this genre was immensely popular in its time, it did not enjoy a particularly good critical reception; yet it marked an important stage in the development of Russian literature and the directions it followed after the heyday of romanticism had passed.[1] Some seminal situations depicted still fairly schematically in society tales, conflicts barely outlined or just hinted at, were to become for the great masters of Russian prose – Tolstoi, for example – the seeds from which their novels grew. One example of such a seminal idea should suffice to illustrate this point. Mariia Zhukova's tale *Baron Reikhman*, published in the cycle *Vechera na Karpovke* (*Evenings of the Karpovka*), depicts a situation where a young and beautiful woman married to an older man, after several years of marriage, falls in love with a younger and more attractive man: a situation which is basically that of Anna Karenina.

R.V. Iezuitova, in her study of this genre, believes that it played an

---

[1] See especially V.G. Belinskii, *Polnoe sobranie sochinenii*, Moscow, 1953-59, vol. 2, p. 133.

important role in the emergence of the Russian novella (*povest'*) in general.[2] Elizabeth Shepard, in an important article devoted to this genre, 'The Society Tale and the Innovative Argument in Russian Romantic Fiction', regards the discovery and depiction of the hidden, the seemingly unimportant 'events of apparently colourless contemporary life' as 'meaningful and *really* real'.[3] Like Iezuitova, she also sees its contribution in the turning of Russian prose from romanticism, with its emphasis on the unique, the extraordinary, the larger-than-life, towards realism, with its interest in the everyday, the mundane and the contemporary.

However, this 'turning', this change of direction, was neither simple nor unilinear; on the road to realistic depiction of real feelings and real people some curious detours were taken, and some hybrids sprang forth which, though they failed to produce any 'offspring', nevertheless are of interest to the student of Russian literature of that period, in so far as they represent attempts to get away from the constraints of the society tale and to create something fresh and original. In this essay I propose to examine one such 'experiment' in generic cross-fertilization, namely I. I. Panaev's *Onagr* (*The Onager*).

The author of this tale, Ivan Ivanovich Panaev, was an important practitioner of the society-tale genre during its period of popularity in Russia. An examination of his evolution towards the end of the decade 1830-1840, which, as we have noted, saw the publication of the best examples of this genre, may therefore be expected to throw a certain light on the development of Russian fiction just before the appearance of the two important prose works of the 1840s: *Geroi nashego vremeni* (*A Hero of Our Time*) and *Mertvye dushi* (*Dead Souls*).

Few readers today, even in Russia, would be familiar with the name of Ivan Panaev; yet in his day he was a popular writer and an influential publicist and journalist, joint editor with N.A. Nekrasov of the 'thick' journal *Sovremennik*, and in general a prominent literary figure. Born in 1812 into a wealthy gentry family, he was sent in 1824 to study in the 'Blagorodnyi Pansion' (the 'Pansion for Nobility'), from

---

[2]R.V. Iezuitova, 'Svetskaia povest'', in *Russkaia povest' XIX veka*, edited by B.S. Meilakh, Leningrad, 1973, p. 199.
[3]Elizabeth C. Shepard, 'The Society Tale and the Innovative Argument in Russian Romantic Fiction', *Russian Literature*, 10, 1981, p. 142.

which he graduated in 1830.

For fourteen years, until 1844, Panaev was employed in the Imperial Civil Service, for the most part in the Ministry of Education. He became interested in literature very early in life, while still a pupil at the Pansion. His first works (which were poems) were published in the 1830s; they were written in the sentimentalist mode, but were unremarkable and showed no real talent for poetry. Panaev soon turned to prose; his early works, though somewhat derivative, did show greater originality and talent than his poetry. In his memoirs, Panaev confesses his youthful worship of Aleksandr Bestuzhev-Marlinskii, one of the most popular fiction writers of the period (the 1830s), and admits that he tried 'slavishly to imitate Marlinskii's manner and style'.[4]

Panaev made his literary debut with a society tale entitled *Spal'nia svetskoi zhenshchiny* (*The Boudoir of a Society Woman*), subtitled 'An Episode from the Life of a Poet in Society'. The hero of this tale, the poet Gromskii, is a typical romantic artist. Panaev mentions that, even in his early childhood, Gromskii was never understood; he was a solitary tormented figure who lived almost exclusively in the world of his imagination. Panaev depicts his hero in the time-honoured romantic style, emphasizing his eyes which burnt with the blinding glow of passion. Following the romantic canon, Panaev makes his poet poor and lacking in social graces. The heroine is, of course, the eponymous 'society lady', Granatskaia. Gromskii falls in love with her but on hearing of her earlier liaison with his friend Verskii attempts to commit suicide in her bedroom. Panaev's first society tale grew out of two strands of romantic fiction, the society tale proper and the tale depicting the fate of an artist in an alien and sometimes hostile world: lonely and misunderstood genius spurned by society. The conflict Panaev tried to depict in his first society tale is the typical romantic clash between an outstanding man and base society governed by bias.

Panaev went on to write several more society tales following the publication of *Spal'nia svetskoi zhenshchiny* in 1835. *Ona budet schastliva* (*She Will be Happy*) was published in 1836. The heroine of this tale, Zina, was forced by her parents into a loveless marriage. After several years she met and fell in love with a young man and eventually died. In this tale Panaev attempted to abandon the highly artificial

---

[4] I. I. Panaev, *Literaturnye vospominaniia*, Moscow, 1988, p. 63.

pompous style of Marlinskii and his imitators, striving to achieve simplicity and directness in his description of feelings, people and events. The tale enjoyed a measure of success and Belinskii noted Panaev's 'true talent, lively feelings, mastery of the language'.[5] Panaev's two society tales brought him to the notice of publishers and readers alike and the former began to solicit work from him. His literary career had begun in earnest.

In this article I intend to examine one of Panaev's most successful tales, *Onagr*, in which he attempted to bring together two diametrically opposed genres: the society tale, with its romantic provenance and all that that entails, and the physiological sketch, one of the early 'realistic' (even naturalistic) genres that for a time became popular in France and later (in the 1840s) in Russia.

Panaev was naturally attracted to satire and later he became one of the better known Russian satirists, excelling in physiological sketches of a type, or genre, which briefly dominated Russian prose in the 1840s and was very popular with the so-called 'Natural School'. Many of Panaev's later works were subtitled '*Ocherk*' (or 'Sketch'), thus emphasizing their 'realistic' (the *ocherk*) rather than imaginative (the *povest'*) thrust.

The originator of this direction in prose fiction was Honoré de Balzac, but his Russian followers, loosely termed 'The Natural School', also owed a great debt to Gogol' and Belinskii. The approach to fiction adopted by the members of this school had its roots in the growing importance and popularity of science in the 1840s, especially the prominence and scientific achievements of zoology, which by that time had progressed considerably in the study of the animal world.

The basic tenet upheld by the writers of the Natural School and derived from zoology was a direct dependence between man and his environment; the method of depiction was scientific in emphasis: the study of a typical phenomenon, class or type and its detailed, meticulous description. The criterion of 'representativeness' (*tipichnost'*) was also important for the writers of the Natural School and was directly opposed to the romantic tendency of presenting an unusual hero. Another important aspect of this movement was the desire 'to show the structure of the social organization, explain its

---

[5]V.G. Belinskii, *Sobranie sochinenii v deviati tomakh*, Moscow, 1976, vol. 1, p. 514.

peculiarities and open up [*vskryt'*] its pathology'.[6] Towards the second half of that decade (the 1840s), a clearer differentiation between the *povest'* (tale or novella) and the physiological sketch proper had begun to evolve: the *povest'* had to have a plot; it united objective depiction with subjective views; it spurned pure photography; but at its very inception these demarcations were far from obvious and, for that reason also, *Onagr* is an interesting example of an early 'mix' rather than a proper 'fusion' of elements typical for the two genres.

The ironic strand so prominent in Panaev's work is also evident in the Russian romantic fiction to which the society tale belongs, and is very pronounced, for example, in Senkovskii's tales. A full analysis lies outside the scope of this article, but satire and, more specifically, irony – especially 'romantic irony' – are important elements in *Onagr*.

Since this tale is not very well known, a brief summary of its plot, flimsy as it may be, seems necessary. The tale presents some episodes from the life of a young man from the provinces, who came to St Petersburg in search of fortune and a good position. The hero of the tale, Petr Aleksandrovich Raznatovskii, is the son of a provincial landlord, brought up by a doting mother. In St Petersburg, instead of working hard to achieve success, he whiles away his time in coffee-houses, theatres and visits, tries to start an affair with a society lady, and in general does not do very much. He is constantly short of money and is pursued by his creditors. Fortunately for him, his rich uncle dies, suddenly leaving him all his fortune. Raznatovskii is thus saved from disaster, and at the end of the tale marries a colonel's daughter who is in love with someone else. The plot is barely sketched and the force of the story does not derive from it. The plot is only a vehicle for the depiction and analysis of a type whom Panaev calls an 'onager'.

The structure of *Onagr* is fairly loose; its fundamental structural principle is consonant with the 'physiological sketch', which imitates the scientific mode of writing; that is to say, it dispenses with plot in favour of a series of descriptions whose end-product is the depiction of a certain social type. Yet the structure of *Onagr* also relies heavily on elements borrowed from the society tale; though loose and episodic, it is based on a series of scenes held together by a rudimentary plot, largely based on the pattern of a society-tale plot. The tale begins with the presentation of the hero and ends with his marriage. In various

---

[6]*Istoriia russkoi literatury*, Moscow, 1956, vol. 7, p. 522.

chapters Panaev portrays a typical day in Raznatovskii's life, his attempt to start a liaison with Katerina Ivanovna, whom he regards as an ideal society lady. Panaev tells us about his money problems, sketches portraits of his friends, and describes his courtship and marriage. Many of the scenes depicting his activities and presenting his social side, so to speak, belong to the canon of the society tale: the visit (in fact several visits), the ball, the masquerade, the conversations with a society lady. All these fixed generic elements play an important role in moving forward the plot of a society tale.

On the thematic plane, Panaev retains some elements central to the society-tale genre: for example the loveless marriage. Raznatovskii marries a girl who loves someone else and hates him. This theme is central to the society tale, yet Panaev inverts the situation: the hero, instead of having an affair with an unhappily married society lady, marries a woman who is in love with someone else and who is forced into the marriage by her parents.[7] The romance (in a society tale this usually takes the form of an extra-marital affair) happened before the tale had begun: Ol'ga, the girl Raznatovskii marries, has fallen in love with her music teacher, who returned her love. The music teacher is perhaps a pale echo of the artist (also a frequent figure in society tales) and represents the poor but noble lover. Thus the structural framework and the thematic elements extant from the society tale endow this work with the dynamics and a progression that a mere series of scenes would lack.

The tale was published in 1841 in *Otechestvennye zapiski* (number 5). It was begun around the end of 1840 and the beginning of 1841. *Onagr* is considered one of Panaev's best works and one which earned him a place in the history of Russian literature.

As has already been pointed out, the tale attempts to bring together, or 'join', two popular but very different genres of nineteenth-century prose: the society tale and the physiological sketch. The plot of *Onagr* follows, without much attempt at originality or invention, the typical plot of a society tale: a young man from the provinces arriving in the capital, bent on achieving success and making his way. The young man chosen by Panaev as the hero of the story is not the individualistic and strong-willed hero of the romantic variety, the usual hero of a society

---

[7]In the sequel to *Onagr*, entitled *Akteon*, Panaev describes the married life of Ol'ga and Petr. This tale is, however, less closely connected to the society tale.

tale. Raznatovskii is neither a strong character, nor is he really ambitious and ruthless. With his provincial upbringing, he is a type who may almost be called degenerate: a *pomeshchik* (landowner) without breeding, with vulgar taste and manners, lacking in sensitivity and understanding. The epigraph to the story, from Blumenbach's *Natural History*, taken from the chapter on onagers, wild asses and donkeys, signals to the reader the kind of young man that Raznatovskii is. Blumenbach describes the type as follows:

> The onager is found nowadays in particular in Tataria, from where numerous herds of onager migrate to India and Persia. This animal runs very fast and is satisfied with grass unfit for other animals; the tame or domesticated ass is his offspring. It is forbidden to export onagers for breeding to Spain under the threat of capital punishment.[8]

It is clear from this epigraph that the hero of Panaev's tale is far from being a strong romantic type; his aspirations are of the basest kind and reflect what he reads, which is mostly trash: his friends' tastes and his own predilections. The element of taste is important, because taste implies choice and is a hallmark of a real member of high society. Indeed impeccable taste is a *sine qua non* for such a man. The fact that the onager feeds on grass unfit (or rejected) for other animals by analogy implies that Raznatovskii is unable to choose the best; he is satisfied with second or even third rate. In short, he lacks discernment, a key characteristic of any true member of high society. Taste plays an important role in the tale because Raznatovskii vaguely feels that it is important but fails to acquire it.

His aim in life, his most cherished dream, is to belong to the 'real high society'. This desire is one of the central motifs in the story, its lynch-pin almost, and is connected with the idea (somewhat in the Platonic sense) of what is 'true' high society. In the society tale, 'true' high society is the milieu in which the action takes place and any outsider is immediately spotted by those belonging to 'the real thing'. In Panaev's tale, however, a central ambiguity – as to what *real* high society is (and I use the term here to indicate the behaviour, attitudes and way of life of a particular social group) and how one knows what

---

[8] I. I. Panaev, *Sochineniia*, Leningrad, 1987, p. 173. The quotation is taken from Blumenbach's *Natural History* but has been adapted by Panaev to give the reader a few hints about his hero.

the real thing is and what it is not – underlies much of the work's irony. Raznatovskii pays visits to certain houses and goes to balls which he assumes are those of high society. The distance between a genuine social reality and the second-hand one perceived as real by the unsophisticated provincial protagonist therefore endows the tale with an interesting ironic dimension. It seems that Panaev's hero is forever striving half-consciously for some ideal; he wishes to belong and makes numerous efforts to become a real man-about-town, learning to dance for example, but never fulfils his ambition and in the end is not even aware of the fact that, like the onager, he has accepted a false imitation as the real thing. Raznatovskii, even though at times experiencing vague stirrings of doubt in his mind, is too gross a creature, too vulgar, ever to see his mistake.

Panaev the writer is an ironic observer who skilfully interweaves two points of view in the story. Foregrounded is that of Raznatovskii, who has very few doubts, if any, that he is behaving as a genuine member of high society; but his knowledge of this élite group is fragmentary, flimsy and derived from flawed sources. The point of view of the omniscient narrator, on the other hand, is that of a man who really does know high society and its ways and who, from time to time, shows Raznatovskii up for the ignoramus that he is. Thus Raznatovskii is a dupe of his own notions and ideas and he ironically confirms what the epigraph to the story states: 'This animal [the onager] runs very quickly and is satisfied with grass which is unfit for other animals'. The onager accepts something inferior; Raznatovskii accepts an *ersatz* high society, the *demi-monde*, as the real thing.

The motif of high society life introduced at the beginning of Chapter Two comes to dominate the conversation of the three young men in the coffee-house, where Raznatovskii holds forth on his idea of a high society liaison: 'With an extra [in a ballet] it is impossible to think about exalted [*vozvyshennaia*] love; the society lady is quite a different matter: clever, sweet, a flirt...'.[9] Carried away by this subject matter, Raznatovskii goes on to describe the mechanism of conquest, stating that daring is the key as it ensures victory, and adds: 'After all, I've experienced all this'. It is of interest to compare Pechorin's reflections on the same theme – an important one in the society tale, which explores relationships between men and women, and especially

---

[9]Ibid., p. 179.

the war of the sexes: 'One thing always seemed strange to me: I never became a slave of the woman I loved; on the contrary, I always had unvanquished power over their wills and their hearts, without ever trying.[10] Pechorin's musings are those of a romantic hero in a society-tale setting; his is a charismatic personality; he is well skilled in power games in his relations with women and men; his knowledge derives from first-hand (and rich) experience. Raznatovskii's knowledge is not personal; he merely attempts to strike the pose of a romantic lover, donning the mantle of an experienced seducer. The war of the sexes, dangerous and fatal in Pechorin's case (for his victims, at least), is brought down to a shallow skirmish in the case of Raznatovskii. The tragic dimension is entirely absent in *Onagr* and this in itself shows its movement away from society tale.

The theme of the strong lover can also be seen as highlighting the importance of the society tale as a literary model for *Onagr*, but one from which Panaev is actually distancing himself: at times implicitly, at other times explicitly. The whole code of behaviour, dress, amusements and opinions followed by high society serves in *Onagr* as a foil, in order to achieve a poignant, comic and ironic effect. Panaev, as the plot unfolds, presents the chasm between the ideal life of high society and the real life of Raznatovskii, the boorish young *pomeshchik* who aspires to it and tries in vain to imitate it.

After the meeting with his friends, Raznatovskii decides to visit the Bobynins. Madame Bobynina is the married woman with whom he yearns to have an affair:

> Nowadays in high society everyone chooses ladies; nobody wants to look at unmarried women [*devitsy*]. I couldn't dance the mazurka so well before ... but now after I've had ten lessons things are quite different... It means a lot to dance the mazurka well.[11]

The central theme of the society tale is love and the relationship between the sexes, unfolding in a range of surroundings appropriate to the genre: the salon, the ball, the garden. According to Iurii Lotman, 'at a ball the nobleman [*dvorianin*] was neither a private person... nor a servitor [*sluzhivyi*] serving the state – he was a *dvorianin* at an

---

[10]M.Iu. Lermontov, *Polnoe sobranie sochinenii*, Moscow, 1948, vol. 3, p. 169.
[11]Panaev, *Sochineniia*, p. 180.

assembly of *dvoriane*, a man of his estate among his equals'.[12] The ball
was a freer event than service, but it was also a social organization with
its own rules and norms; it had a structure, a hierarchy (Lotman calls it
'a grammar'); each dance had its own behaviour and conversation to
match. Panaev devotes a whole chapter to the description of a ball
which his hero attends. Except for Chapter Nine ('The Conclusion'),
this is the only chapter in the story devoted to a single theme, and it has
both structural and artistic significance in *Onagr*. The ball, so often
described in Russian classics (it is to be found in the works of Pushkin,
Tolstoi, Gogol' and many others) is central to the life of high society
and it is perhaps the most consummate expression of the ideal of the
beautiful life. The ball at Madame Gorbacheva's house, which
Raznatovskii attends, is supposed to be a high society ball; it is
perceived as such by the hero; but certain details indicate that it is not,
that at best it is a *demi-monde* ball.

For instance, the number of differing carriages standing in front of
her house amounted to about nine and some guests (probably the
poorer ones) had come by sledge. This compares unfavourably with
Tolstoi's description of Natasha's first ball in *Voina i mir* (*War and
Peace*), where carriages constantly came and went, and the police kept
order in front of the house. The musicians at Madame Gorbacheva's
ball are stationed in the entrance hall, while in a real high society ball
they would have had a special place in a gallery above the room.
Panaev's use of such small but telling details indicates that this ball
does not take place in genuine high society. The behaviour of the
people present there, and especially that of the hero, is in contrast to
the behaviour of true *svetskie liudi* (society people). For example,
Raznatovskii's friend, the officer, who greets him as he comes in, roars
with laughter while dancing and shouts to the new arrivals. Another
episode at the ball is a scene with a fallen fan (another classic emblem
of the society tale), which emphasizes Raznatovskii's lack of
aristocratic ease and poise. Raznatovskii blushes at awkward moments
and fiddles with his tie to cover his embarrassment. In short, he is
representative of the boorish uncouth provincial, lacking real manners.
His conversation is as trite and as devoid of brilliance as his behaviour
and clothes.

The ball apart, there are other events depicted in this tale that often

---

[12]Iu. M. Lotman, 'Bal', in his *Besedy o russkoi kul'ture*, St Petersburg, 1994.

feature in the society tale and which pursue the same objective, to demonstrate that the society frequented by the hero is not true aristocratic society. The ironic attitude of the omniscient narrator serves to unmask this pretence. A good example of Panaev's use of irony comes in his short description of Madame Bobynina's boudoir:

> In Madame Bobynina's boudoir coloured glass half covered the window panes; between the windows stood a massive cabinet adorned with the figures of Amor; a flame was smouldering in the fireplace. She [Bobynina] dressed in a wide peignoir and sat on a damask sofa, *having adopted one of those graceful poses* which Russian authors of society tales describe so well.[13]

What follows in that scene is an imitation of a high society conversation during which Petr Raznatovskii unsuccessfully tries to confess his passion to Madame Bobynina, and is interrupted in mid-sentence. The declaration scene, another important structural element in the society-tale genre, remains unconcluded, emphasizing once more the vain attempts of the hero to assume the role of a society lady's lover.

However, this story also has the classical 'from rags to riches' turning point: the inheritance which in one fell swoop changes the situation of the Onager. One day, besieged by creditors and in despair, he is handed a letter from his mother announcing his uncle's death and making him a rich landowner. From that point on (the end of Chapter Five) the motif of high society undergoes a subtle change. Panaev now describes not a pretender, but somebody who has made it (or almost made it) – at least in his own view. Doubts about his being a real member of high society (a *svetskii chelovek*), which earlier in the story from to time beset him, now disappear almost completely. Once he has become rich, he goes to the best shops and buys the best furniture (from such as Gambs, supplier to the court). The attitude of those around him also undergoes a change. Mr Bobynin, who earlier had barely condescended to talk to him, now treats him as an equal and offers him various services; his wife, whom he meets at a masquerade, makes an assignation with him. Even his own thoughts of what a *svetskii chelovek* should do are lifted to a higher level:

> Ahem! – thought the Onager – very opportune! I will have a liaison in high

---

[13]Panaev, *Sochineniia*, p. 195.

society and a liaison on the stage [he wants to make a ballet dancer his mistress - R.S.]: this is necessary for a real man of the world; Balzac also writes about it and all the young men who belong to high society in St Petersburg follow this fashion.[14]

The pinnacle of his dreams is to become a man of fashion; this dream is fulfilled when he becomes the idol of the young men 'of medium quality' (*srednei ruki*) in the capital, who start to copy him. Rumours about him begin to fly all over St Petersburg. His dreams have come true. His story ends with his marriage to a girl who does not love him – but he fails even to notice it.

Alongside the society tale elements, Panaev uses – and these predominate and set the tone of the story – elements from the physiological sketch. The incongruity of these two strands combined together accounts for a great deal of the comedy in the story. These elements are used to satirize the genre of the society tale by employing its own elements. It is very difficult to classify the genre of this story precisely; however, perhaps due to this unusual mixture, it works well as a satire.

It must be said in conclusion, however, that *Onagr* had no offspring (unlike even the eponymous animal itself, which produced 'the tame or domesticated ass'), probably because, for one thing, the genre of the society tale was on the way out; and, for another, the mixture of society tale and physiological sketch proved unworkable. This attempt may not, then, have produced a line, but it remains an interesting experiment which deserves examination.

---

[14]Ibid., p. 215.

THE SOCIETY TALE AS PASTICHE: MARIIA ZHUKOVA'S HEROINES MOVE TO THE COUNTRY

HILDE HOOGENBOOM

> *O provintsialki, provintsialki! Vy na vse smotrite kakim-to strannym obrazom....!*
>
> Oh provincial women, provincial women! You look at everything in some strange way....!
>
> Mariia Zhukova, *Provintsialka* (1838)

Early in *Provintsialka* (*The Provincial Woman*, 1838), Mariia Zhukova's heroine Katia expounds in a knowing way on the vagaries of friendship in high society. Katia, introduced to Countess V. as an unknown young bride of an important general, is later not recognized by her when they next meet. However, now they are friends because, as Katia matter-of-factly explains, the countess's memory was jogged once Katia had been recognized at court. The problem of recognition, of really being seen, echoes throughout and beyond Zhukova's literary debut with the cycle *Vechera na Karpovke* (*Evenings on the Karpovka*, 1837-38), in which *Provintsialka* is the fifth of six tales set in an elaborate frame narrative.[1] In an interesting discussion of Zhukova's later *Naden'ka* (1853), Irina Savkina analyzes this predicament as the marginality of provincial women: 'One might say that all her main heroines experience some kind of "tragedy of disembodiment"'.[2] Savkina sees this marginality as having a dual nature:

---

[1] [M. S. Zhukova], *Vechera na Karpovke*, 2 vols., St Petersburg, 1837-38; republished Moscow, 1986. References to the later edition appear as page numbers in the text.

[2] Irina Savkina, 'Kategoriia *provintsial'nosti* v proze Marii Zhukovoi (povest' "Naden'ka")', *Slavica Tamperensia: Aspekteja*, vol. 5, Tampere, 1996, pp. 289-94. My thanks to Aleksandr Belousov at IRLI, who passed on Savkina's fine article, which inspired the present essay.

the heroine is marginalized both as a woman and as a provincial woman. Yet, to judge by the ability of provincial women to view things differently or strangely, Zhukova senses the advantages of a life begun at the margins: because of her outsider's viewpoint, Katia is socially astute in a way that recalls Pushkin's Tat'iana. Likewise, Zhukova uses the margins to find her literary persona's voice, as the provincial woman writer who narrates *Vechera na Karpovke*, in a wry, knowing self-representation as the insider who is an outsider with a faintly skewed perspective.[3] It is in *Provintsialka*, I believe that Zhukova most clearly expresses the aesthetic credo that she has developed in the course of writing *Vechera na Karpovke*.

Zhukova's passion for provincial Russian life permeates her writings from the very beginning of her literary career. Detailed descriptions of provincial towns and nature provide the settings for some works, and serve as digressions in others; *Ocherki Iuzhnoi Frantsii i Nittsy, iz dorozhnykh zametok. 1840 i 1842 gg.* (*Sketches of Southern France and Nice, from Travel Notes 1840 and 1842*, of 1844) is perhaps her best work. The frame of *Vechera na Karpovke* is situated outside St Petersburg; within this setting, the first story, *Inok* (*The Monk*), begins in a small provincial town that Zhukova's lone biographer, Konopleva, posits is Arzamas, where Zhukova grew up; the third story, *Medal'on* (*The Locket*), takes places in the countryside of Simbirsk, following 'the fashion of emigration' from St Petersburg for health reasons; *Provintsialka* is divided between St Petersburg and a regional town. The last story published in her lifetime, *Naden'ka*, opens with an essay on the narrator's love for the very distant countryside, on the Volga and far from the capital. On the basis of this story, Savkina examines the conception of distance from the capital in Zhukova's works as an essential, though unexamined, opposition between the provincial and the capital in Russian culture. Thus Zhukova's clear love

---

[3] Both Konopleva, in her biographical essay (p. 24), and Beletskii (p. 245) call Zhukova a '*provintsialka*' in life, which is not the same as in literature: M. S. Konopleva, 'Mariia Semenovna Zhukova', *Golos minuvshego*, 1913, 7, pp. 19-38; A. I. Beletskii, 'Epizod iz russkogo romantizma: Russkie pisatel'nitsy 1830-1860 gg.', (unpublished dissertation, Khar'kov, 1919) 240-90, in IRLI, R. I, op. 2, No 44a, 1 and 2.

for Russian nature has cultural and literary, as well as personal, significance.

Not surprisingly, in response to the implied superiority of the city over the country in this opposition, Zhukova at times couches intense, extensive expressions of love for provincial life defensively, as in *Provintsialka*:

> This is not attractive. Would these passing beauties, if someone told them, believe that in these little homes with little windows, with pots of balsam and wide shutters, people live cheerfully and even very happily; that in this monotonous and quiet life there is both love and poetry? (Zhukova, p. 207)

Yet, perhaps as she expected, in her time and again today, Zhukova has been understood mainly as a writer of society tales.[4] Beletskii (p. 244), who samples her depictions of nature at great length, is still right today: 'Criticism has not explained for us her writerly profile in either its fullness or its originality...'.

When we read Zhukova, we have not really encountered her. This failure goes to the heart of a problem in realist aesthetics, and ultimately one of gender, that she expresses most fully and artfully in *Provintsialka*. Her interest in provincial life was more than a love or a nostalgic weakness for her past, or a botanist's and artist's keen appreciation of nature (for example, *Naden'ka* contains many footnotes with the Latin names of plants). Through it she expressed an essential part of her realist aesthetics, a prosaics of daily life, which she broadly defined not by its subject matter, but as the quiddity of real life: change and its opposite, stasis. The prosaics of daily life that is unpoetic can be found in the works of such other Russian writers as Pushkin and Gogol', and, while her work shows their

---

[4]For example, Belinskii justified his criticisms of Zhukova by saying that he wishes not to be patronizing: 'now compliments in livings rooms have also become bad taste, and in literature they are decidedly tawdry' (2:574): V. G. Belinskii, *Polnoe sobranie sochinenii*, 13 vols. Moscow, 1953-59; on Zhukova see vol. 2, pp. 566-75, plus 4:410-18 and 8:422-6. See also: Joe Andrew, *Narrative and Desire: Masculine and Feminine in Russian Literature 1822-1849*, New York, St. Martin's Press, 1993, pp. 139-83; Hugh Anthony Aplin, 'M. S. Zhukova and E. A. Gan: Woman Writers and Female Protagonists 1837-1843', unpublished PhD dissertation, University of East Anglia, 1988; Catriona Kelly, *A History of Russian Women's Writing, 1820-1992*, Oxford, Oxford University Press, 1994, pp. 79-91.

influence when she explores the tensions between prose and poetry (Beletskii, p. 271), I want to suggest that she shaped these particular views via another literary route: one that can account for her clear preoccupation with gender.[5] In *Provintsialka*, Zhukova's male narrator Gorskii argues that it is provincial women rather than men who have the time to feel rather fully the meandering flow of daily life.

Zhukova's realism echoes that of the society tale, with important modifications that amount to a strong critique of the very principles of the genre. The society tale itself represented a move towards stories about day-to-day life, in a rejection of the improbable heroics, adventures, and excesses of romanticism and of historical novels, such as those of Walter Scott. Yet Zhukova finds this supposedly truer version of daily life equally improbable, for the simple reason that it appears in a book: novels 'choose one event in a person's life, stop at the dénouement and go no further, where another feeling, another life already destroys that unity' (Zhukova, p. 243). She experiments with this idea in *Provintsialka*, where she replays and recasts the romance between Katia and the Count three times: first as a passionate, youthful and true love that includes the Count fainting (with Zhukova's characteristic humour) and a failed elopement; then as a more mature, unidealized relationship; and, finally, as an unknown quantity beyond the end of the story and within the frame, where one of the listeners has 'actually' met them.

Zhukova also derides the society tale's special emphasis on feelings – for example, in the increasingly dispassionate romance between Katia and the Count. Elizabeth Shepard traces the development of the society tale into the 'decoloration and privatization of life' as one from description to analysis, from an external to an internal emotional life of characters, and from representations of events to ocular, medical metaphors for getting beneath the surface of life.[6] The feelings of the human heart, often a

---

[5]In a view that reflects his theoretical apparatus, Andrew, in *Narrative and Desire*, finds gender in the form of irreconcilable differences between men and women to be the defining themes of Zhukova's works. Another literary route not taken is the pastoral in George Sand's novels (see Beletskii, p. 279).

[6]Elizabeth C. Shepard, 'The Society Tale and the Innovative Argument in Russian Prose Fiction of the 1830s', *Russian Literature*, 10, 1981, pp. 111-62 (p. 116). On the society tale

woman's, motivate this deeper life. Zhukova is interested not in spying on the secrets of the human heart, which in any case is 'inscrutable', but in showing the instability of feeling. Again, novels cannot adequately represent this flux because they must end, and closure creates the illusion of something more whole than life can be (see Zhukova, p. 243).

Moreover, Zhukova considers the society tale's great interest in feelings to be simply excessive. In a digression on provincial life in *Provintsialka*, Zhukova's male narrator notes that it is the women, more than the men, who embody the true spirit of the provincial, because they have nothing to do:

> And likewise in the life of a provincial, if his days are poor in events, nevertheless they are overflowing with feelings; there feelings are deeper, more religious, where it is more concentrated, and if one can reproach the society dweller with occasional lightness of feeling, the provincial woman sins in their excess and pomposity. (Zhukova, p. 222)

In fact, Zhukova thumbs her nose at the romantic dichotomy between thought and feeling that is a constant theme in, for example, the works of Elena Gan or Karolina Pavlova. This opposition was often used by such critics as Belinskii to deny women the capacity for thought. Zhukova, like Gan and Pavlova, was sensitive to critics and, for example, rebutted N.N Verevkin's satire *Zhenshchina-pisatel'nitsa* (*The Woman Writer*, 1837) in her *Moi kurskie znakomtsy* (*My Acquaintances from Kursk*, 1840). The third chapter of *Provintsialka* begins with a digression on the progress of mankind from feeling to thought that should be read tongue-in-cheek:

> When people, shaking off the rude envelope of sensibility that dominates in youth, come of age, when a mental life begins to develop and thought, that giant of the world, takes charge over the soul of man, his mental eye [*oko*] turns upon himself, and he is astounded by his own greatness. (Zhukova, p. 195)

---

as a precursor to realism, see also R.V. Iezuitova, 'Svetskaia povest'', in *Russkaia povest' XIX veka: Istoriia i problematika zhanra*, edited by B.S. Meilakh, Leningrad, 1973, pp. 169-99.

Her rhetorical flourishes are an implicit argument against excess as such –
of emotion, or of thought for that matter. With the exception of Catriona
Kelly, critics have missed Zhukova's double-edged use of emotions
because, after all, feelings are a central *topos*. In a review of Zhukova's
second collection, *Povesti* (*Tales*, 1840), Belinskii noted that 'the author
has much soul, much feeling, and their burdensome fullness seeks self-
expression in something external' (Belinskii, 4:111). Like Belinskii,
Beletskii concludes that her feelings dictated her aesthetics (Beletskii, p.
254).

Zhukova rounds off her critique of the society tale's aesthetics by
explaining her views on nature, which she feels has more than the token
role it plays in society tales. In such tales the action moves from the
country to urban interiors, where rooms evoke spatially the narrow
smallness of a life hemmed in by social rules. Nature, no longer the scene
of romantic or narrative excess, has been transformed into a rare place
outside the strictures of society, where the individual can recover some
measure of a truer self. A character's capacity to respond fully to nature
can be a litmus test of virtue. It is easy to see why critics overlooked the
omnipresence of nature in Zhukova's works, viewing her as a society-tale
writer because she wrote *Baron Reikhman* and *Medal'on*, both included in
Vechera na Karpovke.[7]

Yet, in her works as a whole, Zhukova's vision of the Russian
countryside and provincial life does not work in a sketch-like thematic
way, by attesting to virtue or providing some relief from and contrast to
society. Indeed, in *Provintsialka*, Zhukova's heroine handily quashes this
cliché early on, when her uncle asks sarcastically, 'Of course, in the
provinces friendship is higher, purer, more perfect', to which she opines
that 'Society is the same everywhere', only 'more coarse' in the provinces
(Zhukova, pp. 187, 188). Instead, the provinces evoke a process, a way of

---

[7]Two dissertations argue in different ways for the essential capaciousness of the genre, the
first by a long list of definitions, and the second, by eschewing the laundry list, to focus on a
major theme, the art of conversation: Olga Samilenko Tsvetkov, 'Aspects of the Russian
Society Tale of the 1830s', unpublished PhD dissertation, University of Michigan, 1984;
Carolyn J. Ayers, 'Social Discourse in the Russian Society Tale', unpublished PhD
dissertation, University of Chicago, 1994.

life, a progression rather than a plot, to use James Phelan's distinction between focusing on the beginning and middle of the plot, rather than on the ending.[8]

In Zhukova's aesthetics, a country walk best evokes the large, relatively flat expanse of a real lived life, the standard by which she measured narrative in realist fiction.

> The life of a provincial is like a path that winds among the fields in the flat plains of the Penza or Samara *guberniia*; exhausted by the monotony, the traveller walks and in vain his gaze looks for something new in the distance: everything is the same. (Zhukova, p. 221)

This kind of progression actively resists the eventfulness of a literary plot, which in some way revolves around a beginning, a middle, and an end. In her most subtle critique of the society tale, Zhukova uses a narrative strategy that subverts a linear narrative and closure. By way of contrast, the narrative of society tales is exceptionally linear, relentlessly moving towards recognition and dénouement, the better to emphasize the mechanistic, automatic nature of high society.

Zhukova deploys her anti-narrative strategy most completely in making the boundary between the frame and the stories in *Vechera na Karpovke* porous. With the exception of Kelly, who gives Zhukova high marks for professionalism and control in her structure, no critic has felt it necessary to analyze how she manages the frame in relation to her stories and to what purpose. Rather, it is the absence of purpose, or of a familiar plot, that has unsettled critics. Ironically, Belinskii best describes the sensation of reading this work, but, while he sees her rejection of a certain plot structure, he does not recognize what he sees as meaningful. Nancy Miller finds this failure to recognize plots in works by women to be a recurrent phenomenon.[9] In his rather mixed reviews of Zhukova's works, Belinskii develops the idea of *belles lettres* which, in his view, was second-rate literature, and the metaphor of an opera where the parts do not add up to a

---

[8]James Phelan, *Reading People, Reading Plots: Character, Progression, and the Interpretation of Narrative*, Chicago, University of Chicago Press, 1989.
[9]Nancy Miller, *Subject to Change*, New York, Columbia University Press, 1988, p. 44.

whole: '...there is no commonality or whole, arranged by the necessity of each of its parts, of each feature, but much is said rightly and truly' (Belinskii, 2:566). He keeps returning to this theme:

> Not a single one of Zhukova's tales represents a drama, where every word, every feature appears necessary, the result of a reason, appearing of itself and for itself. No, these are sooner opera librettos, where the drama is necessary not for itself but for the situation and the situations are necessary again not for themselves but for the music, and where the drama is not in the drama but in the music — but where the music would not be understandable without the drama. (Belinskii, 4:111)

To complete his conception of her stories as compiled fragments, he attributes her excessive and boring use of essayistic digressions to Balzac (Belinskii, 4:116). Zhukova might as well have imitated the woman painter (Zhukova's other artistic hat) Laure in George Sand's *Indiana* (1832) and signed her name 'pastiche'.[10] In her discussion of the term 'pastiche', Miller interprets it as a 'female signature of protest' against traditional plots for women's lives (Miller, p. 89).

Yet critics have looked for signs of feminism in Zhukova's works and found her somewhat tepid. They inevitably compare Zhukova with Elena Gan (as did Belinskii in his major review of women writers) and agree that Zhukova does not challenge the social system that restricts women, and thus she appears resigned before the consequences.[11] But they have looked for protest in the details of the plot, a reductive appoach that Phelan,

---

[10]Beletskii (p. 249) establishes that, although her heroines do not read Sand's novels by name, Zhukova read them because she quotes and paraphrases Sand's characters. On her aquarelles, see Konopleva (p. 37), who saw them thanks to Zhukova's grandson; on her painterly palette in literary descriptions, see Beletskii (pp. 272-9).
[11]See Aplin, Andrew, and Kelly; see also Barbara Alpern Engel, *Mothers & Daughters: Women of the Intelligentsia in Nineteenth-Century Russia*, New York, Cambridge University Press, 1983, pp. 33-5. Only Kelly (p. 85) argues that this is not Zhukova's signature, calling for 'the necessity for a rereading of Zhukova's work, one which would not simply search for manifestos of liberation and find them lacking, but which would see her work in terms of broader issues of representation and autonomy'. By autonomy, Kelly means that Zhukova's professional identity as a woman writer (unlike Gan's) lay not in 'melodramatic representations of the oppression of women', but elsewhere, in her productivity (pp. 90-1), and, I would add, her artistic range.

among others, calls 'thematism', and not in the structure of the plot. It is here that Miller, in her chapter entitled 'Emphasis Added', argues we must overread women writers, because their plots are not recognizable as such:

> the plots of women's literature are not about 'life' and solutions in any therapeutic sense, nor should they be. They are about the plots of literature itself, about the constraints the maxim places on rendering a female life in fiction. (Miller, p. 43)

With the exception of a brief dismissal by Beletskii of Zhukova's aesthetic ponderings in *Chernyi demon* (*Black Demon*, 1842) as derivative, no one has paid attention to the various artistic manifestos embedded in her works. As we have seen, Beletskii is both right and wrong when he writes: 'Zhukova approaches her own works simply, apparently not considering them creations of high art' (Beletskii, p. 254).

The logic of Zhukova's metaliterary digressions is conveyed by her narrative progression, and in particular by her handling of closure in *Provintsialka* and in *Vechera na Karpovke* as a whole. Typically, closure in a society tale revolves around variations of the heroine's marriage or death. In her study of eighteenth-century French epistolary novels, Elizabeth MacArthur argues that the nineteenth-century novel is very focused on closure as a way to resolve the tensions and instabilities that drive the plot, in 'an attempt to preserve the moral and social order which would be threatened by endlessly erring narratives'.[12] In contrast, eighteenth-century epistolary novels emphasize the problematic nature of closure and, in some, 'the fact that ... inconclusive plots are accompanied by feminist commentary on society suggests that the failure to close might represent a protest against the "closures" generally imposed on women' (MacArthur, p. 6). Similarly, in Zhukova's collection, the closure of the six stories is modified by the open-endedness of the frame.

At the end of *Provintsialka*, Zhukova directly raises the problem of closure, when the hostess complains that there is no ending. Katia has

---

[12]Elizabeth J. MacArthur, 'Devious Narrative: Refusal of Closure in Two Eighteenth-Century Epistolary Novels', *Eighteenth-Century Studies*, 21, Fall 1987, pp. 1-20 (p. 5).

rejected the Count and moved to the countryside to raise his illegitimate child; the Count is travelling; his mistress Laureta is dead.

> — I don't like your tales without an end, — said Natal'ia Dmitrievna, — what is this? She plays the pianoforte and lives somewhere and now, how is it, perhaps, it happens that some day she will meet him! I would like to know what else happens with him.
> — *That is, you need to dance at a wedding or cry some at a funeral?* [my emphasis: HH]
> — Well yes, I like that better.
> — In the world that does not happen: in the life of each individual there are minutes, hours, years of truly poetic existence; they pass, and a person enters into the usual circle of life, completely prosaic, not attracting any attention — like these specks of dust. (Zhukova, p. 249)

In this and her other explanations of aesthetic issues, Zhukova betrays some anxiety that her strategy will not be recognized as sufficiently literary.

From this point on in *Vechera na Karpovke*, Zhukova plays with the possibilities of closure. At the conclusion of *Provintsialka*, within the frame, Zhukova creates a *second* ending, in so-called real life, that undoes this ending of the interior tale. Doctor Ivan Karlovich claims that, when he was called to an elderly woman's bedside last year, her niece Katia appeared with a young boy, and behind them entered a handsome man (the Count, we can assume). Gorskii, the male narrator of *Provintsialka*, explains that 'if people change today what they said yesterday, then one is forced to lie, in order to give them character' (Zhukova, p. 251). While these two male narrators provide different closures, their narratives are disrupted by female questioners who not only question their veracity, but do not like the story, and want to know such apparently unrelated things about Katia as whether she writes letters and are they good letters. With a nod at the epistolary art, Zhukova here plays and works with her realist ideas about the absence of closure, in the flux between story and frame: life is a state of change and life is static, ideas that are contradictory and true. Again, she uses a metaphor from nature to make her aesthetic point:

'... in this monotonous picture there is life and fascination ... the secret activity of nature' (Zhukova, p. 222).

Zhukova further complicates the issue of closure by creating a literary closure within the open-ended frame. Natal'ia Dmitrievna's niece and ward, Liubin'ka and Vel'skii, indicate that they are in love and want to marry. This is the kind of ending the listeners have desired but never got, a couple happily in love and able to marry. Zhukova highlights the precariousness of this happy ending when the doctor precedes it by telling the tale of how he interrupts the doomed love of a certain Olen'ka and her officer, a thinly veiled reference to Liubin'ka and Vel'skii. This is another double ending. More clouds of literary doom overshadow the future of the happy couple when we learn that the middle-aged bachelor Pronovskii, the narrator of *Baron Reikhman*, is none other than the tragic Aleksandr in the tale the doctor has just finished narrating, *Poslednii vecher* (*The Last Evening*). Pronovskii's nephew Vel'skii turns out to be the son of Elena, Aleksandr's beloved, who jilted him for another man, bore his child (Vel'skii) and died miserably. In one more indication of the literariness of this frame ending, Zhukova rewrites a literary tradition in which wards rarely marry and are frustrated in love.[13] *Poslednii vecher* is not in fact the last tale in the collection. This fabricated interrelationship of life and literature underscores how powerfully the plots for literary heroines echo in what Zhukova represents as real life, and the capacity of literature to change those plots.

Why does Zhukova develop this love story within a frame that until now has been a progression, without emphasizing closure? The effect is to highlight the framing role of the narrator of the tales as a whole: restricted to the frame, she nevertheless turns into a storyteller and writer herself. At various points in the frame, we find the narrator of *Vechera na Karpovke* walking around the setting of the tales, as she does before telling *Provintsialka*:

---

[13]See Svetlana Slavskaya Grenier, '"Everyone Knew Her and No-One Noticed Her": The Fate of the *Vospitannitsa* (Ward) in Nineteenth-Century Russian Literature', unpublished PhD dissertation, Columbia University, 1991; also Kelly, pp. 82-3.

> For a quarter of an hour I wandered along the paths, admiring the play of sunbeams
> between the thick vegetation of trees and drinking in the smell of flowers, until
> finally in the arbour made from acacias, woven with the aromatic peas, flickered
> Liubin'ka's dress: I entered. (Zhukova, p. 185).

We have already encountered this activity of a country walk as Zhukova's metaphor for realism. The narrator enters a scene that she will write (what she sees is the love story she reveals at the end) that occurs at the borders (in the frame) in several ways: in a pastoral setting; secluded, yet shared; unstructured, yet structured.

The motif of entering the arbour, or gazebo, lends itself to Miller's metaphor for coming to writing from George Sand's *Valentine* (1832) – the pavilion, located within a female pastoral (Miller, p. 205). In the arbour, Liubin'ka wants to confide her secret to the narrator, whom Pronovksii assures her, she can trust. In *Poslednii vecher*, it is Pronovskii's trust that was betrayed, and he seeks to spare his nephew a similar fate. The question of trusting the narrator arises after several stories, especially after *Provintsialka*, when the doctor's postscript in fact discredits Gorskii's claims to veracity. The doctor suggests that Gorskii lied to please the ladies, but, since he clearly has not pleased his listeners, it appears that neither man understands what these women want. By implication, through several double endings, Zhukova simply, perhaps whimsically, suggests that here is a narrator with a (narrative) strategy to whom women and men can entrust their plots of love.

Zhukova's playful and purposeful digressions on aesthetics have not been recognized as such by her readers, despite the fact that her metaliterary concerns in and of themselves are firmly Russian and nineteenth-century.[14] Moreover, her specific concerns with narrative, closure and open-endedness, with literary pastiches, and the boundaries between life and literature, likewise belong squarely to her literary era.[15] Finally, Zhukova had some good company in her real love for Russian

---

[14]See Michael C. Finke, *Metapoesis: The Russian Tradition from Pushkin to Chekhov*, Durham, North Carolina, Duke University Press, 1995, pp. 18-20.
[15]On this see Lidiya Ginzburg, *On Psychological Prose*, translated and edited by Judson Rosengrant, Princeton, Princeton University Press, 1991.

nature. While I have argued, therefore, that the origins for some of Zhukova's solutions to aesthetic problems can be found in her realist and feminist critique of the society tale, this is clearly only part of the rather more complex picture of her creative life.

Yet, in an important way, the society tale and an unimposing, loosely structured set of tales in a pastoral setting provided an accessible form and an apparently adequate disguise for Zhukova's certain literary ambitions, which are voiced in the opening of *Vechera na Karpovke*. Natal'ia Dmitrievna explains that the first works by great writers are not great and she lists a mixture of pastiches and small genres: Lomonosov's imitations of Trediakovskii, Bogdanovich's madrigals and poemas, and Karamzin's tale *Bednaia Liza* (*Poor Liza*). In his study of Russian metapoesis, Michael Finke suggests that writers reacted to pressures to reveal their metaliterary concerns by hiding them and that specific circumstances further shaped particular manifestations of this phenomenon. In attempting to see, yet not be seen, Zhukova and other such Russian women writers as Elena Gan, Nadezhda Sokhanskaia, Marko Vovchok, and Nadezhda and Sof'ia Khvoshchinskaia were able to find their literary and critical voices on aesthetic issues when they constructed themselves at the margins as provincial women writers.

TOLSTOI'S ALTERNATIVE SOCIETY TALES

W. GARETH JONES

Literary artifice, rather than life itself, often provided the impetus for Tolstoi's literary creation. Indeed, his first juvenile essay in fiction 'Istoriia vcherashnego dnia ('A History of Yesterday', 1851) owed as much to Laurence Sterne's analytic method in his *Sentimental Journey* as to Tolstoi's reflections on his own experiences. Tolstoi was endowed with an exceptional ability to grasp the essentials of literary genres, to understand the procedures of other great writers, be they English, French or Russian, but his genius lay in his power to absorb all this literary experience, to make it part of his being and transmute it into an inimitable enriched form. This is well illustrated by Tolstoi's response to the society tale. The general view is that the characteristic features of the society tale of the 1830s and 1840s were subsumed in Tolstoi's mature work, in both *Voina i mir* (*War and Peace*) and *Anna Karenina.* The aristocratic settings, the glitter of the *beau monde*, the social set-pieces of receptions, balls and theatre, the domestic traumas, the complicated games between the sexes, – all these obvious elements of the society tale are apparent in Tolstoi's work and are deployed with his peculiar intensity. It is not only the superficial characteristics that are subsumed, but also the society tale's essential concerns, particularly the acute recognition of Society's abiding presence and its authoritarian hold over the individual. The popularity of the society tale has indeed been attributed mainly to its portrayal of 'the dependence of men and women's private life on a dominant social setting.'[1] It may be recalled that one of Dostoevskii's criticisms of Tolstoi was that his characters were in danger of lacking individual autonomy, and tended to be determined by their social provenance.[2] Other concerns of the society tale, replayed particularly in *Anna Karenina,* were the dominant role of women in governing the rules of society, and the paradox of their

---

[1] R.V. Iezuitova, 'Svetskaia povest'' in *Russkaia povest' XIX veka: istoriia i problematika zhanra*, Leningrad, 1973, p. 173.
[2] F.M. Dostoevskii, *Polnoe sobranie sochinenii*, 30 vols, Leningrad, 1972-90, vol. 25, pp. 52-4.

personal vulnerability. The first reference to Tolstoi's conception of
Anna Karenina suggests some of these elements of the society tales.
His wife, S. A. Tolstaia, noted in her diary on 24 February 1870:

> Yesterday evening he told me that he had imagined a type of married woman
> from high society but who had ruined herself. He said that his task was to make
> this woman only pitiable and not blameworthy...[3]

Some of the situations of *Anna Karenina* had been anticipated in the
society tales; in Zhukova's *Baron Reikhman*, for example, the mistress
of the main character Levin is Nat'alia Vasil'evna, like Anna, mother of
a child and wife of an idealized, forgiving husband. R.V. Iezuitova,
discussing Pushkin's fragment of a society tale, beginning 'In the
corner of a small square ...' (1830-32), comments that 'in the
description of Zinaida, her pale weary face, her sickliness and
tiredness, the tragic outcome of her spiritual drama is presaged,
anticipating L. Tolstoi's *Anna Karenina*.'[4]

'In the corner of a small square...' may well be seen as a
continuation[5] of an earlier fragment by Pushkin, beginning 'The guests
were arriving at the dacha...' (1828-30), readily identified as a sketch
for a society tale, and the chance reading of which has been recognized
as the literary impulse that propelled Tolstoi into his writing of the first
draft of *Anna Karenina*.[6] The correspondences between that sketch and
the early drafts of *Anna Karenina* were exhaustively analysed by N.K.
Gudzii in his study of the early drafts and the relationship between
them and the final version of the novel. According to Gudzii it was F.I.
Bulgakov who recorded Tolstoi's immediate reaction to his reading of
Pushkin's fragment, by quoting his supposed words to a person who
had happened to interrupt his reading:

[3]*Dnevniki Sof'i Andreevny Tolstoi, 1860-1891*, edited by S.L. Tolstoi, Moscow, 1928,
pp. 35-6; quoted by N.K. Gudzii, 'Istoriia pisaniia i pechataniia "Anny Kareninoi"' in
L.N. Tolstoi, *Polnoe sobranie sochinenii*, 90 vols, Moscow, 1928-58, vol. 20, p. 578.
[4]Iezuitova, op. cit., p. 188.
[5]David Budgen, 'Pushkin and the Novel', in *From Pushkin to Palisandriia*, edited by
Arnold McMillin, Basingstoke and London, Macmillan, 1990, p.13.
[6]Gudzii, op. cit., pp. 577-8.

Here's a gem. This is how one should write. Pushkin goes straight down to business. Anyone else would have begun by describing the guests and the rooms, but he takes us immediately into the action.[7]

Accordingly, Pushkin's masterly economy of expression, the fragment's salient feature, apparently acknowledged by Tolstoi, provided the impetus for the first drafts of what would become *Anna Karenina*.

Gudzii, however, was not wholly convinced that the fragment's sole lesson for Tolstoi would have been to prompt him into eventually beginning his novel *in medias res* with the words, 'Everything was upset in the Oblonskiis' house'. The novel was initially planned to begin with the episode describing Princess Betsy Tverskaia's reception, after a night at the opera in the French theatre, which corresponds with chapters 6 and 7 of the second part of the final version of *Anna Karenina*. Although the episode's eventual position might mask its debt to Pushkin's fragment, the formal correspondences between the two in matters of dialogue, setting and characterization, as Gudzii demonstrated, are obvious.[8] However, in Gudzii's analysis, the question of Tolstoi's possible reaction to the particular dynamics of society presented by Pushkin in his society tale sketch is not raised. Yet it is the dominant role of society, its overwhelming presence in individual lives, that is the striking feature of the sketch; it is precisely this that qualifies 'The guests were arriving at the dacha...' as a society tale. As Iezuitova explains: '"Society" accompanies the characters, participates in their relationships, dictates its conditions to the characters, propels them towards various actions'.[9]

An entry in S.A. Tolstaia's diary suggests that one reason why her husband would have reacted so keenly to the examination of Russian high society in Pushkin's fragment was that questions of the nature of Russia's nobility were uppermost in his mind at the time. With Annenkov's edition of Pushkin open in his hands, Tolstoi told his wife, 'I am learning a great deal from Pushkin, he is my father and one has to learn from him'. S.A. Tolstaia then goes on to say:

Then he read over aloud to me about the bygone days, how the landowners lived and travelled on the roads, and here he found many explanations for the

---

[7] Ibid., p. 578.
[8] Ibid., p. 584.
[9] Iezuitova, p. 187.

way of life of noblemen even in the time of Peter the Great, a matter that had
particularly tormented him; but in the evening he read various fragments and
under the influence of Pushkin began to write.[10]

His wife's reference to Tolstoi's 'torment' is suggestive. When
discussing the Russian society tale, one should not take it for granted
that the image of 'Society' was firm, even for men of apparently
unchallenged inherited nobility such as Pushkin and Tolstoi. When
reading Jane Austen there appears to be little doubt about the
constitution of her Society; her heroes have estates and incomes which
define their social position.[11] Russian society, however, had since the
time of Peter the Great differed from that of Western Europe in its lack
of definition by landed estates. Much of Russian eighteenth-century
literature – and this was epitomized by the experience of that century's
moral journals – was concerned with the need, felt even by noblemen,
to define the Russian nobility; that self-conscious need for demarcation
was inherited by the writers of the society tale. Indeed it might have
been made more acute by the contemporary influence of those French
writers in the 1830s who were also unsure about the delineations of
their Society in post-revolutionary France. Stendhal, for example, has
been seen as regretting the loss of *le monde* of the Old Regime with its
'public system of values and rules, gestures and codes'.[12] What had
replaced it was a society which, despite its attempts to refashion a
Restoration aristocracy in country *chateaux* and Parisian *salons*, was in
Stendhal's perception 'mostly a rather ludicrous fake'.[13] The phoney
aristocratic 'de' adopted by Balzac in 1831 was one sign of the
sensitivity to the fluidity of *le monde,* and the ambivalence of the
writer's position within it. It was that 'fake' that Tolstoi found
tormenting.

---

[10]Gudzii, p. 578.
[11]See the comment by Oliver MacDonagh, *Jane Austen: Real and Imagined Worlds*,
New Haven and London, Yale University Press, 1991, p. 135: '*Emma* presents a
comparatively self-enclosed and static social organism with clearly understood
principles of stratification.'
[12]Peter Brooks, *The Novel of Worldliness: Crébillon, Marivaux, Laclos, Stendhal*,
Princeton, New Jersey, Princeton University Press, 1969, p. 225.
[13]Ibid., p. 227.

An excellent case has been argued by Elizabeth Shepard for the 'innovative' nature of the society tale.[14] But her advocacy should not blinker us from seeing in Russian writers an abiding and continuing impulse to define the Russian nobility – not by estate, wealth and rank, but by cultural appendages and marks.[15] Attention is drawn by Iezuitova to the debt owed by the society tale to the literature of the Russian enlightenment, particularly its satire. As was the case in the eighteenth century, the centre of attention for the society-tale author of the 1830s, she maintains, was often 'the sins and shortcomings of contemporary noble society which are exposed to satirical mocking.'[16] It is the eighteenth-century enlightenment rationalism that she sees at work in the authors' approach to contemporary social problems and their striving to affect social mores directly. What she did not fully acknowledge, however, was the need felt by those authors to present a nobility that would be clearly defined and demarcated. The purpose of their satire was not to be purely negative, rejecting the presumptions of a higher stratum in the social organism, but to suggest the possibility of a positive, exemplary pattern of social behaviour.

It is this that is apparent in Pushkin's fragment 'The guests were arriving at the dacha...', where Pushkin has a visiting Spaniard ask the vital question:

> ...what is the Russian aristocracy? In studying your laws, I can see that a hereditary aristocracy based on the indivisibility of estates does not exist with you. It seems that there is civic equality amongst your nobility, – and that access to it is limited to nobody. On what then is your so-called aristocracy based? Can it be solely on the antiquity of the lines of famous Russian people?[17]

The Russian replies by stating that the Russian nobility (*dvorianstvo*) descended from Riurik and Monomakh had degenerated into a kind of third estate. The present-day aristocracy, he complains (and it was a complaint shared by both Pushkin and Tolstoi), hardly knew who their grandfather was, and their line went back only as far as Peter I and

---

[14]Elizabeth C. Shepard, 'The Society Tale and the Innovative Argument in Russian Prose Fiction of the 1830s', *Russian Literature*, 10-2, 1981, pp.111-161.
[15]Ibid., p. 130.
[16]Iezuitova, p. 170.
[17]A.S. Pushkin, *Polnoe sobranie sochinenii*, 6 vols, Moscow-Leningrad, 1936-38, vol. 4, p. 339.

Catherine II.[18] The Russian had to admit that for people like himself the past might as well not exist: 'We do not take pride in the glory of our forefathers but in the rank of some [idiot] uncle or in a ball given by a female cousin.'[19] This urge to define Pushkin's contemporary society, the new Petrine aristocracy, is clearly articulated in 'The guests were arriving at the dacha...' and it would have been a problem to which Tolstoi was particularly attuned. It was a very Russian problem. (It is striking that no English rendering can quite capture the full significance of Tolstoi's introduction of representatives of the old Muscovite nobility in *Anna Karenina*: '*Doma Levinykh i Shcherbatskikh byli starye dvorianskie moskovskie doma...*'; Maude's translation, 'The Levins and Shcherbatskys were two old aristocratic Moscow families...' will not quite do.)

That Russian literature had for many decades sought to demarcate Russia's nobility may be the answer to Belinskii's sardonic rhetorical question, in response to Shevyrev's coining of the term 'society tale' (*svetskaia povest'*) in 1835: 'Are there such things as peasant, petty-bourgeois and minor-officialdom tales?'.[20] None of these three estates had hitherto persuaded writers that they were in need of careful definition; a *chinovnik* was a *chinovnik*, a peasant a peasant. But there had been a long tradition in Russian literature of attempting to define the elusive Russian nobility, of determining the contours of what 'noble society' should be. The aftermath of the Decembrist uprising and the Nikolaevan regime which had marginalized the flower of the Russian nobility had given that tradition a new edge, as was apparent in Pushkin's fragment.

* * *

Three moments in *Anna Karenina* stand out as passages where it seems that Tolstoi is attempting to define Society; in all three cases the patterning of the society tale of the 1830s in discernible.

---

[18]Budgen, op. cit., p. 34, indicates '...the degree to which Pushkin's writing is prompted, particularly around 1830, by his feeling of social resentment, of being usurped by the "new" aristocracy.'
[19]Pushkin, loc. cit.
[20]V.G. Belinskii, *Polnoe sobranie sochinenii*, 13 vols, Moscow, 1953-59, vol. 2, p. 133.

It is most obvious in the scene [part II, chapters 6-7] in Princess Betsy Tverskaia's house after the opera, where she had barely had time to powder her face and order tea before '...one carriage after another began to arrive at the door of her immense house on the Great Morskaya'.[21] So begins the episode which is most indebted to Pushkin's 'The guests were arriving at the dacha...'. In its transference to the second part of the novel, its link with Pushkin's fragment, as Gudzii suggested,[22] may be less obvious. Yet if the two pieces are read side-by-side, the debt is unmistakable; and it is remarkable that most of the correspondences listed by Gudzii relate to distinct features of the society tale. Indeed many features of the society tale were exploited here, and Joan Delaney Grossman has drawn particular attention to its 'innovative use of the society tale's conventions of discourse.'[23]

The setting, in both cases, is that of a society tale; a *soirée* following a visit to the opera house. Pushkin's narrative is developed by the appearance in the drawing room of Vol'skaia, a married woman in love with Minskii, who is already present among the guests; Tolstoi's initial draft breaks off with the arrival of Anna Karenina and her husband. In the final version, however, Vronskii makes his appearance in Betsy's *soirée*, first towards the end of the sixth chapter, to be followed by Anna's entrance at the beginning of the seventh. It is the conventional society background that propels Anna and Vronskii closer to their adulterous union. The movement in the episode is of an Anna, at first at odds with this setting, towards an Anna who is adapted to society's mores. As in Pushkin's fragment, Society shapes the characters. The arbiters of this Society are its women: at the samovar the presiding genius, Princess Betsy Tverskaia, dispenses tea, while at the other end of the room an ambassador's wife – a society beauty – is the nucleus of another centre. The stylized grouping of the characters gathered about a round table in both Pushkin's fragment and Tolstoi's initial draft was another common feature that Gudzii had seized upon. He noted too Tolstoi's reflection of the malicious gossip, particularly

---

[21]Leo Tolstoy, *Anna Karenina*, translated by Louise and Aylmer Maude, Oxford and New York, 1995, p. 132. Future references will be made in the text to pages in this 'World's Classics' edition.
[22]Gudzii, p. 585.
[23]Joan D. Grossman, '"Words, Idle Words": Discourse and Communication in *Anna Karenina*', in *In the Shade of the Giant: Essays on Tolstoy*, edited by Hugh McLean, Berkeley, University of California Press, 1989, p. 117.

about women, described by Pushkin. In the final version, the dialogue of gossip is splendidly deployed and Joan Grossman has highlighted the abundance of double meaning and ambiguity used by Tolstoi to illustrate the 'small talk' (Tolstoi uses the English expression) at which the ambassador's wife was so adept.[24]

The small talk turns to society wit. In Pushkin's fragment it was the Spanish guest who retold a foreign lady's *risqué* joke about Petersburg winter nights being too cold and the summer nights too light for amorous affairs.[25] Here it is the Ambassador who asks if there isn't something Louis XV about Tushkevich, inviting the rejoinder, 'Oh yes! He matches the drawing-room; that is why he comes here so often!' (133)

Just in case the reader has not mastered the code of society discourse, the narrator intervenes to provide an elucidation; this was another common feature of the society tale.[26]

> This conversation did not flag, since it hinted at what could not be spoken of in this room, namely, at the relations existing between Tushkevich and their hostess. (133)

The intrusive narrator, ready to guide the reader in retailing each detail, not only of the linguistic code but also of demeanour and deportment, is also present when Anna enters in Chapter 7, approaching her hostess 'with that quick, firm yet light step which distinguished her from other Society women' (136). But she does not infringe the code of polite social discourse and, when asked her view in a lighthearted, sophisticated exchange on extra-marital affairs, she displays – with just a touch of hesitation – the society lady's sophisticated skill in hinting at experience in sexual relations, without admitting her own vulnerability:

> 'I think,' replied Anna, toying with the glove she had pulled off, 'I think...if it is true that there are as many minds as there are heads, then there as many kinds of love as there are hearts.' (137-8)

---

[24]Ibid., pp. 119-22.

[25]Pushkin, op. cit., vol. 4, p. 334.

[26]See Carolyn Jursa Ayers, 'Social Discourse in the Russian Society Tale', unpublished PhD dissertation, University of Chicago, 1994, p. 216: 'Tolstoy illuminates several society tale scenes with authorial commentary to expose the sordid aspects of Anna and Vronsky's relationship in *Anna Karenina*.'

Anna struggles to use that skill in society conversation to maintain a decent distance between herself and Vronskii, even when they have removed themselves, contrary to the rules of the society drawing-room, from the other guests. But conversation here expresses its old meaning of social intercourse rather than an exchange of words. It is wordlessly that Anna admits her feelings to Vronskii:

> She exerted all the powers of her mind to say what she ought; but instead she fixed on him her eyes filled with love and did not answer at all.
> 'This is it!' he thought in rapture. 'Just as I was beginning to despair, when it seemed as though the end would never come... here it is! She loves me! She acknowledges it!'
> 'Do this for me: never say such words to me, and let us be good friends.' These were her words, but her eyes said something very different. (139)

As it becomes apparent that Vronskii and Anna have broken Society's rules by isolating themselves from the company (just as Zinaida Vol'skaia does in Pushkin's fragment), Princess Betsy Tverskaia intervenes and brings them back on side according to the rules of the game. And again it is noticeable that the umpires in the society game are women.

There is little doubt about the general satiric undertone to the description of Princess Betsy Tverskaia's society, which Iezuitova saw as one of the main features of the society tale. But does the satirical portrayal succeed in hinting at the possibility of a contrary form of society with honest, noble relations? Princess Betsy Tverskaia's false St Petersburg society seems irredeemable. If there is a suggestion of alternative social relationships, it is perhaps through the presence of Princess Miagkaia, who plays a role not unlike that of Hans Christian Andersen's boy who could not see the Emperor's clothes.

Her role is to deconstruct the social discourse expected of the society tale. Her Russian name in itself sets her apart from Princess Betsy and the ambassador's anonymous wife. So does her unprepossessing appearance and dowdy dress, features which tend always to be a positive indicator of moral probity in Tolstoi: she is introduced as a 'stout, red-faced, fair-haired lady who wore an old silk dress and had no eyebrows and no chignon' (132-3). Her placing is also significant: she occupies an isolated position in the drawing-room, belonging neither to the coterie gathered around Princess Betsy's samovar nor to the one surrounding the ambassador's wife at the other end of the room. Her first intervention is to show up the pretentiousness of the oft-repeated, fashionable cliché that the Swedish diva Nilsson had learnt her operatic poses by studying Kaulbach's engravings of Shakespearean scenes. It would have been the kind of superficial reference to a common high culture that was characteristic of society tale discourse, often 'suffused with literary references and clichés'.[27] Miagkaia's observation brings conversation to a halt. Not for nothing has Miagkaia ('Gentle' or 'Mild' is an ironically telling name) become 'notorious for her simplicity and the roughness of her manners, and nicknamed *l'enfant terrible*' (133). A second time she interrupts the elegant 'small talk' to chatter about a visit to the Schuzburgs who are bankers, and, it is implied, outside the strict social pale. Miagkaia proudly states that the Schuzburgs' 1,000-rouble sauce served at their dinner was inferior to her 85-kopeck recipe. What produced Miagkaia's effect, explains the narrator at this point, was that exceptionally 'her words were simple and had a meaning'.

> The effect produced by the Princess Myagkaya's words was always the same; and the secret of that effect lay in the fact that although she often – as at that moment – spoke not quite to the point, her words were simple and had a meaning. In the Society in which she lived words of that kind produced the effect of a most witty joke. The Princess Myagkaya did not understand why her words had such an effect, but was aware that they did and availed herself of it. (134)

It is fitting, therefore, when the scurrilous small-talk turns to the casting of witty aspersions on the Karenins, that Miagkaia swims resolutely against the general tide of society's opinion by defending Anna bluntly and declaring that Karenin is stupid: 'Anna Karenina is a splendid woman. I don't like her husband, but I am very fond of her' (135).

The general view is that the society tale was motivated by a clash between independent human emotions, aspirations for individual happiness and the oppression of social mores. That collision, however, is not what Tolstoi wished to inherit from the society tale. He was less interested in the freeing of the individual from Society than in the restoration of a good society in which individuals could thrive.

---

[27]Ibid., p. 83.

Princess Miagkaia within Betsy's salon is more than the somewhat inert 'counterforce' identified by Grossman as a means to highlight the artificiality of the other guests.[28] She is rather a positive pointer to an alternative society, which should be like her: plain of face, plainly dressed, and, above all, plain speaking. It would be a homely, and so truly noble society. Significantly Princess Miagkaia's authority is later invoked in Part 3, Chapter 17, when Anna is invited to a croquet match involving two ladies and their admirers from 'a choice new Petersburg circle, called, in imitation of an imitation of something *Les sept merveilles du monde*' (297). When Anna fails to understand or accept the conventions of her 'cosy chat' (again the English phrase is used) with Princess Betsy Tverskaia, the latter laughingly compares her to an '*enfant terrible*', reprimanding her with the mocking charge: 'You are encroaching on the Princess Myagkaya's domain!' (297).

Princess Miagkaia's role alone might not justify the contention that Tolstoi is intent on insinuating the image of an alternative 'Society' into his novel at the expense of the conventional *monde* evoked by the society tale. But there are other considerations. Had the conventional society tale setting of the *soirée* after the opera remained in its original position, at the beginning of the early draft of *Anna Karenina*, it would have been given particular force. But it is moved from that position of prominence. By postponing it to its eventual less conspicuous place in Chapter 6 of the second part of the novel, Tolstoi had lessened its impact.

In Chapter 6 of the novel's first part, precedence is given to another picture of society that might well be perceived as 'Princess Miagkaia's domain'. Here Tolstoi presented his reader with a Society more in keeping with the older noble traditions whose passing Pushkin had regretted in his fragment. The perception there of a truly noble society is from the point of view of a Levin who is inherently plain-speaking, as is made evident from his embarrassment at being frustrated by convention from telling Oblonskii that he has come to Moscow to propose to his sister-in-law. What charms him about this society is its age, good education and sense of honour. There is no doubt about the irony with which Tolstoi insinuates his own deprecating view of the modern manifestation of the marks of nobility in the long period

---

[28]Grossman, op. cit., p. 119.

beginning with the plaintive '*dlia chego?*' ('for what reason?' or 'why?') which is then repeated as a refrain:

> Why these three young ladies had to speak French and English on alternate days; why at a given time they played, each in turn, on the piano (the sound of which reached their brother's room where the students were at work); why those masters of French literature, music, drawing, and dancing came to the house; why...etc. (21)

There is an echo of Pushkin's regret at the transformation of the Russian nobility into a kind of third estate in the listing of those approved social positions which Levin has not achieved: 'his former comrades were already colonels, aides-de-camp, Bank and Railway Directors, or Heads of Government Boards like Oblonsky...' (22). There is irony again in the exclusion of the country squire, the '*pomeshchik*', from the noble ranks 'in the opinion of Society' ('*po poniatiiam obshchestva*'). The irony may indicate the brittleness of even the remnants of Russia's true noble society. Yet this is a passage that might have confirmed James Joyce's suspicion which he once voiced that, under the rough, rustic image presented by the writer, was a Tolstoi who 'speaks the very best Russian with a St Petersburg accent and remembers the Christian name of his great-great-grandfather.'[29] Here is an intimation of that mysterious, truly noble society, that could sustain and enhance individual aspirations.

A third moment in *Anna Karenina* that might be recognized as a miniature society tale within the novel is the episode set in the German spa where Kitty is taken to recover from the depression brought about by Vronskii's rejection of her. It has a distinctive place in the novel concluding the second part, Chapters 30-35. It begins by drawing attention to the society background in a 'little German watering-place'. Spa settings such as this were typical of society tales and one of Pushkin's fragments was headed '*Roman na kavkavskikh vodakh*' ('A Romance in a Caucasus Watering-place').[30] Under the presidency of a real Western aristocrat, a German Fürstin, the 'usual crystallisation ...of Society...assigning to each person a definite and fixed position'

---

[29]James Joyce to Stanislaus Joyce, July 1905, *Selected Letters of James Joyce*, edited by Richard Ellmann, New York, The Viking Press, 1975; quoted in McLean, *In the Shade of the Giant*, p. 73.
[30]Pushkin, vol. 4, pp. 364-5.

(213) is ensured. The enclosed society of the spa regulated by its Kurliste (from which Kitty recognizes Nikolai Levin and his mistress) does indeed provide the constricted canvas on which society tales could be drawn.[31] There are other features of this section reminiscent of the society tale. Women predominate, not only the German Princess but also the aloof Madame Stahl belonging to the 'highest Society'. The dubious artificiality of her position is suggested by the ironic comment that 'Some people said that she had made for herself a position in Society by her pose as philanthropic and highly religious woman' (219). Her adopted ward Varen'ka is that recognizable survival of the heroine of sentimentalist literature with her innocent, good heart and positive moral example. Despite her low breeding as the daughter of a *chef*, Varen'ka possesses all the conventional society attributes: she speaks French and English admirably and is an excellent singer of Italian songs. Like a sentimental heroine she is plain speaking and possesses 'the secret of what was important, and to what she owed her enviable tranquillity and dignity' (222). Another feature of the society tale are the frank confidences exchanged between Varen'ka and Kitty about their disappointment in love affairs.

Chapter 33 begins with the characteristic 'education scene' which Carolyn Ayers has told us is almost invariably present in the society tale.[32] Madame Stahl, whose position in Society has resulted from her pose as a highly religious woman, instructs Kitty in Pietism. 'This was a lofty, mystical religion connected with a series of beautiful thoughts and feelings, which it was not only possible to believe because one was told to, but even to love', explains the narrator (223). In the light of that encomium, the instruction from Madame Stahl runs counter to the kind of teaching invariably given in the society tale's 'education scene'. There the teacher, according to Ayers, invariably paints a picture of Society as an immoral, image-obsessed group into which the novice is invited to be initiated by a cynical mentor. Consequently readers of society tales, sensitive to the subtext of the conventional 'education scene', might well feel uneasy at Madame Stahl's teaching, as indeed does Kitty. The true alternative high society, Tolstoi suggests, is not in high moral and religious living. It can lead in practice to the jealousy

---

[31] Ayers, op. cit., p. 216, indicates how Turgenev would emphasize the sense of social confinement by removing 'society' to the isolation of a country estate.
[32] Ayers, p. 55.

that Kitty's ministrations to the consumptive artist Petrov arouses in his wife.

What then is the true noble society? In this pastiche of a society tale, it is the return of Prince Shcherbatskii that intimates it. He is unashamedly a man who comes from 'Princess Miagkaia's domain' with its rough frankness, and is a Shcherbatskii, from the long line of Shcherbatskiis, whose behaviour demonstrates the wholesomeness of that traditional Russian noble society so appreciated by Levin in Part 1, Chapter 6. In the spa of Soden he breaks the female dominance, speaks 'excellent French which so very few people speak nowadays' (229), is replete with infectious good spirits, generous to a fault, and is demonstrably Russian in his utter disdain for the German view that 'time is money' (232) and for any social or religious pretence.

Tolstoi undoubtedly draws on the society tale in showing the coercive and stifling effect of social conventions on a sensitive individual such as Kitty, who declares to Varen'ka that 'I can't live except by my own heart' (234). But Tolstoi would disagree with Kitty's self-centredness; his characters cannot 'live by their own hearts'. Individuals for him can only prosper in a supportive Society, which is utterly unlike the superficial society portrayed in the typical society tale but which, nevertheless, may be implied by those tales.

The Soden 'society tale' ends with a coda in which the society that will sustain Kitty is indicated:

> ...with her father's return the world in which she had been living completely changed for Kitty. She did not renounce all she had learnt, but realised that she had deceived herself when thinking that she could be what she wished to be. It was as if she had recovered consciousness...
>
> ...she longed to get away quickly to the fresh air, back to Russia, to Ergushevo...
>
> ...The doctor's prediction was justified. Kitty returned to Russia quite cured! (235)

Her new society would be the genuine Russian society of Levin's estate at Pokrovskoe. But to cast full light on Pokrovskoe – where Levin was 'merely a country squire, spending his time breeding cows, shooting snipe, and erecting buildings – that is to say, a fellow without talent, who had come to no good and was only doing what in the opinion of Society good-for-nothing people always do' (22), Tolstoi had to provide the contrasting shadows of that opinionated Society. In that he was assisted by the society tale, whose well-worn conventions were exploited and subsumed into *Anna Karenina*. And the germ of a novel suggested in Pushkin's society tale fragment 'And the guests were arriving at the dacha...' – 'an attempt to portray the social experience of his age through contemporary characters'[33] – may well have come to its fruition in Tolstoi's masterpiece.

---

[33]Budgen, p. 10.

SVETSKAIA POVEST' AND THE 'WORLD' OF RUSSIAN LITERATURE

RICHARD PEACE

In any attempt to view the 'society tale' in the context of Russian literature, certain problems inevitably arise. First of all the question must be asked if such a thing as the Russian 'society tale' really exists. Are the boundaries of the genre sufficiently clear? Thus although both John Mersereau Jr. and Neil Cornwell amply attest its existence, it is, nevertheless, interesting that several of the tales mentioned by Mersereau appear in a collection published in 1980 under the title *Russkie romanticheskie povesti*, and Neil Cornwell has published some of Odoevskii's 'society tales' under the rubric *Romanticheskie povesti*.[1] For the purposes of the present article, we must assume that any short novel or tale, which is set principally in 'polite society', may qualify as a 'society tale'.

A second, and more fundamental, question concerns the 'Russianness' of the genre. After all, *svet* is merely the Russian calque of the French word *'monde'* in its restricted sense of *'le beau monde'* – 'Society'. In a Russian context, the foreignness of this concept is only too apparent, as the heroine of Marlinskii's *Ispytanie* (*The Test*) complains: 'But can one imagine how intolerable copies of the Parisian world [*parizhskogo mira*] are in Russia'.[2] The members of this *svet*

---

[1] See: John Mersereau Jr., 'The Nineteenth Century: Romanticism, (1820-400)', in *The Cambridge History of Russian Literature*, revised edition, edited by Charles A. Moser, Cambridge, Cambridge University Press, 1992, pp. 162-6; and Neil Cornwell, *The Life, Times and Milieu of V.F. Odoyevsky, 1804-1869*, London, Athlone Press, 1986, pp. 51-5. See also: *Russkaia romanticheskaia povest'*, Moscow, 1980; and V.F. Odoevskii, *Romanticheskie povesti* (introduced by Neil Cornwell, reprint of Leningrad, 1929 edition, edited by O. Tsekhnovitser), Oxford, Meeuws, 1975.

[2] A.A. Bestuzhev-Marlinskii, *Sochineniia v dvukh tomakh*, Moscow, 1981, vol. l, p. 230 (hereafter '*Sochineniia*'). See also N.F Pavlov's *Iatagan* (*The Dagger*, 1835): 'All the passions, desires and proclivities of man are easily accommodated in the narrowest of space, and this little world, a copy of the large one, contained within itself the initiation of many varied emotions of the heart. For some there was something to be

speak only French and their behaviour is conditioned by the
conventions and taboos of French 'polite society'. Into this narrow
world no lower order of human being is allowed to enter, except for the
fleeting appearance of a servant. We are dealing here exclusively with
what N.G.Pomialovskii would later define as 'cleaned up humanity'.[3]
The word *svet* itself, with its other connotation of 'light', seems to
suggest the insubstantiality and external brilliance of this world.
Indeed, many of its denizens seem almost to be endowed with the
properties of light themselves – they are '*svetleishie*' and '*Vashe
siiatel'stvo*'. It is a society marked by the playful use of language, and
Marlinskii, who has a claim to be the father of the genre, himself plays
with this concept, when one of his characters says of his aristocratic
mistress: '*Ei zhal' luchei svoego siiatel'stva*' ('She regrets the rays of
her illustrious title').[4]

From the perspective of the early nineteenth century, the historical
roots of this *svet* are not very deep – they go back less than a hundred
years, to the 'century of enlightenment'; and thus, linguistically, this
'polite society' is once more linked to 'light': its very origins associate
it with *prosveshchenie*. Yet this élite is no élite of the mind, such as we
may find in the later development of Russian literature – this is no
intelligentsia.[5]

---

glad about, to hope for; for others... something to envy, a person to be sought, and
someone to glance at.' (*Russkaia romanticheskaia povest'*, p. 333).

[3]In the original, '*podchishchennoe chelovechestvo*': see N.A Blagoveshchenskii,
'Biograficheskii ocherk,' in N.G. Pomialovskii, *Polnoe sobranie sochinenii*, edited by
I. Iampol'skii, Moscow-Leningrad, 1935, vol. 1, p. xli. Nevertheless, there are
anticipations of the 'Natural School' of the 1840s in Marlinskii's description of *Sennaia
ploshchad'* in *Ispytanie* (Bestuzhev-Marlinskii, *Sochineniia*, vol. 1, pp. 201-02); the
brief street scene in M.S. Zhukova's *Baron Reikhman* (*Russkaia romanticheskaia
povest'*, p. 529); and the Jewish quarter depicted in E.A. Gan's *Ideal (The Ideal*: ibid.,
pp. 445-6).

[4]Bestuzhev-Marlinskii, *Sochineniia*, vol. l, p. 246.

[5]Cf. N.F. Pavlov on the values of *svet*: 'Society does not forgive natural behaviour;
society cannot suffer freedom; society is offended by concentrated thought. It wishes
that you should belong only to itself, that you should squander your sympathy and your
life only for it; that you should divide and rend your heart in equal parts for each
person. Bury any elevated thought deep within you; conceal a tender passion, if these
prevent you from smiling, laughing or grieving at the will of the first person who
approaches you. Society will torture you, and it tortured the princess.' (*Russkaia
romanticheskaia povest'*, p. 341).

There is a significant passage on *prosveshchenie* ('enlightenment', or 'education') in Odoevskii's *Kniazhna Mimi (Princess Mimi)* – a work I take to be almost the quintessence of the society tale:

> 'Yes,' Skvirskii replied, 'I will say, that as far as I am concerned, I think that morality *is* necessary, but also education...
>
> 'Oh, you too, count, are on the same tack!' the princess objected. 'Nowadays everybody goes on about education and education! Wherever you look, it's all education. Merchants are educated, peasants are educated. There was none of this in the past, and everything went better than nowadays. My views are those of old: they say education, but it turns out to be ruination!'
>
> 'No, please, princess!' Skvirskii replied, 'I cannot agree with you. Education is necessary, and I will prove it as twice two equals four. Well, what is education? For example, my nephew: he has finished university, he knows all areas of learning – mathematics – Latin. He has a certificate and all doors are open to him. He could become a collegiate assessor or an actual state counsellor. But you know, allow me to say, elightenment takes many forms. Here, for example, is a candle. It shines and without it we wouldn't be able to play whist. But if I took the candle and brought it up to the curtain, the curtain would catch fire... '
>
> 'Allow me to note it down', said one of the players.
>
> 'What I am saying?' enquired Skvirskii with a smile.
>
> 'No, the rubber!'
>
> 'You have revoked, count! How could you?' Skvirskii's partner said in vexation.
>
> 'What?.. I?.. Revoked? Oh dear!.. Is it true? There's education for you!.. Revoke! Oh! Oh dear, revoke! Yes, I have indeed revoked!'[6]

Here the ironies are subtle but pointed. Cards have taken the place of ideas; education could be dangerous for the lower classes; for a candle can shed light in order to play whist, but it could also set alight the whole aristocratic décor. One could be forgiven for thinking that in this gallicized society, such a metaphor and such *ésprit* might be noted down (*pozvol'te zapisat'*), yet all that this interlocutor wishes to write down is the score at cards, and even the technical card term '*renonce*' becomes an ironic comment on Skvirskii's championship of education.

Odoevskii presents his narrow world critically, but through irony and always from inside the genre's own frame of reference. The main negative protagonists of this story, and the guardians of 'society's' values are *kniazhna* Mimi herself and her mother, the *kniaginia*, of whom Odoevskii writes, with obvious irony: 'In a word, the princess

---

[6]V.F. Odoevskii, *Sochineniia v dvukh tomakh,* Moscow, 1981, vol. 2, p. 236 (hereafter '*Sochineniia,* 1981')

was a kind, sensible and charitable lady in all respects'.[7] Whether
consciously or not, Gogol' seems to have picked up this ironic formula
in Chapter 9 of *Mertvye dushi* (*Dead Souls*), to differentiate the two
gossips of local society: the 'simply pleasant lady' and the 'lady
pleasant in all respects'. But, whereas Odoevskii's irony is restrained –
as befits the conventions of polite society – Gogol''s satirical portraits
are boldly caricatured and devastating.

Kniazhna Mimi contains references to *Gore ot uma* (*Woe from Wit*)
and in many respects any critical note to be found in the *svetskaia
povest'* may be seen as having been hugely preempted by this play of
genius.[8] One has to ask why *Gore ot uma* is an undoubted classic,
whereas the *svetskaia povest'* is still struggling for recognition. One
answer lies in the fact that Griboedov's criticism of *svet* comes from
outside – from Chatskii, the forerunner of a type that would be so
meaningful for Russian literature. Chatskii comes into this narrow
world '*s korablia na bal*' ('[straight] from a ship to the ball') to expose
it through his criticism, then to leave it for the wider world beyond.
Although in *Kniazhna Mimi* society condemns Granitskii as: '...some
sort of near Jacobin or other, *un frondeur*, he doesn't know how to
live',[9] he is obviously no Chatskii, nor even a Evgenii Onegin. His
limitations are suggested in his very name – Granitskii (cf. *granitsa* –
'boundary', 'border').

It is not only the foreignness of this world of the *svetskaia povest'*,
but the narrowness of its horizons which is so un-Russian. In *Idiot* (*The
Idiot*) Dostoevskii's prince, in spite of his title, is not 'cleaned up
humanity', and is yet another figure who comes to Russian society
from outside. He tries to appeal to his 'peers' in polite society, but fails
to communicate. He appears comic, and breaks the Chinese Vase. The
leaders of *svet* are unresponsive to his ideas – but yet, as he tells
Rogozhin: 'There is something to be done, Parfen! There is something
to be done in our Russian world [*svet*]. Believe me!'[10] For Dostoevskii

---

[7]Odoevskii, *Sochineniia*, 1981, vol. 2, p. 230.

[8] Ibid., pp. 233, 245.

[9]Ibid., p.235. Cf. comparable views of Chatskii and Evgenii Onegin in *Gore ot uma*,
Act 2 scene 2 (and *passim*); *Evgenii Onegin*, II: 5.

[10]F.M. Dostoevskii, *Polnoe sobranie sochinenii v tridtsati tomakh*, Leningrad, 1972-
90, vol. 8, p. 184 (hereafter '*PSS*'). For a fuller interpretation of this story, see Richard
Peace, 'Dostoevsky's *Little Hero* and "The Knight of the Sad Countenance"', in *Life
and Text: Essays in Honour of Geir Kjetsaa on the Occasion of his 60th Birthday*,

the concept of *svet* is wider than that narrow social stratum of the princes and the counts – it is an all-embracing, Russian world.

Nevertheless, Dostoevskii had himself written a *svetskaia povest'*. The circumstances surrounding it are perhaps significant. He wrote *Malen'kii geroi* (*The Little Hero*) as a prisoner in the Peter and Paul Fortress, having just undergone interrogation. He later wrote to Vs. Solov'ev:

> When I found myself in the fortress, I thought that this was the end of me, I thought that I would not last out three days. Then suddenly I calmed down completely. Well, and what did I do there?.. I wrote *The Little Hero*. Read it! Is there any bitterness or torment in it? I had such quiet, good, benign dreams'.[11]

It is as though in such conditions Dostoevskii can only resort to the most innocuous of social criticism in that most innocent of genres – *svetskaia povest'*. Yet, of course, he does manage to endow it with his own. He carries on the theme of adolescent sexuality, which he had been pursuing in *Netochka Nezvanovna,* and, despite his protestations to Solov'ev, he includes a lengthy section of polemic against those who had refused to recognise the originality of his own literary talent. In his mature works Dostoevskii turns his back on the values of *svet*. Not only is this apparent in Myshkin's behaviour in *Idiot* and Zosima's conversion in *Brat'ia Karamazovy* (*The Brothers Karamazov*), but the foreignness of such 'society' and its bogus claim to leadership is parodied in *Besy* (*The Devils*), in his biting satire on the Von Lembkes.

For all that Dostoevskii's hero Myshkin conceives the word *svet* as national – *russkii svet* – the compass of Russian literature itself is even broader. Events in the world outside were to leave their impact on Russian society and produce a literature of world significance – '*mirovogo znacheniia*'. The first shock wave of the French Revolution tended merely to reinforce the values of *svetskaia povest'*: French émigrés found a welcome in Russia, and real representatives of *le beau monde* now haunted the salons of Russian high society. The revolution's second shock wave – Napoleon – was more dramatic. The values of polite society (*svet)* were directly challenged by the political realities of the world outside (*mir)*. At the opening of Tolstoi's *Voina i*

---

edited by E. Egeberg *et al.*, Oslo, Universitet i Oslo [= *Meddelelser*, 79], 1997, pp. 221-37.
[11]Dostoevskii, *PSS*, vol. 2, p. 506.

mir (*War and Peace*), St Petersburg society (the salon of Anna Scherer, whose very name emphasizes the non-Russianness of this society) is shocked at the news of an upstart assuming a title – Napoleon has just crowned himself emperor. A society that looked to France for its values is disorientated, and worse is to follow: with the Napoleonic invasion the French are clearly the enemy; Moscow society actually institutes fines for the speaking of French.

Yet there is another invasion in Tolstoi's novel, another attack on the values of *svet* – the peasant as ideologue and teacher. It is as though *svet* in both its meanings – of 'society' and Myshkin's wider concept of *russkii svet* – is under pressure from *mir*, both in its wider sense of 'the world', and its more restricted sense of the 'peasant commune'. For all that the wealth and glitter of the *svet* of the *svetskaia povest'* depended on that other restricted world – the *mir* of the peasants, such figures were never allowed within its narrow walls. Tolstoi, that great rejector of the values of *svet* in its narrow meaning, became increasingly concerned with the values of *mir* in this other sense, though not – like the Slavophiles and others – with the peasant institution as such, but with the philosophy and spirituality developed by the peasant through his communal approach to life and his attitude to nature.

Spirituality exists at a purely superficial level in *svetskaia povest'*. Before the duel in Odoevskii's *Kniazhna Mimi* Granitskii says to the baron: 'Before we send one another to the other world [*na tot svet*], I am curious to know, why we are duelling';[12] and earlier Granitskii himself had been likened to 'some sort of apparition from the other world' ('*kakoi-to vykhodets s togo sveta*').[13] It was left to Pushkin to develop such possibilities, though without any element of spirituality, in his version of the *svetskaia povest'* – *Pikovaia dama* (*The Queen of Spades*). Yet spirituality, linked with the existence of 'other worlds', as in Dostoevskii, and with the possible existence of 'the other world' (*tot svet*) in Tolstoi, is an important feature of the main stream of Russian literature.[14] Thus it is possible to see a unique development of *svetskaia povest'* in Tolstoi's *Smert' Ivana Il'icha* (*The Death of Ivan Il'ich*). His hero moves away from the narrow values of 'society',

---

[12]Odoevskii, *Sochineniia*, 1981, vol. 2, p. 255.

[13] Ibid., p. 235.

[14]However, religion does come into the writings of E.A Gan, as in *Ideal*: see *Russkaia romanticheskaia povest'*, pp. 477-8, 480.

represented by the civil service hierarchy, towards the even narrower tunnel of death and the *svet* which enigmatically beckons him at its end: 'Instead of death there was light' (*'Vmesto smerti byl svet'*).[15] *Mir* also may be viewed from a religious perspective if its inhabitants are seen as *miriane* – the laity.[16] Dostoevskii's Zosima, imbued as a younger man with the values of *svet,* faces a sudden crisis in pursuing these values. Not only does he renounce *svet,* he also renounces *mir* to become a monk. Yet, significantly, at the end of his life it is into the world (*v mir*) that he sends his disciple Alesha.

It is, perhaps, Turgenev, with his interest in polite country-house society and his friendship with Henry James, who may be seen as the real society novelist, and therefore, of all major Russian writers, closest to *svetskaia povest'.* Yet Turgenev sets up these small havens of society to have them disrupted from without. Their world is shaken by a figure not allowed into the drawing rooms of the *svetskaia povest'* proper – the intellectual *raznochinets* as exemplified by Rudin, Bazarov, or even the revolutionary foreigner, Insarov. There is here a feature which clearly distinguishes the Russian society tale from its French models, where the 'intruder' is a young man bent on social advancement through the erotic exploitation of women (Julien Sorel in *Le Rouge et le Noir*, Rastignac in *Le Père Goriot*). Such a figure is notably absent in the Russian society tale. The closest the Russian variant comes to it is in Pushkin's *Pikovaia dama* – but it is not very close. Hermann feigns love for a mere companion, but with her mistress, the Countess, he resorts to threats. The young male intruder in Turgenev's novels is more interested in ideas. Indeed, Rudin actually runs away from a love which might better his lot.

The sort of intellectual debate that is typical of Odoevskii's writing in other genres – e.g. *Russkie nochi* (*Russian Nights*) is absent from his *svetskie povesti,* yet it is the intrusion of such debate into the polite atmosphere which marks out the innovation of Turgenev. The philosophical and the social *povest'* are welded together, and in some

---

[15] L.N. Tolstoi, *Polnoe sobranie sochinenii,* Moscow-Leningrad, 1928-64, vol. 26, p. 113 (hereafter '*PSS*').

[16] Nevertheless, in E.A. Gan's *Ideal,* God is seen as having sent out his children '*v stranu vremennogo izgnaniia*' ('to the land of temporary exile'); and, in M.S. Zhukova's *Baron Reikhman,* we encounter a similar idea: '*mir est' strana izgnaniia, gde nichego ne sovershenno*' ('the world is a country of exile, where nothing is perfect'): see *Russkaia romanticheskaia povest',* pp. 478-9 and 521.

sense it is actually as though Turgenev is rewriting Odoevskii. Thus, in *Kniazhna Zizi*, the strange, not fully disclosed, relationship between Princess Zinaida and an older man, which presents the younger Radetskii with such an enigma, seems to look forward to another Princess Zinaida in Turgenev's *Pervaia liubov'* (*First Love*) and the mystery surrounding her relationship with the narrator's father. Yet significantly, in Turgenev the relationship is presented more in psychological than social terms – the *svetskaia povest'* has become a psychological study.

In Odoevskii's *Chernaia perchatka* (*The Black Glove*), Ezerskii, the uncle and guardian of the young count and his future bride, is not a typical representative of 'society', and after an excessively formal education, he has been immersed in the values of a 'new world': 'After such a strange education he was thrown by fate into England... he could not help but be struck by this new world'.[17] He drinks in its values and conforms to its narrowness:

> In all his actions was clearly reflected that English narrowness [literally 'onesidedness'] which, thank God, is unintelligible to the Russian, [A narrowness] on which all the merits and all the deficiencies of English products depends and because of which an Englishman knows a couple of wheels in a machine, and a couple of thoughts in life, and knows them extremely well, but beyond that has no concept of anything else in the world.[18]

His wards are educated in this spirit and the young count is encouraged to run his estate on English lines. Nevertheless, the young couple abandon their estate for the *svet* of St Petersburg, then part from one another. It is almost as though Turgenev has reversed this plot in *Dvorianskoe gnezdo* (*A Nest of Gentlefolk*). The spartan and English education of Lavretskii makes him unfitted for the life of society, which he leaves, after being abandoned by his wife, in order to find true values, Russian values, on his estate.

The flight from the values of *svet* is typical of all major Russian writers. It characterizes Goncharov's *Oblomov*, whose hero criticises St Petersburg society and withdraws from it into a state of mind, seen by others as *oblomovshchina* ('Oblomovitis'). It is a prominent feature of Tolstoi's world, and, in a different sense, that of Dostoevskii too.

---

[17]Odoevskii, *Sochineniia*, 1981, vol. 2, p. 59.
[18]Ibid., p.60.

Love is a central issue in the *svetskaia povest'*. Yet it was Tolstoi who, in expanding the horizons of the genre in *Anna Karenina*, fully exposed the moral inadequacy of the rules by which society lived, when confronted by the reality of genuine love:

> Vronsky's life was particularly fortunate in that he had a code of rules which defined without question what should and should not be done. The code covered only a very small number of contingencies, but, on the other hand, the rules were never in doubt, and Vronsky, who never thought of infringing them, had never had a moment's hesitation about what he ought to do. The rules laid it down most categorically that a cardsharper had to be paid, but a tailor had not; that one must not tell a lie to a man, but might to a woman; that one must not deceive anyone, but one may a husband; that one must not forgive an insult but one may insult others, etc. All these rules might be irrational and bad, but they were absolute, and in complying with them Vronsky felt that he need not worry, and could hold his head high. Only quite lately, in regard to his relations with Anna, Vronsky had begun to feel that the code of his rules did not cover every contingency and that the future presented doubts and difficulties for which he could find no guiding principle.[19]

The *svetskaia povest'* may have had redeeming features: its questioning of the role of women in society; its criticism of the obscurantism, the triviality, the very 'un-Russianness' of such a society.[20] Yet, like the novels of Jane Austen, irony on such matters comes from within. It is a doomed genre because, both in content and in form, it smacks of foreign implantation – it is not the reality of Russian society at large. Social criticism in the mainstream of Russian literature is far more fundamental: it is the ringing scorn of Chatskii; the soul-searching of Levin;[21] the nihilism of Bazarov; and the ideas

---

[19]L. Tolstoy, *Anna Karenina*, translated by David Magarshack, New York, Signet, 1961, p. 313.

[20]The question of the role of women in society is a question raised in E.A. Gan's *Ideal* and is present in M.S. Zhukova's *Baron Reikhman* (see *Russkaia romanticheskaia povest'*, pp. 442, 444, 445, 454-5, 480; 539); whereas, N.F. Pavlov's *Iatagan* makes numerous slighting references to women (see ibid, pp. 338, 340, 342, 356).

[21]The Levin of M.S. Zhukova's 'Baron Reikhman' is not Tolstoi's hero: 'Levin belonged neither to the generation of Werther, sighing without joy, nor to the sons of Young France, youths strong in muscle and passion, who only lacked opportunity to be Napoleons and will to become the equals of Tasso, Schiller, Humboldt; youths, whose love was capable of setting the whole globe aflame, even beginning with the Behring Straits'. We are told that he read from Ecclesiates: 'With a glass of bright wine/Converse with wise men – etc...' and was known in town as *"mauvais sujet"*,

and actions of Dostoevskii's revolutionaries, determined to overthrow the self-satisfied assumptions of society itself.

In our linguistic pirouette around *svetskaia povest'*, there is yet another meaning of *mir* not yet touched on – '*mir*' differentiated in the old orthography as 'peace'. It too has relevance for the Russian literary tradition. Myshkin tells Rogozhin that there is something to be done in the 'Russian World' (*svet*), yet his own role in this world is connected with *mir* in this other sense – he is the embodiment of *smirenie* and seeks to bring reconciliation (*primirenie*) to a fractured Russian world. This pole – the pole of *primirenie* – is just as important to the Russian novelistic tradition as that other pole of rebellion and rejection.[22] In Dostoevskian terms it is Zosima versus Ivan, but it is there, too, in Gogol', whose ultimate hopes for that socially explosive *poema, Mertvye dushi*, lay in reconciliation. These two poles are brought together at the end of Turgenev's *Ottsy i deti* (*Fathers and Sons*):

> However passionate, sinning, and rebellious the heart hidden in the tomb, the flowers growing over it peep serenely at us with their innocent eyes; they tell us not of eternal peace alone, of that great peace of 'indifferent' nature; they tell us, too, of eternal reconciliation and of life without end.[23]

The title of Tolstoi's *Voina i mir* neatly captures a dichotomy at the heart of the great Russian literary tradition: on the one hand 'war' in its many forms, ideological, metaphysical, social; but, on the other, a yearning for reconciliation which is often almost mystical, a reconciliation with all and everything, a peace that can actually be identified with the world itself. The first epilogue of Tolstoi's novel concludes with the young Nikolenko's feelings towards his dead father, Pierre and his French tutor – all are good and wonderful: it is an emotional note of reconciliation with one's superiors. The second 'philosophical' epilogue ends with a rationalist version of *smirenie* –

---

particularly by those who were religious'. See *Russkaia romanticheskaia povest'*, p. 527.

[22]Though, in as much as the duel is a central feature of the *svetskia povest'*, the concept of *primirenie* at a socially conventional level is also a possibility: see Bestuzhev-Marlinskii, *Sochineniia*, vol. l, pp. 251, 252.

[23]I.S. Turgenev, *Polnoe sobranie sochinenii i pisem v dvadtsati vos'mi tomakh*, Moscow-Leningrad, 1961-68, vol. 8, (*sochineniia*), p. 402. The translation is from: Ivan Turgenev, *Fathers and Sons*, edited and translated by R.E. Matlaw, New York and London, Norton Critical Edition (2nd edition), 1989, p. 166.

the abdication of the ego in the face of superior forces: 'It is equally necessary to renounce a conscious freedom and acknowledge the dependence which we do not feel'.[24]

For all that the *svetskaia povest'* is typified on the one hand by military values, and on the other by the falsely reconciling flattery of polite society, it nevertheless lacks the true 'war' and the true 'peace' of the great Russian literary tradition.

---

[24]Tolstoi, *PSS*, vol. 12, p. 341.

ANOTHER TIME, ANOTHER PLACE: GENDER AND THE CHRONOTOPE IN THE SOCIETY TALE

JOE ANDREW

1. Preamble

Virtually since the term was first coined,[1] the society tale has posed a number of problems of definition. As Elizabeth Shepard has shown in her seminal article:

> Not the least of these is the typological problem: as V.G. Belinskij queried polemically nearly a century-and-a-half ago, 'What in the world is a "*society*" tale? We do not understand: in *our* aesthetics nothing is said about "*society*" tales'.[2]

The purpose of the present piece is to build on Shepard's fine work by examining the use of a number of important defining features, especially chronotopes,[3] in some of the most significant society tales of the 1830s and 1840s, as well as in some works, such as *Evgenii Onegin*, which are not society tales properly speaking, but which exhibit some of the crucial ingredients of this genre.[4] I feel that an

---

[1] The term was first used by Shevyrev in 1835: *Moskovskii nabliudatel'*, I, 1, March 1835, p. 124.

[2] See Elizabeth C. Shepard, 'The Society Tale and the Innovative Argument in Russian Prose Fiction of the 1830s', *Russian Literature*, 10, 1981, pp. 111-61 (111). Belinskii made these remarks in 1836.

[3] For the basic introduction to this term, see M.M. Bakhtin, 'The Forms of Time and the Chronotopos in the Novel. From the Greek Novel to Modern Fiction', *PTL. A Journal for Descriptive Poetics and Theory of Literature*, 3, 1978, pp. 493-528.

[4] The list of works covered is as follows:

BY MEN	BY WOMEN
Pushkin:	**Gan:**
Evgenii Onegin (1830)	*The Ideal* (1837)
'The Guests Were Arriving at the Dacha ...' (1828/30)	*The Locket* (1839)

examination of the chronotope will be especially fruitful. Self-evidently it is a 'typological' feature. More substantively, many of the society tales I will be discussing are organized around a series of 'set-pieces', virtual *tableaux vivants* which are usually chronotopic in essence, and so this seems to me a particularly good way of getting to the heart of the 'typological problem'. Moreover, the use of setting is often not neutral in this genre. As Shepard puts it:

> setting is not simply an exotic backdrop which imparts color to the narrative; it is also viewed as a sociological category which has a conditioning or determining effect on character and incident.[5]

While discussing the uses of chronotopes in the works in question, I will also seek to address issues of gender. In particular, I hope to establish how chronotopes are used differentially by male and female writers, and to ask whether male and female characters inhabit different chronotopes, or the same chronotopes differently. I begin on the level of meta-setting, with a consideration of the use of the city, especially St Petersburg.

2. The City

In her discussion of the shifts in Russian literature around 1830 which would lead to the society tale proper of the 1830s and 1840s, Shepard

The Shot (1830)	*Society's Judgement* (1840)
The Queen of Spades (1833/34)	*The Numbered Box* (1840)
Odoevskii:	**Zhukova:**
Princess Mimi (1834)	*Baron Reikhman* (1837)
	The Locket (1837)
Katia, or the Story of a Young Ward (1834)	*A Provincial Girl* (1838)
	Self-Sacrifice (1840)
Princess Zizi (1836/39)	*Dacha on the Peterhof Road* (1845)
Lermontov:	**Pavlova:**
Princess Ligovskaia (1836)	*A Double Life* (1848)
'Princess Mary' (1840)	

As will be seen, this represents an equal sample between male and female authors, and covers the heyday of the society tale, between 1830 and 1848. I should emphasize, however, that this sample should not be considered to be in any way 'scientific', but is more of a 'greatest hits' approach.

[5]Shepard, op. cit., p. 130.

notes: 'Two notable instances of these changes of narrative venue are the actualization of the theme of the Nineteenth Century and the "discovery" of the City.'[6] Certainly, it would be hard to imagine nineteenth-century Russian literature without these 'discoveries', nor for that matter the society tale. Of the eighteen works in my sample ten are set in whole or in part in St Petersburg, while only one, *Vystrel* (*The Shot*), has no real urban motifs. This metropolitan locale is, indeed, one of the defining features of the society tale, although it would be an overstatement to term it a *conditio sine qua non*.

From the outset we can note a gender differentiation. In the works written by men, the use of the St Petersburg, or, occasionally, Moscow, may be said to be largely semantically neutral. Thus, in *Evgenii Onegin, Pikovaia dama* (*The Queen of Spades*), *Kniazhna Mimi* (*Princess Mimi*), *Katia, ili istoriia vospitannitsy* (*Katia, or the Story of a Young Ward*), *Kniazhna Zizi* (*Princess Zizi*) and *Kniaginia Ligovskaia* (*Princess Ligovskaia*) the main characters inhabit the metropolitan world, and, to an extent, are 'conditioned and determined' by it; the life of high society may even be reproached, as in *Evgenii Onegin* or *Kniazhna Mimi*, but in these works the city is not presented as a place of danger for women *per se*, as it is in equivalent tales by women writers. (Equally, in the male-authored tales, the male characters tend to be thoroughly at home in the society of these twin capitals: see especially *Evgenii Onegin* and *Kniaginia Ligovskaia* – Onegin may be bored, but he is not alienated, at least not in Chapter 1). In works by women writers quite a different picture emerges, as we will see from a brief examination of four works: one by Elena Gan, and three by Mariia Zhukova. (Pavlova's *Dvoinaia zhizn'* [*A Double Life*] is an exception to this gender orientation).

Thus, in Gan's *Ideal* (*The Ideal*) the main plot is initiated when the idealistic, pure heroine, Ol'ga, is thrown into the metropolitan world, and is nearly ruined by her liaison with the cynical poet, Anatolii. Equally, her recovery and eventual redemption only begin when she and her husband leave St Petersburg. In Zhukova's *Baron Reikhman* the plot has a reverse motion, beginning and ending in the capital, and it is in the latter sections that the unfaithful wife of the Baron, Natal'ia receives her narrative exclusion. In a sense, these stories imply that

---

[6]Ibid., p. 114. It should be noted that Shepard is here talking about chronotope ('narrative venue'), although this term as such is not employed.

women have no place in the corrupt and corrupting world of St Petersburg. Zhukova's slightly later *Samopozhertvovanie* (*Self-Sacrifice*) offers another variation of the theme of innocent maidenhood corrupted in the big city. Here young Liza is plucked from the idyll of her happy country childhood to be educated as the ward of Countess Aleksandrina, and is at once forced to confront the cold vanity of the *svet*.[7] This confrontation will also lead to a dysphoric conclusion, even if she is not spiritually damaged by the clash.

In general, then, it would seem to be the case that a recurrent theme in society tales written by women is the collision between a pure, warm, idealistic heroine and the cold corruption of the St Petersburg *svet*. Zhukova's *Dacha na Petergofskoi doroge* (*The Dacha on the Peterhof Road*) offers yet another variant of this. At first her tale is more within the male version of the St Petersburg chronotope. We encounter Prince Evgenii, who is cast as a deliberate reprise of his more famous namesake. He, like Onegin, is a man of the *svet*, indulging in the 'tender science' of womanizing, as well as gambling. He is identified with St Petersburg, that is. In a flashback, however, we learn that he had exported, as it were, the world and values of St Petersburg to the unnamed provincial town, where he had seduced, and destroyed one of the two contrastive heroines of the tale, Zoia. Although the chronotopic mechanism works by reverse action, the effect is the same: the idealistic, pure young heroine is destroyed by the values of St Petersburg.

3. The Spa Town
The spa town, whether Russian, Caucasian or German, acts as a kind of sub-set, but also an intensification, of the St Petersburg chronotope. Like its metropolitan equivalent Piatigorsk, Lipetsk and Baden-Baden are places of exclusivity, of intrigue and gossip. We also see male enclaves, such as the restaurant scenes in Gan's *Medal'on* (*The Locket*) and Lermontov's 'Kniazhna Meri' ('Princess Mary'), where young men gather, either to discuss women, or to conspire with each other against another man. (Both Gan and Zhukova wrote works entitled *Medal'on*, although Zhukova's version is not a society tale as such; to avoid confusion, each subsequent reference will have the author's name

---

[7]For a discussion of this point, see Shepard p. 133.

attached.) In the same way that Nevskii Prospekt operates in Gogol''s story,[8] the boulevards and other public spaces of Piatigorsk and the other towns act as a kind of parade-ground, an area for display and observation of others. In a certain sense, then, the spa town operates as an *al fresco* ballroom.

The major distinguishing feature of the spa town relative to St Petersburg is summed up by Pechorin, when he remarks that he had gone to see Mary unchaperoned 'by taking advantage of the freedom of the local manners.'[9] This is precisely the point about 'Kniazhna Meri' and the other stories which use this setting. Elizabeth Shepard has noted the prevalence of a kind of surveillance of the characters in society tales.[10] By 'taking advantage of the freedom' of this more relaxed atmosphere, men and women may escape the vigilant gaze of mothers and other appointed guardians. The narrator of *Dvoinaia zhizn'* sums up this point when the heroine indulges in a little hand-holding: 'And you, Vera Vladimirovna, in the fateful moment you were calmly getting out of the carriage. Where was your sharp eye, watchful mother? Where was your inevitable lorgnette?'[11]

This incident occurs during a *promenade de plaisir*. As it happens, it takes place in Moscow, but illustrates well the general point that this kind of freedom is especially available to gullible young women, and their seducers during the cavalcades and other outings which are a prominent feature of the spa town society tale. There are examples of this in Gan's *Medal'on, Samopozhertvovanie*, and, especially, 'Kniazhna Meri'. In her *Medal'on* Zhukova subverts the rake's progress, in that Baroness Engel'sberg foils every attempt of Prince Iurevich to best her, but when the tale flashes back to Lipetsk, we see the same man seducing and destroying her sister, once more taking advantage of the spa town's more relaxed code to be alone with Olimpiia. And Pechorin, of course, takes the opportunity to be alone with Mary on more than one cavalcade, first to win her heart with tales of his childhood suffering, and then to embrace her during her dizzy

---

[8]Shepard also makes parallels between the Gogol' story and the society tale proper (p. 134).

[9]M.Iu Lermontov, *Sobranie sochinenii v chetyrekh tomakh*, Moscow-Leningrad, 1959-62, vol. 4, p. 415.

[10]Shepard, p. 135.

[11]Karolina Pavlova, *A Double Life*, translated by Barbara Heldt, Oakland, California, Barbary Coast Books, 1986, p. 37.

spell. By and large, then, the spa towns, with their sub-set of the *promenade de plaisir*, have specific gender implications, in that they provide opportunities for the seducer more easily to go about his business. This applies to both male- and female-authored work.

4. The Provincial Town

In most regards this chronotope has an opposite semiotic significance to that of St Petersburg or the spa town. Bakhtin himself draws our attention to the significance of this chronotope, which was about to become one of the dominant features of the emerging Russian realism:

> The small bourgeois provincial town with its stuffy way of life as a location for the accomplishing of novelistic events is widespread in the nineteenth century (both before and after Flaubert). ... Such a town is a place of cyclic domestic time. There are no events here, only 'recurring occurrences'. ... Day after day the same domestic actions repeat themselves, as do the same topics of conversation, the same words, etc. In this time people eat, drink, sleep, have wives and mistresses (without romance), make petty intrigue, sit in their shops or offices, play cards, gossip. *This is mundane, everyday cyclic domestic time.*[12]

The use of this chronotope would seem to be much more favoured by women writers. Of those covered in this paper, and written by men, only *Vystrel* has any elements of this setting, and the case is decidedly marginal.[13] The provincial town features very negatively in Gan's work, while Zhukova offers a more mixed impression. Gan's first work, *Ideal*, offers a bleak picture of the lot of the woman of talent trapped in the provinces. In particular, gossip is even more petty and vicious than in the capitals. *Sud sveta (Society's Judgement)* reinforces this view, and it is, indeed, the power of gossip that leads, at least in part, to the death of innocent people. In *Dacha na Petergofskoi doroge*, however, Zhukova takes a less romantic, less passionate view. In fact, Zoia's wild romanticism is seen as a very exotic growth in her sleepy provincial town, which is certainly shown to be a place of little culture, but, for the most part, is treated with affection. In sum, it is a cosy Larinesque world into which the values of the *svet* and romance come as

---

[12]Bakhtin, op. cit, p. 493.

[13]This chronotope would, however, become extremely important in Russian realism, as in Gogol"s *The Government Inspector*, and *Dead Souls*, as well as Dostoevskii, Leskov, Saltykov-Shchedrin and other writers.

dangerous, pathological invaders. In an earlier work, *Provintsialka* (*The Provincial Girl*), an even more positive view emerges. The title implies, perhaps, that such an approach will be taken. Certainly, the town in which the main heroine, Katia, has grown up is presented as a place of deep and abiding affection, both between father and daughter, and between man and woman. Looking at her work as a whole, Zhukova privileges the provinces over the metropolis, as can also be seen in works other than her society tales, such as *Medal'on* and *Inok* (*The Monk*).

5. Nature and Isolation

Moving yet further from the centre, as it were, we come to another, opposite chronotope to that of the city, namely the use of nature and/or isolated places. As Shepard has noted, nature is almost an antithetical principle to the whole ethos of the society tale. She comments: 'Not infrequently nature is banished from the society tale writer's purview, its absence heightening the sense of high society's artificiality and constrictiveness.'[14] Indeed, what we usually encounter is a kind of quasi- or semi-nature, the dachas on the edge of town or country estates where idealistic *devushki* spent idyllic girlhoods with perfect mothers. As these remarks imply, this is a chronotope preferred by the women writers in my sample. That is to say that, although nature is, of course, a very important (and valorized) chronotope in *Evgenii Onegin* and, in a different key, in 'Kniazhna Meri', for the most part, the society tales written by men considered here conform to Shepard's model. In the works by women writers, it is a very different story. In all but one of these tales, *Nomirovannaia lozha* (*The Numbered Box*), we see examples of this chronotope, although it has different values in different contexts.

One of the more common chronotopes, especially favoured by Gan and, to a lesser extent, Zhukova, is the flashback to the idyllic childhood of the pure heroine. In *Ideal* this is to an all-female enclave in the warm south; in her *Medal'on* it is also an all-female setting, gathered on a country estate. In both these stories the sentimentalist, pastoral traditions of the eighteenth century are explicitly evoked. *Sud sveta*, *Provintsialka* and *Samopozhertvovanie*, also utilize this

---

[14]Shepard, pp. 134-5.

chronotope, although in these instances the idyllic childhood involves fathers as well as mothers. But in all five cases, the primary function of this chronotope, as it was in Karamzin's *Bednaia Liza* (*Poor Liza),* and as it was to be in Dostoevskii's *Bednye liudi* (*Poor Folk*) – as well as in many other works, of course – is to provide an enclave of peace and security in which the girl was reared before she is plunged into the corruptions of the urban *svet.*

A related chronotope is the use of nature as a pathetic fallacy connoting intimacy, purity and genuineness. We see this in an early scene in *Ideal,* where the contrastive heroines discuss their contrasting feelings and beliefs while walking 'in the lap of nature', and this scene is reprised by Zhukova in *Dacha na Petergofskoi doroge.* Nature, in conjunction with the Gothic chapel, is the scene for Ol'ga's redemptive epiphany in *Ideal,* while the narrator of *Baron Reikhman* explicitly contrasts the vivacity of nature with the emptiness of *svet.*[15] Equally often we encounter a domesticated form of nature, or nature as spectacle. This is true of the natural Caucasian scenes visited in both Gan's *Medal'on* and 'Kniazhna Meri', as well as in the descriptions of the environs of Baden-Baden in *Samopozhertvovanie,* especially the scenes in the picturesque, ruined *schloss* with which the tale opens. This society view of nature is encapsulated by the narrator of *Dvoinaia zhizn',* who observes the heroine, Cecily, and her mother drinking their morning tea, gazing upon and 'enjoying what they imagined was nature.'[16] Combining several of these chronotopes is 'suburbanized nature', the scene at the dacha where young women, and sometimes men, stroll amid 'what they imagine' is nature. There are such instances in *Ideal, Dvoinaia zhizn',* and, of course *Dacha na Petergofskoi doroge* itself. This last story encapsulates what seems to be the essential view of nature taken by the society tale. Nature is tamed, gentrified, although perhaps still charmingly wild. The dacha here and elsewhere (which is utterly different from its Soviet equivalent, it should be noted) is a hybrid chronotope, the scene of the passionate melodrama of poor, mad Zoia, but also of the mercenary transactions *à la mode* of Evgenii and the woman who marries him to become the second Princess Mary. As such, and given its location on the edge of town/on the edge of country, the eponymous building can

---

[15]See ibid., p. 135, for a similar point.
[16]Pavlova, op. cit., p. 43.

be said to symbolize the victory of the prosaic *svetskaia povest'* over its earlier romantic equivalent.[17]

6. Army Life

This chronotope is closely related to sub-sets of the previous two, in that, predominantly, it is to be found in isolated places, and provincial towns. Perhaps surprisingly, it is just as common in female as in male writers. That said, it is only stating the obvious to note that it is a world inimical to women and female values, and which often has tragic consequences for both men and women.

Thus, in *Ideal*, part of the basic structure of the story is predicated on how alienated, and unhappy, the heroine Ol'ga feels in the military world she inhabits after her arranged marriage to Colonel Gol'tsberg. (It is also an autobiographical theme). Gan's slightly later *Sud sveta* develops these ideas both in the prologue, and in the flashback to Zenaida's arranged marriage. In neither of these two instances is the military chronotope central to the stories' thematics. Nor is it, perhaps, in *Pikovaia dama*, although it is still of significance that the story has a military setting.

More commonly, however, the military life theme acts as a distillation of the more negative values of the *svetskaia povest'* in general, and of masculine values in particular. We see this tendency in works by both male and female authors. In Gan's *Medal'on*, for example, the military theme is decidedly marginal, but even here it is significant that the all-female enclave begins to collapse, and the first steps to the eventual tragedy are taken, when a company of hussars arrives in their area. In *Sud sveta* the tragic events that befall Vlodinskii and Zenaida are shaped long before the story proper begins, when Vlodinskii is immersed in the exclusively male world of 'bivouac life', and all its false sense of honour that will lead to death. In reverse, Vlodinskii is only humanized when he is *feminized*, when illness detaches him from his regiment. Gan uses this chronotope in the same way in *Nomirovannai lozha*, where the hero Vseslav is also humanized by being feminized after he has left the army. (As in *Medal'on*, this is

---

[17]Another critic, in fact, sees society tales arising 'in the process of the evolution of romantic prose': R.V. Iezuitova, 'Svetskaia povest'', in *Russkaia povest' XIX veka. Istoriia i problematika zhanra*, edited by B.S. Meilakh, Leningrad, 1973, pp. 169-99 (169). This is probably the best 'Soviet' account of the society tale.

only a background theme in this story).

In *Baron Reikhman* the whole story is imbued with military values. Moreover, the critical events of the plot take place in a specifically military setting, and the values of male honour and duty, this time to each other, determine the eventual social tragedy for Baroness Reikhman. In *Vystrel* the military setting is also critical in shaping the story's values. Once more, it is a world in which men are prepared to kill each other for the flimsiest of reasons, even if the treatment here is ironic and parodic. Finally, in 'Kniazhna Meri' the military context is not foregrounded, but is, I feel, a critical ingredient of the whole story, as a determining background force.

Within the chronotope of 'army life' we commonly encounter two sub-chronotopes or themes, namely, card-playing and its analogue, duelling, and I now turn to these features.

7. Card-Playing[18]

In the stories in which card-playing features as a theme (there are five such in my selection), the links between card-playing and duelling are usually made explicit. In all versions, card-playing is treated as an all-male event, although there are also generalized references to whist and other more social games, in which women were involved. But wherever an author chooses to give this theme any detailed treatment at all, it is the games of chance variety that is chosen. As with army life (and indeed, duelling) this theme is also dealt with by women. Thus, in Gan's *Medal'on* Prince Iurevich has recourse to the gaming-hall after Baroness Engel'sberg proves a difficult conquest, and promptly loses 30,000 roubles. Here, the implication is that men will have recourse to 'duelling' with each other over the table, when women are unavailable or unwilling. Gan returns to these interconnections in a similar vein in *Sud sveta*. Vlodinskii's revenge against the seemingly perfidious Zenaida is thwarted when she decides not to attend the ball, so he retreats to the gaming-room, where his cavalier treatment of her parting gift (yet another locket) leads directly to the fatal duel. *Baron Reikhman* handles these interconnections in a very similar way,

---

[18]For a masterly account of this theme, see Jurij Lotman, 'Theme and Plot: The Theme of Cards and the Card Game in Russian Literature of the XIXth Century', *PTL. A Journal for Descriptive Poetics and Theory of Literature*, 3, 1978, pp. 455-92. My approach is, however, rather different.

although on this occasion the duel does not take place.

In all three of these tales, the card-playing/duel motif is set within a military context, and this also applies, of course, to Pushkin's *Vystrel* and *Pikovaia dama*. In the former work, the insult at the gaming-table does not, as we know, actually lead to a duel, as Sil'vio is, as it were, already in the middle of one. In the latter, there is no suggestion of a real duel, but when Hermann is locked in conflict with Chekalinskii on the fateful third night, the narrator is moved to remark: 'It was like a duel.'

8. Duelling

By definition, this *topos* is completely all-male. Moreover, perhaps because they could not write from direct experience, it is rarely used by women writers. As we know, however, there is a fatal duel in Gan's *Sud sveta*. The overall context and plot significance of the *topos* is not markedly different from the instances in male writers, except to say that Gan, through the first person narrator, Vlodinskii (the survivor of the duel), emphasizes the tragedy, and awful waste of the situation rather more than is the case in Pushkin, Lermontov or Odoevskii. In her *Nomirovannaia lozha* Gan also mentions a duel, but this is dealt with in an extremely perfunctory way, in that the vicious, oppressive husband of the spiritual heroine, Korneliia, is simply removed from the plot, off-stage, as it were, by means of a duel – significantly over a gambling debt – so that Korneliia may join her soul to the equally admirable hero, Vseslav. Zhukova brushes against the idea of a duel in *Samopozhertvovanie*, only to reject it, in that pragmatic Count Antonii decides not to fight de Nolle over his wife's honour.

There are famous duels, as everyone knows, in Pushkin and Lermontov, which have been so exhaustively discussed that there is no need here to do more than mention them briefly. In *Evgenii Onegin* Pushkin, as Gan was to do, dwells on the stupidity and pointlessness of the whole affair, but he laces his treatment perhaps more with farce than tragedy. In *Vystrel* duelling might be said to be one of the central themes (the *Blade Runners* of its day?), with the insane logic of masculine honour again being laid bare. At the same time, however, albeit through the 'romantic imagination' of the narrator, duelling is depicted as the very essence of masculinity. In the overall context of the gender implications of chronotopes, it is significant that it is the intervention of the feminine, and domesticity, in the shape of Countess Masha, which prevents the duel reaching its potentially fatal terminus. In *Kniazhna Mimi* Granitskii is killed in a duel. The emphasis once more is on the stupidity of this male convention, although it should also be noted that it is the malicious gossip of the eponymous 'heroine' which sets off the chain of events which will lead to his death. It is 'Kniazhna Meri', however, which offers the fullest society tale treatment of duelling (in this sample at least). The circumstances leading up to Grushnitskii's death are dealt with in great detail, as is the event itself. Here the duel acquires an existentialist aura, in keeping with the overall themes of the novel.[19] But, although Lermontov does not, I feel, emphasize the stupidity of the male code of honour, many of the gender implications remain as in many other treatments of this chronotope. Two men, here supported by other men, fight to the death, over the sexual honour (or, at least, ostensibly) of a woman.

With the exception of the gaming-room, all the chronotopes discussed so far are large-scale, and primarily with outdoor settings. I would now like to move for the rest of this paper indoors, to consider a series of settings which are, perhaps, more quintessentially typical of the society tale, although all of them may be found in other genres of the time. As Shepard has noted: 'Typically the society-tale narrative unfolds indoors.'[20]

9. The Church

Given the fundamental ethos of the *svetskaia povest'* (precisely so – *svetskaia*), it is perhaps unsurprising that this chronotope is little used. Its semantic significance, however, varies, although in all three instances I have found it is primarily, and intimately, connected with female characters. In *Ideal*, as we have already seen, Ol'ga rediscovers her vital spirituality in a wayside chapel, and this scene provides a fitting climax to the narrative proper. In *Medal'on* Gan uses this setting quite differently. Here the victim-heroine, Olimpiia, retreats to a

---

[19]It should also be noted that 'duelling', in a more metaphorical sense, is one of the central themes, and structural principles of other sections of *A Hero of Our Time*, as in Pechorin's battle with Kazbich in 'Bela'; with Ianko in 'Taman''; and with Vulich, and then the marauding Cossack. in 'The Fatalist'.

[20]Shepard, p. 134.

church to find consolation, only to be pursued into her sanctuary by the man bent on her seduction. The scene becomes the occasion for his lustful gazing on her suffering form, as Gan deliberately evokes, to lay bare, the Sadeian *topos* of sacrilege. Odoevskii uses the chronotope in similar fashion in *Kniazhna Zizi*, where Radetskii follows the eponymous Zizi into church, where he observes her, this time more neutrally, as she weeps. This motif of a kind of ocular rape of the victimized heroine is also found in a much more typical society tale chronotope, the theatre (or opera) scene.

10. Theatre/Opera

The treatment of this chronotope is markedly different in male as opposed to female writers. In *Evgenii Onegin* the theatre is a relatively semantically neutral social space, where Onegin goes to see and to be seen, although his intrusive training of his lorgnette on 'women he does not know' sets the tone for Gan's development of the motif. Pechorin goes to the theatre in *Kniaginia Ligovskaia* really only to see who is there, leaving indeed after only one act.

Gan acknowledges that she will be resonating with *Evgenii Onegin* in this regard by introducing her first theatre scene, in *Ideal*, by a (slightly incorrect) quotation from the equivalent scene in Pushkin's novel. But the treatment is utterly different and the theatre becomes a place of real danger for the innocent heroine. The theatre, that is to say, becomes a place of spectacle, but in the sense that it is the pure heroine who is the object of the male gaze. Moreover, once Anatolii, the rake poet, realises the effect all this has on the susceptible Ol'ga he sets off in a more literal and relentless pursuit. Gan returns to this scene in *Medal'on*, when Olimpiia attends a performance of *Hamlet* in Moscow. Not only does she dangerously identify with Ophelia (whose name her own echoes), but she too becomes the target of the phallic lorgnette, this time wielded by Prince Iurevich. Gan gives this chronotope her fullest attention in the slightly later *Nomirovannaia lozha*, which, as the title suggests, has the theatre, or rather the opera house, as one of its main settings. Indeed, the story opens in the Odessan opera house where a group – or rather a gang – of men gather to ponder on the mystery of what lies behind the eponymous box's permanently drawn curtain. Here, however, Gan will be in more redemptive mood, as the theatre becomes not a place of seduction and tragedy, but the scene of

true, requited love (a rarity in her *oeuvre*) when Vseslav and Korneliia
return at the end to her box, united in their deep spiritual love for each
other. As so often, in fact, Gan uses a masculinized *topos* in order to
reinvent and/or subvert it.[21]

11. The Morning Visit

This really is at the very heart of the society-tale world. At the 'round
table', as Odoevskii ironically dubs it in *Kniazhna Mimi*, men and
women – or sometimes just women – gather with the almost explicit
purpose of gossiping. This both moves the plot along and thereby helps
speed some stories to their tragic conclusions. In Zhukova's *Baron
Reikhman*, for example, the gathering in the chapter entitled 'Morning
Visit' is absolutely critical in spreading the stories about the Baroness's
liaison with Levin which eventually reach the Baron's attention. Here
both men and women are gathered at Lidiia Ezerskaia's music lesson. It
is also a mixed gathering in *Dvoinaia zhizn'*, where men and women
meet to exchange information about others, but also so that they can
observe others, thus collecting more material for future such
gatherings; or else to be alone, but in public, so that they may exchange
confidences and do things unobserved. In these regards, the morning
visit is the diurnal equivalent of the ball.

The 'round table' scene in Odoevskii's story opens with Mimi
sitting with her sister and mother gossiping nastily about the alleged
activities of a fourth female, and generally being unpleasant to each
other. Guests arrive, which gives the women the opportunity to share
their malice and, ultimately, this scene will lead to the death of
Granitskii in a duel. Odoevskii uses another variation on this theme
when Mimi meets her hated enemy Eliza at an acquaintance's house,
and this gives Mimi the chance to observe Eliza's every move, thus
giving her ammunition for later use. The use of this chronotope, from
such (perhaps limited) evidence, suggests that male and female writers
used it in essentially the same way.[22]

12. The Library

The library, either in the physical sense of the room, or the more

---

[21] For further discussion of this tendency in Gan, see my *Narrative and Desire in
Russian Literature, 1822-49*, Basingstoke and London, Macmillan, 1993, pp. 85-138.
[22] Shepard, p. 135, also discusses the role of observation and gossip.

general sense of reading-matter, also plays an important role in the society tale. Again, it is used by both male and female writers, and once more *Evgenii Onegin* seems the inspiration for later authors. Tat'iana's reading, and the effect it has on her psyche and role within the novel, has become such a commonplace in Pushkin criticism that there is no need to dwell on it here. Suffice it to say that her entry into the adult world through her encounters with the exciting, but dangerous, world represented in the rhyme *roman / obman* ('romance / deception') was to become the blueprint for similar rites of passage for a whole generation of enthusiastic young heroines. As Pushkin notes in Chapter 3 of his novel, she wanders 'with a dangerous book [in her hand]' and, paradoxically, several of Pushkin's followers were also to write of the dangers for impressionable young women of reading, or rather of believing too literally what they read.

Echoing Tat'iana, Princess Zizi is defined by her reading. But this identification is to have decidedly ambivalent resonances. Zizi herself introduces this motif by remarking: 'as before I continue to steal books from Father's library: this is my one joy.'[23] Tat'iana had been deeply influenced by her mother in acquiring her taste for 'dangerous books'; here an opposite nexus is established in that Zizi steals these 'masculine books', despite her mother's prohibition. Amongst the books she illicitly reads is an incomplete edition of *Clarissa*. This too is significant, in that, if she had been able to read the novel to its conclusion, she might have avoided the mistake of falling in love with the first man she sees, Gorodkov. He turns out to be a seducer, although for almost entirely mercenary reasons.

That the library, or, more broadly, the world of books is a dangerous space for the idealistic young Russian woman is a theme which female writers of society tales also developed. In her first published work, *Ideal*, Elena Gan takes an ambivalent view. Ol'ga and her confidante Vera are given free access to Ol'ga's mother's library and, from the works of de Staël and Genlis, as well as Plutarch, they learn many valuable lessons. Later on, Ol'ga will argue that the *inner space* provided by her immersion in the world of books is a great consolation to her in the harsh, military world she is forced to inhabit. But, as the more worldly Vera will point out, and as Gan implies throughout her *oeuvre*, the lofty 'ideal' (or is it 'a dream [*mechta*]'?) inspired by such

---

[23]See V.F. Odoevskii, *Sochineniia v dvukh tomakh*, Moscow, 1981, vol. 2, p. 263.

an education may even be counter-productive in a world which will not allow women to fulfill their aspirations. Moreover, Gan also develops a more Oneginesque version of this theme, in that Ol'ga almost allows herself to be seduced by the Lovelaceian Anatolii, precisely because of her tendency, *à la* Tat'iana, to live and love 'by the book'.

Gan returns to these ideas in *Sud sveta*. In her testamentary letter to Vlodinskii, Zenaida also describes an idyllic childhood immersed in books, but she too thereafter enters the mercenary *svet* singularly ill-equipped to deal with its prosaic coldness. Zhukova's main treatment of this chronotope comes in the relatively late *Dacha na Petergofskoi doroge*, in which poor mad Zoia had begun to be detached from reality precisely when she too had had unsupervised access to her mother's library. We should remember that the sensible heroine in this tale becomes Princess Mary, and ensures that she will make none of the mistakes of her victimized predecessor and namesake. Zoia, however, does not learn the lessons of literature, and imitates Lermontov's heroine by reading Byron in the original. She too is seduced by the dangerous books she reads even before Prince Iurevich meets her.[24]

13. The Private Room/Study

If the chronotope of the library is treated in much the same way by male and female writers, then this chronotope has marked gender differentiation. As always, Shepard encapsulates very well the significance of these spaces:

> Thus, the observer's quest for significant detail will lead him [*sic*] to private rooms. Here society tale protagonists nurture their illusions, and here also the dénouement of the the narrative's intimate drama is frequently played out. Typically illuminated by dim lamplight, a single candle, a glowing or flickering fire, or moonlight, these recesses of the domestic setting are the locational counterparts of innerness.[25]

All that said, however, the use of these spaces seems quite different when applied to male or female characters.

As in a number of other ways, *Evgenii Onegin* establishes the trend

---

[24]This theme was to be used later in Russian literature: see my discussions of Gan's *A Futile Gift* and of Dostoevskii's *Netochka Nezvanova*, in *Narrative and Desire*, pp. 131-8 and 214-26.

[25] Shepard, p. 137.

for the male inner space. Onegin is twice characterized by his room: in Chapter 1, and then when Tat'iana visits his deserted estate house. On both occasions the study acts as a mirror of the male protagonist's soul and, strikingly, this space is described in terms of what is there, rather than what the hero does in his room. Effectively, the man is what he *possesses*, rather than what he does. This is especially marked on the second occasion as the owner is physically absent, and this will generally be the case. The man, that is, has a life outside his own inner spaces. (In reverse, one might say that they do not inhabit these inner spaces.) As we shall see, almost the opposite is true for female protagonists.

Both male and female authors continue the pattern established by Pushkin. In *Ideal* we visit Anatolii's study with Ol'ga, when he is out. This is a space of profligate luxury, but it is also empty, devoid of life, as it were. Vlodinskii's study in *Sud sveta* is also viewed when he is absent, and the confused disarray of his books and papers reflect the emotional chaos of his spiritual distress. Zhukova shows Levin's study in a similar state in *Baron Reikhman*, and once more, the owner is absent: men neglect their inner selves is the clear implication of this chronotope. Lermontov's treatment of the motif in *Kniaginia Ligovskaia* is slightly different. Again, the study reflects the man's soul, but at least Pechorin is physically present when his room is viewed!

On the whole, however, interiors are associated with female characters, as Shepard has also observed.[26] But the use made of the distaff chronotope of the inner space has many variants. Seldom is this space seen as one which man and women may inhabit harmoniously together. A rare instance is the main plotline of *Nomirovannaia lozha*, in which Korneliia's home is the locus of the developing deep love between her and Vseslav.[27] Much more commonly women will find this space a potentially dangerous one, unless they are alone, or with other women. Thus, *Baron Reikhman* opens with a seemingly innocent domestic interior, with Natal'ia in her boudoir with the Baron and their son. Their seemingly good-natured sparring has a dark undercurrent, however, and when we next see the two together again at the end of the tale, the former scene's implications are made manifest in the Baron's brutal exclusion of his wife from his future family plans, and this is

---

[26]Ibid., p. 139.
[27]As Iezuitova notes, happy endings are very rare in society tales: op. cit., p. 180.

immediately followed by the equally brutal expulsion of her from the text. Zhukova makes similar use of this scene a couple of years later in *Samopozhertvovanie* when Count Antonii confronts his errant wife Aleksandrina, again at night, it should be noted, and makes plain her choices in the same 'playful' tone adopted by Baron Reikhman at the start of his tale.

When the heroine is alone with her confidante, however, the woman is secure in her domestic interior. As ever, *Evgenii Onegin* sets the scene with Tat'iana's celebrated nocturnal encounter with her dear nanny. Usually, in fact, confidantes exchange confidences in the lap of nature. There are examples of this in *Ideal* and *Dacha na Petergofskoi doroge*, as well as in Zhukova's *Medal'on*. Relatively rare indoor instances of this scene may be found in Natal'ia's *soirée* in *Baron Reikhman*, and in *Dvoinaia zhizn'*. Rather more often, however, we see women alone in their own spaces, even if they are quite regularly soon joined by an unwelcome, aggressive lone male. The connotations of these scenes of women alone are both negative and positive.

Quite commonly, the reader is invited to gaze on the woman caught in a meditative, sorrowing pose, often with explicit fetishized descriptions of her body. There are many such instances, in both male and female writers. For example, Gan writes in *Medal'on*: 'Who would recognise the charming, brilliant Baroness in this sad woman, who with her arms crossed on her chest, with her head thrown back, white and pale, like mountain snow in the moonlight, more resembled a marble carving than an animated being?'[28] As here, and as Shepard implies, these scenes are almost always nocturnal. Zhukova follows suit in her capturing of the similarly posed Natal'ia as she awaits her fate at the end of *Baron Reikhman*: 'Natal'ia Vasil'evna sat, or almost lay ... Her thrown-back head, pale face, her lowered hands, the position of her whole body indicated complete moral destruction.'[29] For women at these times a room of their own represents captivity rather than liberation, a prison cell rather than an inner space where they can be freely alone.

Male writers use this scene in much the same way. As Mary declines, we see her sitting in a similar crushed pose in the early hours as Pechorin passes her window after visiting Vera. Just before Zizi is

---

[28] E.A. Gan, *Polnoe sobranie sochinenii*, St Petersburg, 1905, p. 224.
[29] M.S. Zhukova, *Vechera na Karpovke*, Moscow, 1986, pp. 67-8.

visited by Gorodkov, Odoevskii provides the reader with a very detailed account of how she looks as she sits alone in the *chiaroscuro*:

> Just imagine a little room, with dark-blue wall-paper, rugs; in the corner is a small Turkish divan ... In the room it is dark; the dull light of the lamp illuminates only the divan, on which sits a fine girl in a white blouse ... a darkish ribbon circles her slender waist; her black wavy hair falls over her shoulders in small curls; on her graceful little feet are velvet slippers.

Odoevskii makes explicit the effect of his own description shortly thereafter when he compares her with 'a brilliant insect, nailed to a piece of wood by a cold observer.'[30]

In this last instance the 'fine girl' effectively sits alone waiting to be seduced, and this too is a common motif in the chronotope. In *Ideal* we see Ol'ga alone just before Anatolii arrives, while *Pikovaia dama* provides a deliberate travesty of this as we watch the Countess undressing and sitting alone just before Hermann arrives. And indeed the seducer does usually arrive, to attack the lone woman in the privacy of her own room. We see this in *Ideal*, in Gan's *Medal'on*, when Iurevich assaults Olimpiia, and twice in *Kniazhna Zizi* as Gorodkov attempts to seduce his sister-in-law. Again, *Pikovaia dama* travesties this *topos*, while Hermann's visit to Liza's room immediately after the death of the Countess reveals to her his mercenary motivation. Virtually without exception, then, when a man penetrates the female space, it is with negative consequences for the woman. And these consequences are lasting. In *Ideal* Ol'ga takes many months to recover; Olimpiia is utterly destroyed; Zizi can no longer even pray in her desacralized 'cell'; while, again in travesty mode, the death of the Countess is the resullt. (It should also be noted that Pushkin, a much more playful author than most writers of the tragic melodramas which followed, has the Countess return Hermann the compliment – with almost equally devastating consequences for the male!)

Elsewhere, however, the inner space is depicted as a deeply positive situation for the woman. We see this in a number of works. Thus, even in *Medal'on* and *Kniazhna Zizi*, in the scenes already looked at, the Baroness and Zizi are seen at peace with infants immediately prior to

---

[30]Odoevskii, op. cit., vol. 2, pp. 284-5. See also *Princess Mimi*, ibid., p. 228, for a grotesque equivalent scene as the rather older and rather less glamorous Mimi undresses.

the reader's apprehension of them in their iconographic poses. More generally, there is a common identification of the female with interior spaces, with the reverse connotation that the public domain, the *svet* itself, is a male sphere. This opposition is summed up by a woman in Gan's *Medal'on*:

> In the life of a man there are many collateral adventures which he can communicate to all and sundry, without touching upon a single one of his sincere feelings; a woman's existence, on the contrary, is entirely composed of tones and echoes from her inner world; we do not have external circumstances which would not be intimately connected with it: our entire life is a single harmony, and whichever string you might touch, its sound evokes an echo of the whole chord.[31]

This, of course, takes a largely positive view of the 'two spheres'. Certainly, in this interpretation, a woman's life seems more of a *whole* than that of a man. And, indeed, the ability of the women of the society tale to find peace and tranquillity in their interior spaces, within their very selves, is a consolation to them, and a mark of their strength. We see this especially clearly in *Dvoinaia zhizn'*, where each chapter ends with the heroine Cecily retreating into her room at the end of the day, and then into herself. Pavlova even marks it off generically by writing these passages as poetic prose, and as actual poetry. The rationale of this device is made explicit:

> Tiredness weighed her down more and more. Her thoughts grew still; a dream flew in to her. She forgot everything, but through that forgetfulness, some indistinct memory melted and grew clear in the depths of her soul.[32]

We see this approach in a less explicit way in Gan's Ol'ga and Zenaida, as well as in others. (Indeed, one might say that the choice of *Medal'on* as a title by both Gan and Zhukova is a metonymic realization of this whole theme).

But there are also very real dangers for the women of the society tale in this retreat, however enforced, or however voluntary, into their own private worlds. The price that they are made to pay is that, when they dare to enter the public domain, they enter a world which is, in its very essence, alien to them. Levin, in *Baron Reikhman* sums up this

---

[31]Gan, op. cit., p. 257.
[32]Pavlova, p. 17.

treacherous dichotomy:[33]

> The life of a man is twofold: he is a family man and at the same time the duties of a citizen fall to him. Should he be unhappy at home, he may live his life outside the home; he still has purpose, a sphere of activity which is quite sufficient to occupy his spiritual resources. *Woman is created solely for the family; the area of activity beyond it is alien to her: her entering this sphere is quite inappropriate.* [my italics, J.A.]

And nowhere is this made more evident than in what are the most recurrent chronotopes of the society tale, the ballroom and salon.[34]

14. The Ballroom and Salon[35]

These twin chronotopes appear in fourteen of the eighteen tales covered by this paper. As seems invariably the case, *Evgenii Onegin* is the critical influence, although *Gore ot uma* is also important. As we might expect, there are many variations within these tales, although some strong common threads.

There are three balls of various types in *Evgenii Onegin*. The first occurs in Chapter I, and at once several of the key motifs are established, to be developed by later writers. The ball is a place of intrigue: 'There is no surer place for confessions/And for slipping letters' (I: 29). The ballroom is thus the locus for men and women to be in public, but also to be able to act as if in private. It is significant that for Pushkin there is no suggestion that women are at any disadvantage relative to men; later writers, especially women, will give a rather different impression. Pushkin does, however, suggest playfully that the ball is a place where sexual behaviour needs to be monitored, as he advises 'respected husbands' and 'mamas' to maintain close surveillance over their respective charges: 'Keep your lorgnette straight' (ibid.). The name-day party, with its tragic consequences, intensifies, of course, the note of intrigue, while the ball in Chapter VII

---

[33] Zhukova, op. cit., p. 60. In fact, it is not clear whether these are the thoughts of Levin or of the narrator.

[34] As Shepard notes: 'The ballroom scene, or some close equivalent, is therefore all but mandatory in the society tale' (p. 136).

[35] I recognise that these two chronotopes are by no means identical, and that in some regards they are really quite different in function. Even so, it seems to me that there are sufficient similarities between them to permit a conjoint treatment: at very least, they overlap.

is the microcosm of the 'market for fiancées' which is the *raison d'être* of Tat'iana's journey to Moscow.

Pushkin uses these chronotopes in both the fragment 'Gosti s"ezhalis' na dachu' ('The guests were arriving at the dacha ...') and *Pikovaia dama*. In the former the motif of women observing, and commenting on other women, which is touched upon in *Evgenii Onegin*, is further developed, while the balcony leading from the salon encapsulates perfectly the note of private spaces within a public arena.[36] As in other regards, Pushkin uses the emerging *topoi* of the society tale to playful effect in *Pikovaia dama*. The visit to the ball is really introduced as a convenient pretext for Hermann to be able to gain access to the Countess, while the teasing exchanges between Tomskii and Lizaveta are dismissed as 'mazurka chatter [*boltovnia*]', rather than the much more vicious 'gossip [*spletnia*]' which was soon to become the hallmark of the society ball.

The ball and the salon gathering are not used as a centre-piece in 'Kniazhna Meri', but they do play important plot-advancing roles, as well as repeating the motifs of intrigue. The first ball at the Nobles' Assembly, when Pechorin 'rescues' Mary from the unwanted attentions of the drunk, marks the opening move in his campaign to seduce her, while the following gathering *chez* Princess Ligovskaia allows Pechorin and Vera to be 'alone', though in public, while the same applies to later conversations between Pechorin and Mary, and Mary and Grushnitskii. (Lermontov had also used this chronotope in a somewhat perfunctory way in *Kniaginia Ligovskaia*.)

The main male exponent of the ball-scene in my sample is Odoevskii, in his *Kniazhna Mimi*. Significantly, he begins this society tale with a ball. Moreover, the scene itself opens in dialogue form, declaring that this will be a locus of gossip and intrigue. In particular, it will establish women in general, and Mimi in particular, as 'guardians of morality'. That is, women will be at the centre of this world, both as a kind of moral police-force, and as the unwilling recipients of this unwanted surveillance. The ball is also a space for sexual display. This is most evident in the 'Gynecaeum', a grotesque parody of the private

---

[36] For further discussion of this location in this tale see Joost van Baak, '"The Guests Gathered at the Dacha...": The Dynamics of a Drawing Room', in *Semantic Analysis of Literary Texts. To Honour Jan van der Eng on the Occasion of his 65th Birthday*, edited by E. de Haard *et al.*, Amsterdam, Elsevier Science Publishers, 1990, pp. 51-66.

place for women. Instead of retiring to this room to exchange confidences, and to offer support, perhaps, Odoevskii's women retreat here to primp and preen before the enormous mirror, and to comment, unfavourably, on the behaviour of their latest targets. Odoevskii evidently regarded the ball as emblematic of the society tale,. as he devotes almost one quarter of the whole story to this opening scene, and its immediate aftermath.

By and large, however, women writers seem to have been more conscious of the power of this emblematic chronotope: all but one (*Nomirovannaia lozha*) of the nine tales written by women in my sample have ball scenes. Thus the epigraph to Chapter II of Zhukova's *Provintsialka* reads: '*Le grand monde est un bal masqué*', and this seems to have been the general approach of women writers of the society tale. Here, indeed, they could write from personal experience. There are many types of ball covered. *Provintsialka*, as the title suggests, deals for the most part with the charms of the provincial world, and Zhukova was to give her fullest attention to the provincial ball in *Dacha na Petergofskoi doroge*. Although the ball scene will be a deeply charged erotic encounter between Zoia and Iurevich, Zhukova reveals the absurdity of Zoia's romantic delusions by her deliciously Gogolian parody in her introduction to the scene. To Zoia, the ball is an exciting and magical arena; in reality, it is a prosaic social gathering in the back of beyond. Thereby, Zhukova, writing very near the end of the heyday of the society tale (1845), reveals that the ball is a prime location for silly young girls to indulge in '*romany/obmany*', although this will all end in tragedy for Zoia.

Elena Gan was a very intense writer and her treatment of the provincial ball scene was usually laced with bitter sarcasm rather than playful parody or irony. The very title of perhaps her best work, *Sud sveta* ('Society's *Judgement*'), sums up her approach to these issues. This tale has a ball very near its commencement, and Gan shows this to be the place where petty, malicious women would gather in hostile crowds to pass judgement on any woman who stood out from the crowd. (In some senses, her approach is not dissimilar to that of Odoevskii in *Kniazhna Mimi*, although her motivation was very different.) As the tragedy of this story unfolds, the key events take place at a series of provincial balls, where the false witness borne against the spiritual heroine Zenaida by other much more venal women will lead to death and despair. For Gan the ball is a literally *infernal* chronotope.

Anticipating Lermontov, Zhukova also provides a spa-town ball and, as in her later work, she shows a rather lighter touch than Gan. As in other writers, however, the ball scenes in Piatigorsk (in Gan's *Medal'on*) provide the arena for the battle of the sexes, although here it is the woman who wins. Here too the semi-private, semi-public encounters of the main protagonists are the object of observation, scrutiny (through lorgnettes and telescopes!), and ill-informed gossip. Indeed, the dynamics of the ball seem to be much the same whether provincial, spa, St Petersburg or Moscow. *Dvoinaia zhizn'* is set in this last location and the ball held in honour of Cecily's birthday is full of romance, exchanged confidences and the same blurring of private and public, inner and outer. In turn, Zhukova's *Samopozhertvovanie* treats the ball as a kind of initiation to the cold world of the *svet* for her heroine, Liza, while the dynamics of the ball in Baden-Baden are especially dramatic, in that the eyes of unnamed characters are trained on the activities of other unnamed characters. The social functions of the ball are especially clearly laid bare here.

Of all the tales in my sample, the two which utilize this chronotope in the most striking way are *Baron Reikhman* and *Ideal*. The former work has two critical ball-scenes, around which the whole plot revolves, and Zhukova's narrator, as relatively early as 1837, lays bare the fact that this device was already becoming a cliché. The second chapter opens thus:

> No; I won't describe the ball! The glitter of lights, the glitter of diamonds, of outfits and beauty, the assembly place of passions ... : who doesn't know all this? This simulacrum of life, of our desires, the ball! ... it's as if you're bewitched by the dazzling glitter of the artificial day ... And who, at the end of the ball has not collapsed exhausted into your carriage, sometimes annoyed and almost always dissatisfied, *with an emptiness in one's soul and a feeling of cheated expectations?*[37]

It may be a cliché, but it is still a potentially deadly place for the women who enter this alien sphere. Indeed, immediately after this we witness Natal'ia and Levin embarking on the sequence of events that will lead inexorably to social disgrace. Fittingly, it is at 'Another Ball'

---

[37]Zhukova, p. 46 (my italics).

that she learns that he will be true not to her, but to the masculine code of honour.

Elena Gan's very first published words describe a ball, at the beginning of *Ideal*, and these opening pages capture what was for her, and many others, the terrible force of this chronotope. It is a glittering occasion – indoors, at night, in a provincial town. Men and women will gather, to be alone, but not alone. It is both safe and dangerous, a deeply ambiguous semiotic space. In particular, echoing *Kniazhna Mimi*, and foreshadowing Gan's own *Sud sveta*, it is a place where women gather like a 'swarm of wasps' to condemn the pure heroine merely for being different. The ball is from the outset for Gan the defining locus where women come to be gazed at by men, and to be defined by their fellow women. As Zhukova suggests in the very same year, *svet* and women of feeling are deeply inimical to each other, and the former will mercilessly extirpate the latter. Here too there will be a second ball, at which Ol'ga's fate is sealed. And, as in her later *Sud sveta*, Gan compares the society ball to an infernal place.

* * *

Elizabeth Shepard quite rightly remarks that:

> relative to other Russian short story forms of the romantic period, interest in female character in the society is marked. Indeed, at one level the society tale might be regarded as a feminine equivalent of the *Bildungsroman*, following the rites of passage of a young woman's entry into society and the subsequent trials and tribulations.[38]

This is generally speaking true. At the same time, however, we must note that the society tale depicts the world of high society as hostile to women's interests in many regards. In more purely literary terms, the society tale was a highly ritualized form in which certain chronotopes were recycled, as I hope to have shown. By and large, male and female writers of these tales used the same chronotopes as their counterparts, but often in very different ways. In this regard they mirror the world from which they came, and which they were depicting, a world which consisted of separate, but far from equal spheres.

---

[38]Shepard, p. 139.

L'EDUCATION SENTIMENTALE
OR THE SCHOOL OF HARD KNOCKS?
THE HEROINE'S EDUCATION
IN THE SOCIETY TALE

CAROLYN JURSA AYERS

At first glance, it seems a fool's errand to search narratives with an apparent thematic range from ballroom etiquette to the marriage market for any profound treatment of issues such as the rational development of the mind. Yet, on closer refelection, the society tale's consideration of the rules of propriety naturally concerns the sources of social success. This, in turn, leads to questions of education and learning. Pushkin himself pointed to the logical connection between *svetskost'* and education in a note defending Prince Viazemskii's sophisticated sensibilities, saying, 'A sense of propriety [*prilichie*] depends on upbringing [*vospitanie*] and other sources'.[1] Furthermore, it should hardly be surprising that society tales, which explicitly claim to represent the situation of their contemporary readers, take up this problem.[2] The question of how – and how much – to educate women had been discussed and debated since Catherine took decisive steps in the direction of providing a rational programme by founding the Smol'nyi Institute in 1764.[3] Throughout the nineteenth century, the

---

[1] A.S. Pushkin, 'O stat'iakh kn. Viazemskogo', in *Sobranie sochinenii v desiati tomakh*, Moscow, 1981, vol. 6, p. 88.

[2] The narrator in Count V.A. Sollogub's 'High Society' tale *Bol'shoi svet* claims to be driven by the imperative to represent the people he sees and meets every day: 'Truth, terrible truth, which I dare not disobey, directs me to depict you in your true colours in my faithful narrative': V.A. Sollogub, *Bol'shoi svet*, in *Russkaia svetskaia povest' XIX veka*, Moscow, 1990, pp. 355-428 (364).

[3] For historical surveys of the development of formal education in Russia, including women's education, see J.L. Black, *Citizens for the Fatherland. Education, Educators and Pedagogical Ideals in Eighteenth-Century Russia*, New York, Columbia University Press, 1979; and James C. McClelland, *Autocrats and Academics. Education, Culture and Society in Tsarist Russia*, Chicago: University of Chicago Press, 1979.

issue of education remained relevant, albeit mainly on a theoretical level until mid-century, in part because it served as a focus for a broader discourse on key social issues, such as gender roles and the family, educated Russia's self-image with regard to Western European models, and questions of generation and class.[4] Moreover, different philosophies of learning and education were developed, nurtured, and discussed at length in England and the rest of Western Europe, as eighteenth-century Enlightenment views were challenged by the values of romanticism.[5]

In Russia, there was not yet a standard model of education, or any sort of comprehensive educational system.[6] Rather, the 'principles' of idiosyncrasy and eccentricity ruled, even among the relatively small and homogeneous group of the upper nobility. Claire Clairmont, a transplant from the openly polemical but more systematic educational environment in England,[7] had this observation about her stint as a governess in a wealthy Moscow family:

> ...every child has its governess, and each governess is of a different nation: each pursues her own mode, and such a system affords no center of repose to the eternal jarring of their ideas, manners, and languages...[8]

At the same time, education was always considered a strong 'marker of self' in the Russian literary tradition, and, as Pushkin noted, in the

---

[4]In the years of the society tale (*c.* 1820-50), there was hardly a discussion of any sort of 'education for the people.' Rather, the issue of class at this stage arises in the question of the right of the nobility to obtain an education that would include areas of learning not directly of use to the state, or even what might be considered subversive ideas. See, for instance, Pushkin's 'On Public Education', (in A.S. Pushkin, *Sobranie sochinenii v desiati tomakh,* Moscow, 1981, vol. 6, pp. 28-33) an essay that, despite being written under the coercion of Nicholas II, bristles at the idea that the sons of the nobility should be kept in ignorance.

[5]See Alan Richardson, *Literature, Education, and Romanticism: Reading as Social Practice, 1780-1832,* Cambridge, Cambridge University Press, 1994.

[6]The Lyceum for boys at Tsarskoe Selo and the Smol'nyi Institute for girls stood out as exceptional institutions; they had originally been experimental, and remained exclusive.

[7]Clairmont was the mother of Byron's child, spent much time with the Shelleys, and had lived for a time on the periphery of the intellectual circle surrounding the Godwins.

[8]From a letter of 11 Sept., 1824; see *The Journals of Claire Clairmont,* edited by Marion Kingston Stocking, Cambridge, Mass., Harvard University Press, 1968, pp. 297-8.

social environment out of which the literary tradition grew.[9] All the more interesting, therefore, to investigate how different approaches to education are represented in fictional narrative. Society tales address the problem of education for women on several levels. Of course, different writers offer different perspectives on the issue, and education emerges more or less clearly as a distinct theme. Yet the conventions of the society narrative itself lead in certain directions; links and associations can be found between the form and its representations of education and learning. Reading the tales against the background of certain sets of nineteenth-century social expectations and notions about the nature of learning can open up new meanings in the narratives for the modern reader. This approach not only links the tales with topics of continuing social relevance, but also provides a lens through which we can conceive of the society tale as a coherent group of narratives, and thereby better appreciate their role in Russian literary history.

The education of a superfluous woman

Any heroine old enough to be featured in a society tale would have already completed or abandoned her formal education. It is worth remarking, then, that in this literary form concerned predominantly with the present moment (we could almost consider the fashionable drawing room a chronotope in the tales, as Bakhtin suggests for the salons of Stendhal and Balzac), society narratives consistently refer back to the heroine's early education. Clearly, a woman's upbringing and training are seen as crucial for explaining both her personality and her predicament at the time of the drama. The word used is normally *vospitanie* ('upbringing') and not *obrazovanie* ('formal education'), but for women this tends to be the accepted term for both formal and domestic training; thus it is often the conceptual equivalent of male *obrazovanie*. This may seem an obvious point, but it does not apply equally to the hero, who is more often explained through an accounting of his present financial position or, more likely, of his temperament. For example, in Marlinskii's 1830 tale *Ispytanie* (*The Test*), the hero Strelinskii's naivety is remarked by the narrator in order to give insight into his character:

---

[9]See Sidney Monas's essay, '"Self" and "Other" in Russian Literature,' in *The Search for Self-Definition in Russian Literature*, edited by Ewa M. Thompson, Amsterdam, John Benjamins, 1991, pp. 77-91 (85).

he [Strelinskii] lacked only experience − but that would come of its own accord...in spite of the strength of his passion, his intentions were firm; in the important circumstances of life he knew how to control himself.[10]

Strelinskii's younger sister Ol'ga seems to share her brother's naivety, idealism and determination. In her case, however, these traits are identified not with her character, but with her training as an *institutka*:

Educated in the Smol'nyi monastery, she, *like all her girlfriends*, purchased with her ignorance of the trivialities of social life a redeeming ignorance of the early impressions of vice and the untimely disturbing of the passions [italics mine: C.A.].[11]

This passing comment is typical, both in its assumption that Ol'ga's behaviour directly reflects her upbringing, and in its explicit linking of education to morality.[12]

The term 'education' applies loosely here. The idea that learning was synonymous with pedantry was still in force at mid-century. Pechorin in Lermontov's *Kniaginia Ligovskaia* (*Princess Ligovskaia*, 1836-37) deems it out of the question to be seen actually carrying books at the university,[13] and certainly no family of any social pretensions wanted their daughter branded as an intellectual highbrow. Girls born into fortunate families often received private tutoring at home, or were sent for a stint of several years at one of the institutes or *pansiony* in Moscow or St Petersburg. For members of high society, a good education, like any other advantage money and connections could buy, was prestigious, and desirable at least partly for that reason. Society narratives expose this situation. In *Kniaginia Ligovskaia*,

---

[10]A.A. Bestuzhev-Marlinskii, *Ispytanie*, in *Russkaia svetskaia povest' pervoi poloviny XIX veka*, Moscow, 1990, pp. 15-74 (53). All translations are my own.

[11]Ibid., p. 44.

[12]The question of whether girls and/or society were better served by protecting them as long as possible from exposure to vice (in exchange for the 'charming naivety' that endears Ol'ga to her brother), or by training them in self-restraint, so that they were prepared to confront vice with cultivated modesty, remained unresolved, and is the source of some of the tension surrounding the issue.

[13]*Kniaginia Ligovskaia*, in M.Iu. Lermontov, *Sobranie sochinenii v chetyrex tomakh*, Moscow, 1969, vol. 4, pp. 119-183 (150).

Pechorin's mother is far from unusual in articulating the expectation that her daughter will be able to occupy a high position in society 'with [in the following order] God's help, and her pretty face, and her brilliant [*blestiashchee*] education.'[14] 'Brilliant' is an apt term; the essence of this type of education is training for performance, so that a girl can shine in society. The main subjects taught, both at home and in the institutes, were languages, dancing, music, and drawing.[15] Formal education thus becomes an investment in social success, measured primarily in terms of the quantity and quality of suitors a girl is able to attract.

It is tempting to draw an analogy between a society education and a very nice ball gown, both acquired in order to elicit admiration, but in the world of the society tale the standards might well be higher for the ball gown. When families need to curtail expenses, such investments as the education of their daughters can be sacrificed. In *Kniaginia Ligovskaia*, the narrator provides an ironic account of the reasoning behind Lizaveta Nikolaevna Negurova's upbringing:

> Here in Russia, French governesses have gone slightly out of fashion, and in Petersburg they are not engaged at all... Her parents were not in a position to hire an English governess. ... English girls were expensive – it was also awkward to get a German girl: God knows what kind they would end up with: there were so many here of all sorts ... Elizaveta Nikolaevna remained without a governess at all – she learned to speak French from her mother, but even more from [their] guests, because from her earliest years she passed her days in the drawing room, sitting next to her mother and listening to all kinds of chatter....[16]

Here the description of Lizaveta's (non)education represents the basic opposition of Petersburg society to formal learning. A potentially serious intellectual endeavour is conceived instead in terms of fashion, money, prestige, and convenience: in a word, the values of the *svet*. The narrator's ironic perspective on these considerations helps to

---

[14]Ibid., p. 122.

[15]Fictional representations generally agree with historical sources on the content of girls' education. See Iu. M. Lotman, 'Ocherk dvorianskogo byta oneginskoi pory', in his *Roman A.S. Pushkina Evgenii Onegin. Kommentarii*, Leningrad, 1980, pp. 54-55; and Christine Johanson, *Women's Struggle for Higher Education in Russia*, Kingston and Montreal, McGill-Queen's University Press, 1987), pp. 3-4.

[16]Lermontov, *Princess Ligovskaia*, op. cit., p. 137.

establish a critical commentary on this opposition. Later in the novella, Lizaveta's skill in worldly conversation is contrasted unfavorably with the thoughtful contemplation of which Perchorin and the woman he loves, Vera Ligovskaia, are capable (this in spite of Pechorin's lackadaisical attitude toward his own formal education). The implication is clear: Lizaveta's superficial upbringing is at least partly to blame for leaving her unworthy of the attentions of a serious man such as Pechorin. At the same time, she is incapable of conceiving any other goal.

Odoevskii had made the critical commentary explicit in *Kniazhna Mimi* (*Princess Mimi*, 1834), with the narrator's scathing assessment of Mimi's education:

> At that time she had no definite character of any kind. You know what sort of sensibility, what sort of thinking can unfold with the upbringing that women receive: needlework, the dance teacher, a little bit of cunning, stand up straight, plus two or three anecdotes delivered by their grandmother as reliable guidance in this life and the next – and so much for education.[17]

Odoevskii goes on to explain precisely why this inadequate and unsystematic education has rendered the heroine unfit for any productive life outside of a society marriage. As she becomes more and more desperate to secure a place for herself in society, Mimi cannot visualize any spot outside the conventional opposition 'married/unmarried'. When she eventually puts the only skills she knows – keen observation and interpretation of hidden ballroom dramas – to negative use in the interest of self-preservation, her character becomes poisoned. Here again, because it is represented as falling entirely outside high society's value system, education serves as a point of perspective from which to narrativize critical commentary on those values and norms.

Assuming that a girl's parents do have the means and the commitment to provide her with a formal education, society narratives show that female accomplishment is nevertheless assessed largely by social rather than intellectual criteria. In Mariia Zhukova's tale *Medal'on* (*The Locket*, 1837), the poor and ugly but talented and sensitive heroine Mariia realizes quite painfully the extent to which social values work against recognition of her skills:

---

[17] V.F. Odoevskii, *Kniazhna Mimi*, in *Russkaia svetskaia povest'*, pp. 75-114 (77).

If she [Mariia] played the piano, her gaze read in that of her dear old teacher, 'Lovely, my pet, I am satisfied with you!' ... But society? *'Bravo, ma chère, vous faites des progrès, mais vraiment!'* ... Here *'Vous faites des progrès'* meant: very nice for a pupil, very respectable: keep practising; at least your piano will be a source of joy to you in your solitude. If Sofia played – she was weaker in music; more than once the teacher had stamped his foot with impatience during a lesson; or left the room when at social gatherings she would begin to play an accompaniment to two violins; but the room would bubble with rapture![18]

In recognizing the source of the injustice in society's reactions, Mariia reveals a psychological depth of character that reinforces Zhukova's representation of her as an intelligent young woman. Again, the 'wise' perspective lies outside the *svet*.

And what happens to girls who do meet society's main criteria of beauty and wealth? They actually appear to be impaired – if not corrupted – by the lack of balance in their upbringing. Immediately following the passage above, the narrator in *Medal'on* defends Sofia, Mariia's foil and a mediocre society girl:

Was Sofia really slighted by nature? people will ask me. Why else was she not successful in anything? Absolutely not; she had the finest disposition; but easy successes spoil a person, they make you sure of your talent when it is still just beginning to unfold.[19]

If a typical society education not only fails to enrich a girl's life, but actually excludes her from the standards of thinking men and women (a group presumably including the tales' writers, narrators and readers), alternative approaches to bringing up women disappoint in other ways. Some society narratives – almost all written by women – offer heroines who, by some quirk of fate, acquire more substantial intellectual training. In Elena Gan's 1837 tale *Ideal* (*The Ideal*), for instance, the heroine Ol'ga receives an extraordinarily thorough and classically based education from her mother, who is described as having been 'a

---

[18]*Medal'on*, in M.S. Zhukova, *Vechera na Karpovke*, Moscow, 1986, pp. 75-109 (88). The opposition between high society and learning is reflected as well in the marginal position of the teacher in the aristocratic household.
[19]Ibid., pp. 88-9.

smart, almost scholarly woman, ...something of a free thinker'.[20] Ol'ga's own upbringing, in a closely supervised and controlled nurturing and protective environment, reflects an ideal of education loosely based on ideas championed by Locke. As a child, Ol'ga's mental capabilities have been employed in a very controlled way to guide her moral development. Thus, 'from an early age [she] became accustomed to feeling and thinking after the model of the ancients'.[21] An unexpected parallel in terms of moral development emerges in Zhukova's *Dacha na Petergofskoi doroge* (*Dacha on the Peterhof Road*, 1845). In this tale, the sensitive heroine Zoia encounters culture by accident, thanks to the beneficent attitude of her uneducated guardian aunt, who 'recognizing this as necessary, had her read French and German books aloud every day and, although she herself did not understand a single word, nevertheless listened assiduously, sitting with her knitting'.[22] For Zoia, this is a 'blessed time', when she is allowed to discover moral ideals unencumbered by any attached expectations. Lacking intellectual guidance after the death of her mother, Zoia nevertheless benefits from a protective and nurturing home environment that does not actively *discourage* learning.

A good and/or lucky education such as Ol'ga and Zoia receive may lead to the development of good character and intellectual proclivities in a woman, but it most assuredly does not lead to a happy life. Rather, these heroines' enhanced sensibilities only bring them increased pain when they face the banalities of a life that falls far short of the ideal they have discovered through learning. Indeed, the conditions of society life prevent them from using their refined judgment, even in such matters as the choice of a husband.[23]

The society tales, then, give a rather scathing representation of what learning means for young women in aristocratic Russia. At best, a girl's education, if it is intellectually substantial, is wasted, or even

---

[20]E.A. Gan, *Ideal*, in *Russkaia romanticheskaia povest'*, Moscow, 1992, pp. 215-54 (221).
[21]Ibid., p. 221.
[22]M.S. Zhukova, *Dacha na Petergofskoi doroge*, in *Dacha na Petergofskoi doroge: Proza russkikh pisatel'nits pervoi poloviny XIX veka*, Moscow, 1986, pp. 245-322 (277).
[23]Chatskii, in Griboedov's play *Gore ot uma*, faces the same problem, as do some of Turgenev's heroes. Indeed, frustration at the inability to put learning to use is one of the hallmarks of the 'superfluous man'.

counterproductive in sowing the seeds of discontent. More often, a society education is simply superficial and inadequate to prepare women for any but the most limited role in life. And, at worst, it is a mechanism for corruption, designed to wipe out genuine talent and sensitivity and replace them with shining mediocrity.

It is important to realize that the society tale's representation of overwhelming antipathy on the part of the *svet* toward education and learning does not entirely reflect the range of attitudes that are represented and documented elsewhere in historical and autobiographical narratives. Lina Bernstein, in her essay on salon hostesses in the first half of the nineteenth century, paints a more optimistic picture of the achievements of at least a few highly privileged women (but after all, the society tales are concerned precisely with highly privileged women).[24] Gan herself was extremely well educated and, if her ability to converse intelligently in many languages on many subjects was not always appreciated, and if she did not always find equals in her society, she was nevertheless not actually prevented from acquiring knowledge. We might speculate, then, on how and why the cliché of vacuous high society functions in the society narrative. In a form which relies heavily on just such schematic and non-nuanced representations, intellectual competence seems to be associated with a depth of moral discrimination too individualized, and beyond the range of values linked with the *svet*. Thus a representation which directly opposes *svet* to education serves to reinforce the basic conflict posited between the (moral) individual and (immoral) society.

Acquired worldly wisdom

Two strands of Western European literature with which the society tale has either direct links or affinities represent an approach to learning based not on a systematic programme of guided education begun in childhood, but on the acquisition of experience in the world. First, the eighteenth-century French novel of manners, or what Peter Brooks calls the 'novel of worldliness',[25] represents a model of learning in

---

[24]Lina Bernstein, 'Women on the Verge of a New Language: Russian Salon Hostesses in the First Half of the Nineteenth Century', in *Russia – Women – Culture*, edited by Helena Goscilo and Beth Holmgren, Bloomington, Indiana University Press, 1996, pp. 209-24.

[25] For example, Crébillon's *Mémoires de M. de Meilcour*; see Peter Brooks, *The Novel*

which the characters gradually acquire insight into the prevailing code of social discourse. By becoming masters of that code, they become masters of their own fates. In this sophisticated and competitive social world, pragmatic knowledge both of human nature and of the mechanisms of society is essential in order to avoid becoming a victim of both.

Russian society tales do feature a number of characters in whom we can identify the result of this type of education. The Russian narrative, however, displaces this representation of learning in a couple of crucial ways. First, while it is generally the hero(ine) of the French novel of manners who learns to master the social context, sophisticated characters in Russian tales tend to be peripheral players in the central drama. Vladimir Sollogub's *Bol'shoi svet* (*High Society*, 1840) features two of these sophisticates: the countess Vorotynskaia, and her nemesis Saf'ev.[26] These characters are the 'teachers' in the so-called 'education scenes,'[27] whose worldview the main character – and the reader – must place in perspective with other, opposing value systems; they are not the characters with whom the reader identifies. Moreover, cynical acquisition of this sort of pragmatic knowledge is represented as a completed process which predates the drama at hand. Since we are not exposed to the (often bitter) experience leading to their social skill, we have little sympathy with the emotional price it might require. Sophistication is not a goal in the narrative, but a starting point. Indeed, Pushkin's Onegin undergoes something of a worldly education in reverse over the course of *Evgenii Onegin*. The Russian society tale emphatically does not advocate this pragmatic approach to learning, but rather subjects it to testing against abstract moral values that are represented in terms of family relationships, friendship, and so on.

A second and substantially different model of worldly education can be found in the English 'domestic novel' of the early nineteenth century. Writers such as Maria Edgeworth, Susan Ferrier, and Jane Austen developed a tradition stemming from the female

---

of Worldliness, Princeton, Princeton University Press, 1969. For links between the novel of manners and the society tale, see C.J. Ayers, 'Social Discourse in the Russian Society Tale', unpublished Ph.D. dissertation, University of Chicago, 1994, pp. 95-8.
[26]V. A. Sollogub, *Bol'shoi svet* (see note 2 above).
[27]See G. Bennington, *Sententiousness in the Novel: Laying Down the Law in Eighteenth-Century French Fiction*, Cambridge, Cambridge University Press, 1985, pp. 100-111; Ayers, op. cit., pp. 57-62.

Bildungsroman, 'at once novel, conduct-book, and educational tract.'[28] In these novels, the narrative typically demonstrates the value of mental and emotional flexibility, gained through the gradual process of learning from one's mistakes.[29]

Like the acquisition of worldly wisdom, this organic, experiential education finds very little place in the society tales or, for that matter, in other contemporary Russian narrative forms. In the Russian context learning seems associated not with immediate experience, so much as with the acquisition of a moral and philosophical framework which would prepare one to assess and properly understand experience. Thus characters often do not survive their own mistakes, but they may remain as models of experience for the reader. Zhukova's frame tale in *Vechera na Karpovke* (*Evenings on Karpovka*) indicates that we should read the narratives in the collection precisely in this way; the members of a small social circle aim not simply to entertain one another, but to compare interesting and contrastive examples of human behaviour, which turn out to be relevant for their own lives (these, incidentally, do not end in tragedy, but in a happy union). Of the tales in this collection, *Provintsialka* (*The Provincial Girl*)[30] comes closest to portraying learning through experience in a positive way. Even here, however, the heroine's eventual reconciliation with her life situation, her 'wisdom', is heavily tinged with a nostalgia for the security of her sheltered, guided, and morally unproblematic upbringing.

Even Odoevskii's *Kniazhna Zizi* (*Princess Zizi*, 1839),[31] while apparently portraying just this type of domestic education, represents Zizi's experience framed within several layers of narration, so that it is reported as a completed story, considered as a single 'event' from the perspective of the outside narrator. In fact, the drama in this very complex tale seems to be 'already completed' at every point; there is no development, only discovery, so that the possibility of learning is already precluded at the narrative level.

Gan's Ol'ga is an exception to this pattern, in that she does survive her disastrous encounter with the poet she had idealized, and she does

---

[28]Alan Richardson, op. cit., p. 190.

[29]Susan Morgan discusses this ethos as a historical development in the conception of female learning in her *Sisters in Time: Imagining Gender in Nineteenth-Century British Fiction*, Oxford, Oxford University Press, 1989.

[30]Zhukova, *Provintsialka*, in *Vechera na Karpovke*, pp. 186-251.

[31]Odoevskii, *Kniazhna Zizi*, in *Russkaia svetskaia povest'*, pp. 115-162.

get the opportunity to look back and contextualize this experience in the narrative of her life. Yet, even so, she does not seem to have actually learned from the experience. Ol'ga's closing letter, in which she testifies to her friend that a religious awakening has allowed her to find comfort in her difficult marital situation, reveals that she has never managed to integrate her mistake into a greater understanding of the world. Instead, she has appealed wholesale to moral principle, which enables her to endure without ever compromising or adjusting her ideals. This 'wisdom' seems more simplistic than the fine moral discrimination she should have gleaned from her early education.

It may well be that the society tale is simply too schematic in terms of plot elements to be able adequately to represent learning through experience. The tales, after all, are not novels. If a broader and wiser perspective is indicated, it can only be implied for the reader, who comes to share the narrator's point of view. In this case, learning is based not on experience itself, but on narrative representation of experience.

Books and self-education

Society tales offer numerous examples of independent reading as a model of learning, a sort of 'education of the heart'. Needless to say, representation of reading in literature can hardly be ideologically neutral. All the more interesting, then, that the tales generally do not show reading to be a straightforward, exclusively positive endeavour.

In virtually all cases, the impulse to read is represented as favourable. Often this trait serves to set the heroine's inherent sensibility apart from the material interests of other family members or the rest of society. In this sense, the tales avoid endorsing a Rousseauesque model of female development, in which a woman is best kept in blissful ignorance, so that she can become a willing pupil for her husband. Rather, the heroine of the Russian society narrative often turns to reading as a natural extension of her basic goodness. Like guided formal education, however, independent reading can result in an unbridgeable gap between the concrete conditions in which the heroine finds herself and the sensibility she has acquired through books. More problematically, self-education through reading is always arbitrary, and therefore often incomplete. By the nineteenth century reading no longer corrupts, but it may cultivate a false innocence based on the uncritical expectation that life will reflect literature. In this connection, society tales caution against at least two flawed reading habits to which, the narratives indicate, women are particularly susceptible.

The first bad habit is addressed most directly – if not logically – by Odoevskii in the inserted 'preface' to *Kniazhna Mimi*, in which the narrator whines about society ladies' taste for French novels.[32] In part, this section of the narrative reflects some of the unease still surrounding female readership in Russia. In Odoevskii's preface, this unease is discussed in terms of the schematic society tale pattern of representation; French novels are associated not with reading in any positive sense, but with the familiar corruptions of the *svet:* fashion, slavish imitation of Western European society, and prestige. Appreciation for Russian literature, on the other hand, is invariably represented as positive, if only because it demonstrates good literary taste. In fact, for women with both a 'moral' and a 'worldly' education, such as Lidiia in Panaev's *Spal'nia svetskoi zhenshchiny* (*The Boudoir of a Society Woman*, 1834) the choice to read in Russian can be made only *after* undergoing a learning process of some sort. Women who have been brought up in the *svet* must approach the reading of Russian narratives as an acquired skill.[33] Once again, then, the terms of the argument as it was conducted in Western Europe are shifted in the Russian context. It is not books, but specifically French books, which contain dangerous temptations for young women. Russian literature, on the other hand, represents if not a rejection of, then at least a critical approach toward foreign models.

In *Kniazhna Zizi* Odoevskii cautions against relying on an uncritical, incomplete conception of the world provided by self-education. When Zizi manages to obtain books by stealing the keys to her dead father's locked library (see Joe Andrew's remarks on this classic appropriation of the male realm elsewhere in this volume), she is responding positively to overcome her extremely oppressive domestic environment. This detail sets her apart from her family. It makes her interesting to us, because it is representative of her determination and her inclination for intellectual/moral stimulation.

---

[32]Odoevskii, *Kniazhna Mimi*, in ibid., pp. 99-102.
[33]*Spal'nia svetskoi zhenshchiny*, in I. I. Panaev, *Pervoe polnoe sobranie sochinenii*, vol. I, St Petersburg, 1888-89, pp. 1-46.

Her apparently admirable pastime primes her for her downfall, however, because she never gets to the end of her favourite book, *Clarissa Harlowe* (the last volume falls behind the shelf), and she proves susceptible to her own Lovelace. Meanwhile, the two men in her life act according to different literary prototypes, and no-one's life goes according to plan. The lesson delivered in many of the tales, that unguided reading leads to an unbalanced and therefore false view of the world in literary terms, is reinforced by a tendency to cast the characters' reading choices into stereotypical categories such as Zizi's 'Sentimentalism'.

Despite a proliferation of such cautionary examples, the society tales do nevertheless seem to advocate independent reading as a positive way of learning. The classic paradigm, of course, is Tat'iana in *Evgenii Onegin*. William Mills Todd describes Tat'iana's early, naive application of literary models, and her later insight gained through reading what Onegin has read, as part of her successful integration of different conventional frameworks.[34] Pushkin is not the only writer, though, to put forth the idea that one needs to learn how to read in order to learn from reading. I return to Marlinskii and *Ispytanie* for a final example. The heroine Alina explains to Strelinskii – and it is significant that she is represented as capable of rationally assessing her own upbringing – how her attitude toward life has evolved. Alina admits that if her first love, Gremin, had continued to write to her after they parted, then that 'fidelity, which I worshipped as a worthy adherent of Sentimentalism, could have completely altered my fate'. Since he does not write, she recovers from her loss, and learns:

> Abroad, more often by myself, and more often with educated people [*s liudmi obrazovannymi*], I began to feel the necessity of reading and a thirst for knowledge. Good books and even better examples, and the advice of women who knew how to combine sophisticated qualities with lofty principles, convinced me that ...the greatest of unhappinesses is the loss of self-respect.[35]

There are several conclusions to be drawn even from the rather general preliminary survey I have undertaken here. Learning in the

---

[34] See William Mills Todd, III, *Fiction and Society in the Age of Pushkin. Ideology, Institutions, and Narrative*, Cambridge, Mass., Harvard University Press, 1986, pp. 125-29.
[35] Marlinskii, *Ispytanie*, in *Russkaia svetskaia povest'*, p. 51.

social context represented in the Russian society tale would seem to be a rather risky enterprise, and its benefits dubious. Where there is no accepted standard, education – even reading – is an individual endeavour, usually lonely, and at times subversive. Not only does education fail to impose or reinforce the values of this society,[36] but it exists completely outside the concrete conditions of social life. Thus formal education acts as a separating, rather than a unifying force in society. But worldly wisdom also fails to satisfy, because it cannot provide a moral or philosophical structure compatible with that desired by 'good' people. An 'education of the heart' is what is needed; however, independent reading is too often unbalanced and arbitrary. This is where the society tales seem to offer at least the beginnings of an alternative. By providing narrative examples as lessons, by setting up schematic oppositions in their representations of a complex world, and finally by teaching their readers how to read, society tales move in the direction of creating a community of readers. These readers will not learn everything they need to know from a single narrative. This much is clear at the fictional level (as with Zizi's example), so it would be fruitless to look to the society tale for literary ambition on this scale. Instead, to use a rather anachronistic concept, it may be more appropriate to see the fictional narrative as a sort of 'learning aid', as Alina does in *Ispytanie*. Readers can achieve what the characters – with the exception of Alina – do not; they can come to know what to expect in certain situations, and they can assess a social context in individual terms, from the outside, but with little risk. From this perspective, the eventual demise of the society tale as an independent literary form may demonstrate less about its own weaknesses than about the success of Russian readers in learning their lessons and moving on to the next chapter.

---

[36]As described by Pierre Bourdieu, in his *Reproduction in Education, Society and Culture*, translated by Richard Nice, London, Sage, 1977.

FROM THE SOCIETY TALE TO THE NOVEL:
A MODEL OF GENRE DEVELOPMENT

REBECCA EPSTEIN MATVEYEV

Although the society tale was the most prevalent genre in Russian prose of the 1830s – a transitional period between romanticism and realism – it has received relatively little attention from literary scholars. Traditionally, Soviet scholars, in particular, have considered the society tale a third-rate genre. Only within the past decade or so have western Slavists begun to re-explore the society tale: some of those efforts are represented by the range of essays collected in this volume. The purpose of this particular essay is to place the society tale within a larger context. After discussing stock elements of the society tale, I describe a theoretical framework that allows for the subsequent reappearance and transfiguration of those *topoi* in later works. While limitations of space preclude extensive analysis and discussion of specific texts, this essay posits that the society tale became a primary source for the generic development of the nineteenth-century Russian novel.

The origins of the society tale lie in the 1820s, when A. A. Bestuzhev (Marlinskii) and V. F. Odoevskii wrote several sketches and tales that depicted the mores of high society, focusing on courtship rituals and marriage arrangements within that milieu. By the early 1830s, the society tale had developed as a distinct genre with a fixed set of *topoi*; by the middle of that decade a group of settings, character types, and plot elements had become assimilated under the rubric of 'society tale'. Stock society tale settings include the ballroom, the salon, the boudoir, the theatre, and the opera: all enclosed settings governed by strict behavioural rules and discourse codes that high society's members are expected to follow. Plots revolve around courtship and marriage: institutions under the strict observation and regulation of high society's 'moral guardians', who enforce marital restrictions through gossip and other social deterrents. Recurring character types include: beautiful young *ingénues* who are forced into pragmatic marriage; seductresses who attempt to rebel against high society's moral restrictions, and who are harshly punished for adultery; and scandalmongers who delight in creating and propagating rumours that destroy their social rivals.

The first Western scholar to discuss the society tale at any length, John Mersereau, defines the society tale as a set of conventionalized plots, characters, and settings. According to Mersereau:

> The heroine was typically a beautiful princess or countess unhappily married to a fat and stupid husband, the hero a young man of sensitivity and potential whose talents were scorned by an insensate society. There was often some cynical schemer who manipulated the other characters and brought about a tragic denouement. The plot included clandestine meetings, secret communications, a ball, a duel, death and banishment.[1]

Despite the ironic tone of this definition, Mersereau's statement summarizes some of the basic character types and *topoi* of the society tale. Olga Samilenko Tsvetkov's dissertation,[2] written under Mersereau's direction, greatly expands upon his genre description. Using structural analysis, Tsvetkov catalogues settings, character types, and love plots typical of the society tale. Through her detailed examination of the dazzling ballrooms, rumour-filled salons, and elegant boudoirs in which the society tale's innocent lovers, seducers, adulteresses, spinsters, and scandal-mongers interact, Tsvetkov provides a useful starting point for further work on the genre. While Carolyn Ayers focuses on discourse strategies in the society tale, early in her dissertation she summarizes the primary settings and *topoi* of the genre:

> The label 'society tale' describes ... a complex of thematic and narrative elements ... includ[ing] ... ballrooms, theatres, drawing rooms ... an elegant and sophisticated style that replicates the language of the drawing room ... love triangles, duels, balls.[3]

The formulaic, 'pulp fiction'-style plots of many society tales, and

---

[1] John Mersereau, Jr, 'Yes, Virginia, There Was a Russian Romantic Movement', *The Ardis Anthology of Russian Romantic Fiction.*, Ann Arbor, Ardis, 1984, pp. 511-17.
[2] Olga Samilenko Tsvetkov, 'Aspects of the Russian Society Tale of the 1830s', unpublished PhD dissertation, University of Michigan, 1984.
[3] Carolyn Jursa Ayers, 'Social Discourse in the Russian Society Tale', unpublished PhD dissertation, University of Chicago, 1994, p. 12.

the tendency toward melodramatic, heavy-handed narration that characterizes some tales, have led many scholars to dismiss the society tale as a second-rate, formulaic genre, highly derivative of Western prose. The society tale had thematic limitations, and some tales are, admittedly, not particularly well written. Nonetheless, the genre should not merely be shunted aside.

Virtually all significant Russian prose writers of the 1830s – including Pushkin[4] and Lermontov[5] – worked in the genre.[6] That fact in itself suggests that the society tale deserves closer examination. It is also significant that Pushkin and Lermontov both drew upon the society tale for their best known works, *Evgenii Onegin* and *Geroi nashego vremeni* (*A Hero of Our Time*): the proto-novels which, along with *Mertvye dushi* (*Dead Souls*), became the foundation of the great nineteenth-century Russian novel tradition. Tat'iana's development into a grand society lady and Onegin's disillusionment with high society have clear similarities to the society tale; the plot of Lermontov's 'Kniazhna Meri' ('Princess Mary') is essentially that of a society tale, transplanted to an exotic setting.

The generic development of the Russian novel, then, clearly had its

---

[4]While none of Pushkin's works can be categorized as a society tale pure and simple, some of his texts are extremely characteristic of that genre. In particular, *Evgenii Onegin* shares clear affinities with the society tale. Several of Pushkin's prose fragments - most notably the one entitled 'Gosti s"ezhalis' na dachu', which later played a significant role in the first drafts of *Anna Karenina* - are also within the society tale tradition. For a detailed discussion, see E. Gladkova, 'Prozaicheskie otryvki Pushkina iz zhizni sveta', in *Pushkin: Vremennik Pushkinskoi komissii*, 6, 1941, pp. 305-22. Also see the following two articles by Joost van Baak: 'Pushkin's Prose Fragments: Between Lyrical Nucleus and Societal Chronotope,' *Russian Literature* 26, 1989, pp. 425-40; and '"The Guests Gathered at the Dacha ... ": The Dynamics of a Drawing Room, in *Semantic Analysis of Literary Texts*,' edited by Erik de Haard *et al.*, Amsterdam, Elsevier Science Publishers, 1990, pp. 51-65.

[5]See M.A. Belkina, 'Svetskaia povest'' 30-kh godov i *Kniaginia Ligovskaia* Lermontova', in *Zhizn' i tvorchestvo M. Iu. Lermontova.*, Moscow, 1941, pp. 516-51; V.A. Evzherikhina, '"Kniazhna Meri" M. Iu. Lermontova i svetskaia povest' 1830-kh godov', *Uchenye zapiski. Institut im. Gertsena. Voprosy istorii literatury 219*, Leningrad, 1961, pp. 51-72; and E.M. Mikhailova, *Proza Lermontova*, Moscow, 1957. These critics argue that Lermontov's *Kniaginia Ligovskaia* and 'Kniazhna Meri' overcame the limitations of the society tale paradigm. But, in fact, a number of their statements only serve to establish a closer link between Lermontov's works and the society tale.

[6]See Ayers, op. cit., pp. 2-4; R.V. Iezuitova, 'Svetskaia povest'', in *Russkaia povest' XIX veka*, edited by B.S. Meilakh, Leningrad, 1973, pp. 169-99.

origins in the society tale. Even in the 1830s, the society tale proved flexible enough to interact and blend with other genres. For example, Helena Goscilo has discussed Lermontov's *Kniaginia Ligovskaia* (*Princess Ligovskaia*) as a blend of the society tale and the petty clerk's tale.[7] Karolina Pavlova's *Dvoinaia zhizn'* (*A Double Life*) interpolates sections of lyrical poetry within a prosaic – both literally and figuratively – society tale. From the beginning, society tale elements were often 'integrated or embedded in a larger work' (Ayers, p. 10). And even after the society tale's reign ended, as the novel continued to develop, the society tale remained a significant source of character types, plot elements, and settings.

It seems surprising that connections between the society tale and later Russian prose have received only passing mention in previous scholarship, limited to one or two sentences within much larger studies. For example, Ayers comments that 'many of the [society tale's] characteristic elements – aristocratic settings, domestic traumas, and the like – were subsumed and transformed by later writers like Turgenev,. Goncharov, and Tolstoi (and parodied by Gogol and Dostoevskii)' (Ayers, p. 2). Allan Urbanic mentions that 'when tracing the development of this genre, one finds its echoes ... in the works of Turgenev and Tolstoj'.[8] Elizabeth Shepard states that the society tale may have inspired Russian realist novelists, such as Druzhinin and Goncharov, to undertake a focused analysis of relationships between men and woman, as well as to depict strong female protagonists.[9] In his monograph on Odoevskii, the editor of this volume remarks that the society tale contains 'the basic plot lines, dramatic situations, character types, and configurations, albeit in a relatively primeval form, that were to recur throughout Russian prose for the rest of the century, from the young Dostoevsky to Chekhov'.[10]

As a framework to examine literary reinscriptions of the society

---

[7]Helena Goscilo, 'The First Pechorin En Route to *A Hero*: Lermontov's "Princess Ligovskaja"', *Russian Literature*, 11, 1982, pp. 129-62.
[8]Allan Joseph Urbanic, 'In the Manners of the Times: The Russian Society Tale and British Fashionable Literature, 1820-1840', unpublished PhD dissertation, Brown University, 1983, p. 2.
[9]Elizabeth C. Shepard, 'The Society Tale and the Innovative Argument in Russian Prose Fiction of the 1830s', *Russian Literature*, 10, 1981, p. 140.
[10]Neil Cornwell, *The Life, Times and Milieu of V.F. Odoyevsky, 1804-1869*, London, Athlone, 1986, p. 55.

tale, I have adapted ideas from Russian and western scholars to create a synthesized form of genre theory. During the 1920s, the Russian Formalists began to develop a theory of literary evolution – a task they never completed.[11] Additional contributions to genre theory were made by Bakhtin and his followers, and later by Tzvetan Todorov. More recently, several western scholars have explored genre problems, drawing upon ideas of earlier literary theorists and philosophers. My approach – which is limited to the society tale and its significance for the Russian realist novel – incorporates and adapts aspects of the following theories: Bakhtin's idea of genre memory; Tynianov's concept of the functions of generic elements; Todorov's theory of 'low' and 'high' genres; and the notion of familial genre relations, originally derived from Wittgenstein.

While the Formalists provide a useful foundation for genre study, their perception of genre development as a battle between opposing schools results in an overly hierarchical approach that ignores the possibility of interaction among genres. Furthermore, Formalist theories of literary 'evolution' are, in fact, hobbled by a strongly synchronic approach. By contrast, Bakhtinian genre theory – which proposes that genres leave behind traces or residues that gradually accrete to form other genres – allows for a more open-ended, less hierarchical approach. The diachronic basis of Bakhtinian genre theory also suggests the possibility that society tale elements can be traced throughout the development of the nineteenth-century Russian novel. Finally, analogies between intergeneric and familial relationships provide a concrete, creative way to visualize genre development in a diachronic fashion.

In the early 1920s, Shklovskii created a developmental theory that is binary in nature, and that is characterized by political-militaristic overtones. To Shklovskii, dominant literary forms replace one another by turn, each temporarily maintaining its own hegemony. No genre undergoes a dialectical development, and no synthesis between genres occurs. In his 1921 article, 'Literature Beyond the Plot', Shklovskii explains that, while different genres and movements continually coexist, one literary trend dominates at any given time: 'In every

---

[11]See Victor Erlich, *Russian Formalism: History, Doctrine*, New Haven, Yale University Press, 1965, pp. 118-40, for a discussion of the school's demise, due largely to political circumstances (referred to in the text hereafter as 'Erlich').

literary age there exist not one, but several literary schools... One of them is the canonized crest. The others exist in an uncanonized, muted state'.[12] But, as the demands of a given literary era change, older genres may return from obsolescence, overcoming the current canonical form. 'The conquered line is not destroyed, it does not cease to exist. It simply is thrown off the crest ... and can again be resurrected, as the eternal claimant to the throne'.[13] During the period that one literary form predominates, the others remain in the background – plotting, as it were, a military overthrow of the dominant genre.

Drawing on Shklovskii's ideas, Tynianov developed the concept of automatization: once canonical genres become entrenched, they are forced out by newer, lesser-known forms. In the 1924 essay, 'The Literary Fact', he writes: 'During the time of a genre's decomposition, it is moved from the centre out to the periphery and a new phenomenon from literature's backlog of petty things rises to the centre, taking its place'.[14] As an example, elsewhere Tynianov discusses the ode's initial status as a canonical poetic genre, the 'destruction' of the genre by Derzhavin, and the eventual replacement of the ode by lyric poetry.[15] But even after the end of the ode's reign over Russian poetry, the genre did not entirely disappear: in the 1820s, '[d]oomed to a secret underground life, out of favour, the ode resurfaced during the revolt of the archaists'.[16] Again, in typical Formalist fashion, genre 'evolution' more closely resembles warfare, or political struggle.

However, departing slightly from Shklovskii's view of genre development as a continual struggle, Tynianov differentiates between two forms of literary evolution: he contrasts, on the one hand, the mere avoidance of an established literary tradition and, on the other, a deliberate battle with an established tradition. That is, unlike Shklovskii, he differentiates categories and degrees of competition, rivalry, and co-existence among genres. In his 1921 essay, 'Dostoevskii and Gogol': On the Theory of Parody', Tynianov writes:

---

[12] V. B. Shklovskii, 'Literatura vne siuzheta', in his *O teorii prozy*, Moscow, 1925, p. 228.

[13] Ibid., pp. 227-8.

[14] Iu. N. Tynianov, 'Literaturnyi fakt', in his *Arkhaisty i novatory*, Leningrad, 1929 (reprint Munich, Wilhem Fink, 1967), p. 9.

[15] Tynianov, 'Oda kak oratorskii zhanr', in ibid., pp. 48-86.

[16] Ibid., pp. 84-5.

> When people talk about a 'literary tradition' ... they usually imagine ... a direct
> line connecting the junior representative of a known literary branch with the
> senior representative... But actually it is much more complicated. There is not a
> continuation of a direct line, but more nearly ... a battle. But in regard to the
> representatives ... of another tradition, there is no such battle: they are simply
> circumvented... the battle results from the very fact of their existence.[17]

Similarly, in the 1921 essay 'The Archaists and Pushkin', Tynianov distinguishes between the evolution of literary movements 'friendly' to each other and those 'hostile' to each other – that is, those basically similar in nature, and those fundamentally different.[18] And in the 1924 article, 'The Literary Fact', he describes the principles of literary evolution as 'battle' and 'replacement'.[19]

While some scholars credit the Formalists with defining literary change as a 'dynamic principle of literary evolution',[20] that notion is problematic. According to Jauss, the Formalists – in particular, Tynianov and Shklovskii – created a diachronic model of literary *development*, rather than the synchronic approach of literary *tradition* promulgated by earlier theorists.[21] But, in fact, because Tynianov and Shklovskii examine only the literary school which predominates at any given time, their approach is essentially synchronic. They do not examine literary history or literary development as such; rather, they examine individual cross-sections of literature at isolated points in time.

According to the author[22] of *The Formal Method in Literary*

---

[17]Tynianov, 'Dostoevskii i Gogol': k teorii parodii', in ibid., p. 412.

[18]Tynianov, 'Arkhaisty i Pushkin', in ibid., p. 87.

[19] Tynianov, 'Literaturnyi fakt' , in ibid., pp. 3-29.

[20]Hans Robert Jauss, *Toward an Aesthetic of Reception*, translated by Timothy Bahti, Minneapolis, University of Minnesota Press, 1982, p. 17.

[21]Ibid., p. 17.

[22]Since the 1970s, the authorship of this book has been a matter of controversy (see the 'Foreword' to M.M. Bakhtin / P.N. Medvedev, *Formal'nyi metod v literaturovedenii*, Moscow, 1993, pp. viii-ix). Currently the foremost experts on Bakhtin consider that the book was written by P. N. Medvedev, a member of Bakhtin's circle, and that Medvedev's theories on genre influenced Bakhtin: see Gary Saul Morson and Caryl Emerson, *Mikhail Bakhtin: Creation of a Prosaics*, Stanford, Stanford University Press, 1990, p. 271 (referred to hereafter in the text as 'Morson and Emerson'); for a discussion of Bakhtin's adaptation of Medvedev's genre theory, see ibid., pp. 272 ff.

Scholarship: 'Strictly speaking, the process of historical-literary development, as understood by the Formalists, cannot be called evolution or development, without creating ambiguity'.[23] Taking issue specifically with Tynianov, he declares:

> To show that two phenomena struggle and replace each other does not mean, in any sense, that there is an evolutionary connection between them... In order to reveal an evolutionary connection, one must show ... that two phenomena are fundamentally interconnected, and that one ... fundamentally and necessarily determines the other. (p. 183)

After the publication of *The Formal Method in Literary Scholarship*, with its critique of Formalist genre theory, Tynianov began to consider a more diachronic approach to literary studies. In 1928 he collaborated with Jakobson to compose the terse theoretical guidelines described in 'Problems in the Study of Language and Literature', one precept of which implies that a purely synchronic approach is no longer feasible, hinting at a dialectical approach to literary evolution. But after 1928 Tynianov made no further significant contributions toward a genre theory; and soon afterwards the Formalist movement dissolved. More typically – and in his most thoroughly developed and useful essays – Tynianov treats genres outside a larger historical framework.

By contrast to Formalist theory, Bakhtinian theory explores literature diachronically, positing that genres evolve into higher forms in later, more complex works. In the 1927 essay 'On Literary Evolution', Tynianov states: 'Tolstoi's historical novel is not correlated to Zagoskin's historical novel, but rather correlates to the prose which was contemporary to him [Tolstoi]'.[24] Bakhtin, by contrast, would argue that the roots of Tolstoi's historical novel do, in fact, lie in Zagoskin's work – if not much further back. More significantly, Bakhtin would argue that a historical novel written in the mid-nineteenth century derives not merely from its earlier generic counterparts. For Bakhtin, genres accrete over time, creating a multi-layered literary repository that becomes richer and more complex. Tolstoi was able to draw not only on previous historical novels, but also on other genres that had developed in the interim. Similarly, an adapted form of Bakhtinian genre theory provides a framework to

---

[23]M.M. Bakhtin/P.N. Medvedev, op. cit., p. 175.
[24]Tynianov, 'O literaturnoi evoliutsii', in *Arkhaisty i novatory*, p. 38.

examine the relationship between the society tale and the nineteenth-century Russian novel.

In Bakhtinian theory, genres that became obsolete many centuries ago can be renewed through the phenomenon of 'genre memory'. Over time 'archaic elements are preserved ... thanks to their constant renewal, which is to say, their contemporization... A genre lives in the present, but always *remembers* its past, its beginning'.[25] For example, renewing and reworking Menippean satire, Dostoevskii 'linked up with the chain of a given tradition'.[26] Rather than utilizing specific examples of Menippean satire, his novels contain generalized reflections of that generic tradition. Dostoevskii himself did not even need to be consciously aware of Menippean satire: 'It is ... a case of collective and not individual memory, and its content may even remain unknown to the individual; but this content is inscribed in the formal properties of the genre'.[27] For Bakhtin, genres develop over the course of millennia, marked by 'the residue of past behavior, an accretion that shapes, guides, and constrains future behavior' (Morson and Emerson, p. 290).

In contrast to Bakhtin's example of Dostoevskii and Menippean satire, I would argue that genre memory is not the primary force that shapes the relationship between the society tale and the Russian realist novel. Whereas many centuries separate Dostoevskii from Lucian and Apuleius, there was a relatively small time lag between the society tale and the realist novel. Russia's literary history was tremendously compressed during the nineteenth century, encompassing several major literary movements and numerous genres. Classical Russian literature was created and reached its greatest peak within the course of a half-century, from the time of Pushkin to Tolstoi. That remarkable pitch of literary development meant that Russia's novelists of the 1860s and 1870s were all too aware of their national forebears. That constant self-awareness among Russia's nineteenth-century novelists took precedence over the phenomenon of genre memory.

Russia's nineteenth-century novelists themselves deliberately

---

[25]M.M. Bakhtin, *Problems of Dostoevsky's Poetics*, edited and translated by Caryl Emerson, Minneapolis, University of Minnesota Press, 1984, p. 106.

[26]Ibid., p. 121.

[27]Tzvetan Todorov, *Mikhail Bakhtin: The Dialogical Principle*, translated by Wlad Godzich, Minneapolis, University of Minnesota Press, 1984, p. 85.

resurrected and reworked archetypal character types and situations from the society tale. Also, because of the society tale's recent widespread prevalence, Russia's nineteenth-century novelists may have been influenced not only by the society tale as a paradigmatic form, but also by individual examples of the genre. But even so, the connection between the society tale and the realist novel can be partly defined in Bakhtinian terms: 'Because genres are so often adapted from previous genres, they may carry the potential to ... redefine a present experience in an additional way. Some genres ... recover old contexts or intimate the possibility of new ones' (Morson and Emerson, p. 283).

While a modified Bakhtinian approach toward connections between literary *genres* is more useful than Formalist views, Tynianov's approach to the recurrence of literary *elements* is more productive than Bakhtin's. According to Bakhtin, motifs which appear in different genres – including genres separated by large spans of time – enact the same function in all cases. Those elements 'were ... reinforced by tradition; in their subsequent development they continued stubbornly to exist, up to and beyond the point at which they had lost any meaning that was productive'.[28] Genre memory seems so pervasive as not to allow for variation. For example, Bakhtin remarks on the recurrence of the 'motif of meeting and the chronotope of the road' in many diverse genres – and apparently considers that the function of those motifs never alters.[29]

By contrast, according to Tynianov, when established elements and motifs appear in later genres, those elements play a different function – even if the form is apparently analogous. In 'The Literary Fact', he comments: 'The generic function of one or another device is not something fixed'.[30] In 'About Literary Evolution', he differentiates between two types of literary function: the 'auto-function', a term which refers to different elements within a single literary work; and the 'syn-function', a term which refers to similar elements within different works.[31] Of primary importance for my purposes is the notion of the 'syn-function', for that concept provides a way to describing the

---

[28]M.M. Bakhtin, *The Dialogic Imagination*, edited by Michael Holquist, translated by Caryl Emerson and Michael Holquist, Austin, University of Texas Press, 1981, p. 85.
[29]Ibid., p. 98.
[30]Tynianov, *Arkhaisty i novatory*, p. 8.
[31]Ibid., p. 39.

reappearance of society tale *topoi* in subsequent literary works.

Working under the dual influence of Russian and western theorists, Todorov expanded on certain ideas of the Formalists and the Bakhtin Circle. In the essay 'The Origin of Genres', he states that '[a] new genre is always the transformation of an earlier one, or of several: by inversion, by displacement, by combination'.[32] That statement continues in the spirit of the Bakhtinian tradition, further clarifying that several genres can combine to create a new one, through accretion. Todorov would probably emphasize, more than Bakhtin does, that Dostoevskii's novels contain numerous generic elements apart from Menippean satire. Similarly, the Russian realist novel incorporates generic and literary sources apart from the society tale.

Todorov also expands on Formalist views by reinvisioning a genre hierarchy. To Tynianov and Shklovskii, peripheral literary forms eventually achieve a more substantive state, through the 'canonization of the younger genres' (Tynianov, 'Literaturnyi fakt', p. 9). In Shklovskii's view, everyday linguistic elements and lowbrow genres can be raised to the level of canonical works: 'literature draws upon motifs and devices of sub-literary genres... Products of popular culture, leading a precarious existence on the periphery of literature, are ... raised to the status of literary art' (Erlich, p. 260). But for Todorov, peripheral genres – which he terms 'low art' – can maintain themselves distinctly from canonical genres – or 'high art'. Furthermore, pulp fiction can prove highly fruitful for genre study and definitions: 'the masterpiece of popular literature is precisely the book which best fits its genre'.[33]

While Todorov limits his discussion to detective fiction, a similar argument could be made for the society tale: for the society tales that are most productive – at least for the purposes of my approach – may be those that are most formulaic. In contrast with popular literature, 'high art' avoids typicality and predictability. Genre definitions continually shift, and the canon's boundaries remain neither distinct nor stable: 'every great book establishes the existence of two genres, the reality of two norms: that of the genre it transgresses, which dominated

---

[32]Tzvetan Todorov, *Genres in Discourse*, translated by Catherine Porter, Cambridge, Cambridge University Press, 1990, p. 15.
[33]Tzvetan Todorov, 'The Typology of Detective Fiction', in his *The Poetics of Prose*, translated by Richard Howard, Ithaca, Cornell University Press, 1977, p. 44.

the preceding literature, and that of the genre it creates' (Todorov, 'The Typology...', p. 43).

More recently, several western scholars have attempted to expand the scope of genre theory; but much of their work has simply duplicated that of Bakhtin and Todorov.[34] In other cases, their attempts to polemicize with and move beyond those earlier ideas have been largely unproductive.[35]

One form of genre theory that crops up in the work of recent theorists is the comparison of intergeneric connections to family relationships: an idea that derives from an abstruse Wittgensteinian linkage between linguistic schemata, game systems, and family resemblances. For example, Alistair Fowler compares 'intergeneric relations'[36] to an extended family:

> In literature, the basis of resemblance lies in literary tradition: ... a sequence of influence and imitation and inherited codes connecting works... [T]he family grouping allows for wide variation... [T]he theory of family resemblance also suggests that we should be on the lookout for ... unobvious, underlying connections between ... works.[37]

David Fishelov protests that scholars such as Fowler have:

> ... isolated one element — the family — from [Wittgenstein's] network of analogies and, ignoring its function in the entire conceptual set, used it exclusively to establish the analogy frequently found in genre theory: between a

---

[34]For example, Adrian Marino's distinction between 'the essence of genres (defined by literary *notions* and *ideas*) and the phenomenon of genres (expressed in literary *forms)*', in his 'A Definition of Literary Genres', in *Theories of Literary Genre*, edited by Joseph P. Strelka, 'Yearbook of Comparative Criticism', Vol. 8, University Park, Pennsylvania State University Press, 1978, p. 54), recalls Todorov's idea that a genre's basic literary code can manifest itself differently in individual works (see Todorov, 'The Typology...', pp. 51-52).

[35]In a formulation that destroys the meaning of the term 'genre', Marino states that 'each literary work can be written *only* in its own genre, belongs to its own genre, and starts a *new* genre' (op. cit., p. 51). John Reichart differentiates between genre theory and genre criticism, arguing that genre theory - in particular, as practised by Todorov - is an inadequate tool for literary study: 'More than Kin and Less than Kind: The Limits of Genre Theory', in *Theories of Literary Genre,* op. cit., pp. 66-70. However, he does not provide a working substitute.

[36]Alastair Fowler, *Kinds of Literature: An Introduction to the Theory of Genres and Modes*, Cambridge, Mass., Harvard University Press, 1982, p. 251.

[37]Ibid., pp. 39-40.

'family' ... and a 'genre'.[38]

Some years before the appearance of Wittgenstein's theory of resemblances, the major Russian Formalists incorporated other family analogies into their genre theory.[39] Both Tynianov and Eikhenbaum expressed the notion that a writer, 'in his recoil from the conventions of the recent past, [may] fall back consciously or unconsciously on the pattern of a more remote age' (Erlich, p. 259). In the 1924 article 'The Interval', Tynianov describes Khlebnikov's return to Lomonosov's eighteenth-century poetic principles: 'This is not a return to the old, but simply a battle with the father, in which the grandson turns out to resemble the grandfather'.[40] By contrast, Shklovskii argues that writers may choose to disrupt literary tradition by pursuing an oblique line from 'uncle' to 'nephew'. The established literary precedent is bypassed, and the canonical authority of the 'fathers' is denied (see Erlich, pp. 259-60). However, despite the incorporation of non-literary terminology, those ideas do not venture beyond a purely aesthetic approach to literary development. Polemicizing with Shklovskii, Zhirmunskii argued that '[s]ince literature ... is closely bound up with other human activities, its evolution cannot be accounted for in purely literary terms' (Erlich, p. 255).

My own concept of generic 'family relations' – specifically, between the society tale and the nineteenth-century Russian novel – is both more socially grounded than the Formalist views and more culturally based than the Wittgensteinian approach. Society-tale authors and several of Russia's major nineteenth-century novelists shared cultural and literary concerns. Consequently, their texts reflect similar themes and enact similar scenarios. But the two genres face

---

[38]David Fishelov, *Metaphors of Genre: The Role of Analogies in Genre Theory*, University Park, Pennsylvania State University Press, 1993, p. 56. I quote here from Fishelov only to demonstrate that there is some controversy over the ways in which contemporary genre theorists have appropriated and developed Wittgenstein's ideas of family resemblance. It is outside the scope of this essay to discuss that controversy in any depth.

[39]Wittgenstein's *Philosophical Investigations*, the work containing his ideas about family resemblances and generic, linguistic and game systems, was written from the 1930s to the 1950s. Shklovskii's idea of the uncle-nephew line must have been developed sometime prior to 1923, since he refers back to that concept in his 1923 work *Literatura i kinematograf* (see Erlich, p. 260, n. 37).

[40]Tynianov, 'Promezhutok', *Arkhaisty i novatory*, p. 562.

each other across a generation gap: the novel strives to overcome the society tale, to achieve more than its predecessor could.

Throughout the 1830s, typical plot elements, settings, and character types made a text easily recognizable as a society tale. But those same traits also made the society tale vulnerable. For sarcastically minded writers, the society tale's formulaic themes and stock situations facilitated the creation of parodies on the genre. Even during the height of the society tale's popularity – and even as he published many of the tales in *Biblioteka dlia chteniia* (or 'A Library for Reading') – Senkovskii mocked generic conventions. One has merely to consider the tone of the titles that follow. 'A Woman's Entire Life in Several Hours' (1833), which highly compresses a typical society tale plot, casts high society settings in an absurd light. 'A St Petersburg Lady' (1834) is related by a chatty narrator who sardonically portrays the foolish heroine's arranged marriage. Rakhmannyi's 'One out of Two' (1836) viciously dissects the 'sufferings' of an 'angelic' woman who rationalizes her extramarital affairs by complaining that high society unjustly forced her into an unhappy marriage. According to both Urbanic and Ayers, these are superficial parodies written by authors who failed to understand the society tale's true significance. But more importantly, the act of parodying demonstrates that a genre has achieved a certain measure of renown and that it is widely recognized.

At the same time, parodies of the society tale also displayed the genre's limitations: the society tale was so widespread that it had become trite and overly predictably, and it would have to undergo some transformation if it were to remain part of Russia's literary tradition. By the early 1840s, the society tale as such became obsolete. As the 1840s progressed, the 'natural school' received Belinskii's critical acclaim as an alternative to the aristocratic literature of previous decades. Works by Gogol' and the early Dostoevskii – texts that Belinskii perceived as sympathetically portraying the plight of the lower classes – came to the forefront of the literary canon.

However, the society tale did not simply disappear from Russian literature. Given the society tale's dominance over Russian prose for over a decade, the genre's basic situations, themes, and character types were embedded in the literary consciousness of the next generation of writers. In a Bakhtinian formulation, the society tale formed a significant layer in the accretion of genres that comprised the realist novel. The society tale proved a fruitful source for such authors as Goncharov, Tolstoi, and Dostoevskii, who rediscovered and found new uses for the society tale. As Joan Delaney Grossman comments, 'more interesting than [the] simple presence [of society tale themes] in the works of later authors are the uses these authors sometimes found for the earlier generic forms'.[41]

During the second half of the nineteenth century, the society tale became incorporated into the larger forms of the social novel and the family novel. Certainly the society tale was not the only source for the nineteenth-century novel. Scholars have long since documented that Russia's greatest novelists read widely and extensively, both in their native literature and in western literatures, and that they drew upon those resources in their own work. But a number of well-known nineteenth-century novels can be productively read as reworkings of the society tale. Scenarios of courtship, marriage and adultery that appear in such novels as Goncharov's *Obyknovennaia istoriia* (*A Common Story*), Tolstoi's *Anna Karenina* and Dostoevskii's *Idiot* (*The Idiot*) derive, in various ways, from the society tale. But those novels adapt, revise, and transpose society-tale marriage plots. Sections of each novel unfold in typical society-tale settings, such as the salon and the ballroom; but those texts also extend beyond high society, to include other social classes.

Several examples help demonstrate ways in which those novels transmute settings, character types, and plots drawn from the society tale: the phenomenon that Tynianov described as the 'syn-function'. Society tale *topoi* such as the ball, the salon, and arranged marriages appear decades later, in nineteenth-century Russian novels; but within that context, those elements acquire new functions. For example, ball scenes – a common *topos* of the society tale – appear in *Anna Karenina* as well. But unlike his literary predecessors, Tolstoi uses the ball scene to greater psychological effect, providing insight into the character of his *ingénue* heroine, Kitty Shcherbatskaia. The scenes that unfold in Betsy Tverskaia's salon echo society tale scenes rife with destructive gossip and hypocritical judgements. But the structural distribution of those scenes throughout the novel provides those scenes with a

---

[41]Joan Delaney Grossman, '"Words, Idle Words": Discourse and Communication in *Anna Karenina*,' *In the Shade of the Giant: Essays on Tolstoy*, edited by Hugh McLean, Berkeley, University of California Press, 1989, p. 116.

different significance than their society tale counterparts. Anna's appearances in Betsy Tverskaia's salon occur at varying intervals: at first before her involvement with Vronskii, and then at various stages of her affair. Thus, the reader can trace changes in Anna's psychology as she becomes increasingly affected by that high society milieu. As a consequence, Tolstoi is able to imbue his heroine with greater psychological depth than that normally attributed to society-tale adulteresses. In *Idiot*, Nastas'ia Filippovna's name-day party suggests a chaotic version of salon scenes from the society tale. Similarly, the engagement party scene, in which Myshkin collapses from an epileptic attack, can be seen as the failure of high society to maintain its facade of composure and elegance. In Dostoevskii's hands, the social gatherings of the society tale deteriorate into scandalous scenes.

The *ingénues*, fallen women, innocent heroes, seducers, moral predators and moral guardians of the society tale also reappear – transformed and refigured – in the Russian realist novel. Goncharov's Aleksandr Aduev represents a composite of various types of society tale protagonists: he starts out as an innocent figure who condemns high society's lack of idealism, but he becomes increasingly cynical and finally enters a pragmatic marriage of his own. The heroines of *Obyknovennaia istoriia* also recall various types of society-tale heroines, including the *ingénue* and the seduced 'fallen woman'. In *Anna Karenina*, Kitty Shcherbatskaia, initially infatuated with Vronskii, starts out much like a society tale *ingénue* doomed to seduction. But she steps beyond that paradigm to marry Levin, a character entirely foreign to the society tale. While Anna Karenina's role within high society and involvement with Vronskii recalls the adulteresses of the society tale, her character is psychologically far more complex. Thus Tolstoi takes single stock character types from the society tale, and examines them in greater psychological depth. In *Idiot* the opposing roles of *ingénue* and "fallen woman" become confused and intertwined. Despite her situation as a marriageable young woman, Aglaia has a darker and more complex character than the typical society tale *ingénue*. And while Nastas'ia Filippovna is a fallen woman, Myshkin's perception of her as an icon of purity places her outside the realm of society tale seductresses. One way in which Dostoevskii reworks the society tale is to combine and synthesize paradigmatic society tale figures, finding new depths of character in those combinations.

The society tale's influence on the nineteenth-century Russian novel can be not only theoretically constructed, but, in certain cases, it can also be concretely established: that is especially true for *Obyknovennaia istoriia* and *Anna Karenina*. One of Goncharov's first works was a prose tale entitled *Schastlivaia oshibka* (*A Lucky Mistake*).[42] This tale, written in 1839 – that is, near the end of the society tale's reign – belongs within the society-tale tradition in terms of theme, plot, characterization, and structure. In the mid-1840s, *Schastlivaia oshibka* provided a partial basis for Goncharov's first novel, *Obyknovennaia istoriia*. But even as Goncharov drew upon his own society tale, his novel went beyond that text, and beyond the society-tale genre as a whole. Among his accomplishments in writing *Obyknovennaia istoriia* was the creation of a composite of stock situations and character-types from the society tale. Nearly three decades later, when Tolstoi began to write about a high society adulteress, his first drafts resembled nothing so much as a society tale.[43] However, the relatively short expanse and narrow scope of the society tale did not allow for the complications of plot and character development that characterize the final version of *Anna Karenina*. As Tolstoi continued to work on his novel, he introduced other elements, creating a work far more complex than the society tale. The final version of *Anna Karenina*, although still reliant on the society tale, goes beyond the limitations of that genre.

When compared to the nineteenth-century Russian novel – and especially to the work of Dostoevskii – the society tale appears rather formulaic and stodgy. To conclude with a continuation of the family analogy introduced earlier, the novel may not want to identify itself with its older relatives, much like a teenager embarrassed by his

---

[42]This story appeared in the private manuscript collection *Lunnye nochi* in 1839 and was published in standard form only in 1927: Vsevolod Setchkarev, *Ivan Goncharov: His Life and Works*, Würzburg, Jal-Verlag, 1974, p. 30. Shepard (op cit., p. 157, n. 102) states that in 1839 Goncharov wrote a society tale entitled *Dvoinaia oshibka* ('A Double Mistake') . Since I have found no other mention of a work by that title, I have to assume that Shepard is actually referring to this tale (i.e. *Schastlivaia oshibka*).

[43]See A.H. Keesman-Marwitz, 'The Compositional Evolution of *Anna Karenina*', *Dutch Contributions to the Tenth International Congress of Slavists*, Amsterdam, Rodopi, 1988, pp. 115-37; David Sloane, 'Pushkin's Legacy in *Anna Karenina*', *Tolstoy Studies Journal*, 4, 1991, pp. 1-23.

parents. But the nineteenth-century novel also depends on the society tale, and cannot free itself of that generic, or perhaps genetic, influence. Finally, the connection between the early nineteenth-century tale and the later nineteenth-century novel presents, as well, a curious twist on genre evolution. In the 1830s various types of tales – most notably the society tale – arose in part as a reaction against historical fiction, which had first taken the form of the novel. In the 1860s and 1870s the novel flourished, growing out of the society tale: the very genre which had earlier replaced the first phase of the Russian novel.

NOTES ON CONTRIBUTORS

Joe Andrew is Professor of Russian Literature at Keele University. His main interests are in nineteenth-century Russian literature, feminist approaches to literature and women writers. His most recent books are *Narrative and Desire in Russian Literature, 1822-1849: The Feminine and the Masculin* (Macmillan, 1993) and *Russian Women's Shorter Fiction: An Anthology, 1835-1860* (Oxford University Press, 1996). He is co-chair of the Neo-Formalist Circle and co-editor of its journal, *Essays in Poetics*.

Carolyn Jursa Ayers is a Postdoctoral Fellow in Comparative Literature at the University of Groningen, The Netherlands. Her interests are in nineteenth-century culture and, following her doctoral dissertation on the Russian society tale, she has written on various aspects of representation in narrative.

Neil Cornwell is Professor of Russian and Comparative Literature, University of Bristol. He is the editor of *Reference Guide to Russian Literature* (Fitzroy Dearborn, 1998), the author of two books on V.F Odoevskii, and the translator of a selection of his stories into English. He has also published studies in other areas of nineteenth and twentieth-century Russian literature and on comparative themes. He is the Bristol Classical Press series editor for Russian Texts and Critical Studies in Russian Literature.

Sally Dalton-Brown is Lecturer in Russian, University of Exeter. She has published widely on late twentieth-century Russian literature and is the author of *Pushkin's 'Evgenii Onegin'* (Bristol Classical Press, 1997). She is currently preparing a study of Petrushevskaia.

Hilde Hoogenboom is Assistant Professor in the Russian Studies Program at Stetson University, DeLand, Florida. She has written articles on Maria Bashkirtseva, on George Sand's biographer, and on Varvara Komarova [Wladimir Karenine], and is currently working on both Sokhanskaia and Khvoshchinskaia.

W. Gareth Jones is Professor of Russian at the University of Wales, Bangor. His main interests are the Enlightenment in eighteenth-century Russia and the nineteenth-century Russian novel. His recent publications include *Tolstoi and Britain* (Berg, 1995) and 'Politics and the Novel', a contribution to *The Cambridge Companion to the Classical Russian Novel* (Cambridge University Press, 1997).

Rebecca Epstein Matveyev is Assistant Professor of Russian at Lawrence University, Appleton, Wisconsin. The essay appearing here is based upon the introduction to her doctoral dissertation on reworkings of the society tale.

Richard Peace is Professor Emeritus of the University of Bristol, where he taught Russian from 1963 to 1994 (with an interlude from 1975 to 1984 as professor at Hull University). He has published widely on nineteenth-century Russian literature, including books on Dostoevskii, Gogol', Chekhov and Goncharov.

Michael Pursglove is Senior Lecturer in Russian at the University of Exeter. He specializes mainly in nineteenth-century literature and has published a monograph on, plus a book-length translation of, Grigorovich, as well as articles on Pushkin, Gogol' and Tolstoi. He has also edited four titles in the Bristol Classical Press Russian Texts series.

Robert Reid is Senior Lecturer in Russian, Keele University. He edited *Roblems of Russian Romanticism* (Gower, 1986) and has published monographs on *Pushkin's 'Mozart and Salieri'* (Rodopi, 1995) and *Lermontov's 'A Hero of Our Time'* (Bristol Classical Press, 1997). He is co-chair of the Neo-Formalist Circle and co-edits *Essays in Poetics*. He is also an active translator of contemporary Russian poetry.

Ruth Sobel teaches Russian at the Defence School of Languages, Beaconsfield, having formerly taught at the University of Sheffield. A Member of the Institute of Linguists, she is the author of *Gogol's Forgotten Book: Selected Passages and Its Contemporary Readers* (University of America Press, 1981) and the translator of Pogorel'skii's *The Double, or My Evenings in Little Russia* (Ardis, 1988).

Select Bibliography

1 *ANTHOLOGIES*

Russian Romantic Prose: An Anthology, edited by C. Proffer, Ann Arbor, Translation Press, 1979 (hereafter 'Proffer, 1979')

Russkaia romanticheskaia povest', Moscow, 1980

Russkaia romanticheskaia povest' (pervaia tret' XIX veka), Moscow, 1983

The Ardis Anthology of Russian Romanticism, edited by C. Rydel, Ann Arbor, Ardis, 1984 (hereafter 'Rydel, 1984')

Russkaia romanticheskaia novella, Moscow, 1989.

Stepnaia baryshnia. Proza russkikh pisatel'nits XIX veka, Moscow, 1989

Russkaia svetskaia povest' pervoi poloviny XIX veka, Moscow, 1990

An Anthology of Russian Women's Writing, 1777-1992, edited by C. Kelly, Oxford, Oxford University Press, 1994

Russian Women's Shorter Fiction: An Anthology, 1835-1860, translated by J. Andrew, Oxford, Clarendon Press, 1996 (hereafter 'Andrew, 1996')

2 *MAIN PRIMARY TEXTS*

Bestuzhev-Marlinskii, A.
Ispytanie (1830); translated as 'The Test' (Proffer, 1979)
Fregat 'Nadezhda' (1832)

Durova, N.A.
Graf Mavritsii (1838)
Ugol (1840)

Gan, E.
Ideal (1837); translated as 'The Ideal' (Andrew, 1996)
Medal'on (1839)
Sud sveta (1840); translated as 'Society's Judgement' (Andrew, 1996)
Nomirovannaia lozha (1840)

Lermontov, M.
Kniaginia Ligovskaia (1836)

'Kniazhna Meri'; translated as 'Princess Mary' (*A Hero of Our Time*, various)

Odoevskii, V.F.

Kniazhna Mimi (1834); translated as 'Princess Mimi' (Rydel, 1984)

Kniazhna Zizi (1839)

Panaev, I.

Spal'nia svetskoi zhenshchiny (1834)

Onagr (1841)

Pavlov, N.

Iatagan (1835)

Maskarad (1839)

Pavlova, K.

Dvoinaia zhizn' (1848); translated as *A Double Life* (Ann Arbor, Ardis, 1978)

Pushkin. A. S.

Vystrel (1830); translated as 'The Shot' (*The Tales of Belkin*, various)

Pikovaia dama (1833); translated as 'The Queen of Spades' (various)

Evgenii Onegin (1823-31) translations various)

Complete Prose Fiction (Stanford, Stanford University Press, 1983)

Rostopchina, E.

Chiny i den'gi (1837)

Sollogub, V.A.

Bol'shoi svet (1840)

Tolstoi, L.

Anna Karenina (1877); translations various

Zhukova, M.S.

Baron Reikhman (1837); translation as 'Baron Reichman' (Andrew, 1996)

Medal'on (1837); translation as 'The Locket' (Andrew, 1996)

Provintsialka (1838)

Samopozhertvovanie (1840); translated as 'Self-Sacrifice' (Andrew, 1996)

Dacha na Petergofskoi doroge (1845)

3 *SECONDARY LITERATURE: GENERAL STUDIES*

Andrew, J., *Narrative and Desire in Russian Literature, 1822-49: Feminine and Masculine*, Basingstoke and London, Macmillan, 1992

Aplin, H.A., 'M. S. Zhukova and E. A. Gan: Woman Writers and Female Protagonists 1837-1843', unpublished PhD dissertation, University of East Anglia, 1988

Ayers, C.J., 'Social Discourse in the Russian Society Tale', unpublished PhD dissertation, University of Chicago, 1994

Brooks, P., *The Novel of Worldliness*, Princeton, Princeton University Press, 1969

Brown, W.E., *A History of Russian Literature of the Romantic Period*, 4 vols., Ann Arbor, Ardis, 1986

Cornwell, N. (editor), *Reference Guide to Russian Literature*, London, Fitzroy Dearborn, 1998

Goscilo, H. and Holmgren, B. (editors), *Russia – Women – Culture*, Bloomington, Indiana University Press, 1996

Hingley, R., *Russian Writers and Society in the Nineteenth Century*, 2nd edition, London, Weidenfeld and Nicolson, 1977

Iezuitova, R.V., 'Svetskaia povest'', in *Russkaia povest' 19-ogo veka: Istoriia i problematika zhanra*, edited by B.S. Meilakh, Leningrad, 1973, pp. 169-99

Kelly, C., *A History of Russian Women's Writing, 1820-1992*, Oxford, Clarendon Press, 1994

Lotman, Iu. M., *Besedy o russkoi kul'ture*, St Petersburg, 1994

Matich, O., 'A Typology of Fallen Women in Nineteenth Century Russian Literature', *American Contributions to the Ninth International Congress of Slavists, Kiev, September, 1983: Vol. II, Literature, Poetics, History*, edited by P. Debreczeny, Columbus, Ohio, Slavica, 1983, pp. 325-43

Matveyev, R. Epstein, 'Reworkings of the Society Tale in the Nineteenth-Century Russian Novel', unpublished PhD dissertation, University of Wisconsin-Madison, 1996

Mersereau, J., Jr, 'Yes, Virginia, There Was a Russian Romantic Movement', *Russian Literature Triquarterly*, 3, 1972, pp. 128-47; reprinted in Rydel, 1984, pp. 511-17.

Mersereau, J, Jr, 'The Chorus and Spear Carriers of Russian Romantic Fiction', in *Russian and Slavic Literature: Papers from the First International Slavic Conference,* edited by R. Freeborn *et al.,* Cambridge, Mass., Slavica, 1976, pp. 38-62

Mersereau, J., Jr, *Russian Romantic Fiction*, Ann Arbor, Ardis, 1983

Moser, C. (editor), *The Russian Short Story: A Critical History,* Boston, Twayne, 1986

Moser, C. (editor), *The Cambridge History of Russian Literature,* Cambridge, Cambridge University Press., 1992

O'Toole, L.M., *Structure, Style and Interpretation in the Russian Short Story*, New Haven, Yale University Press, 1982

Shepard, E.C., 'The Society Tale and the Innovative Argument in Russian Prose Fiction of the 1830s', *Russian Literature*, 10-2, 1981, pp. 111-61

Todd, W.M., *The Familiar Letter as a Literary Genre in the Age of Pushkin*, Princeton, Princeton University Press, 1976

Todd, W.M. (editor), *Literature and Society in Imperial Russia, 1800-1914*, Stanford, Stanford University Press, 1978

Todd, W.M., *Fiction and Society in the Age of Pushkin*, Cambridge, Mass., Harvard University Press, 1986

Tsvetkov, O., 'Aspects of the Russian Society Tale of the 1830s', unpublished PhD dissertation, University of Michigan, 1984)

Urbanic, A., 'In the Manners of the Times: The Russian Society Tale and British Fashionable Literature, 1820-40', unpublished PhD dissertation, Brown University, 1983

INDEX

The Society  ture

DATE DUE FOR RETURN

This book may be recalled before the above date.

STUDIES IN
SLAVIC LITERATURE
AND POETICS

VOLUME XXXI

edited by

J.J. van Baak
R. Grübel
A.G.F. van Holk
W.G. Weststeijn